WHAT PEOPLE ARE SAYING ABOUT EL
AND *ENNEAGRAM LIFE*...

Elisabeth's teaching on the Enneagram is insightful and deep. Her focus never wavers from providing biblical insights to assist believers in personal, professional, and spiritual growth. This book gives readers the power to see their stage and season in ways they may have previously overlooked. Elisabeth invites us to look a little longer at the impact our personalities have on all aspects of life.

—*Molly Wilcox*
Blogger, author, and coach

To say that this book is comprehensive is an understatement. I am touched by the depth and breadth that Elisabeth has gone to not only make the Enneagram applicable to an individual's growth across all seasons of life, marriage, and parenting, but also to make each reader feel especially seen and loved.

—*Christa Hardin, MA*
Host, *Enneagram and Marriage*

Enneagram Life by Elisabeth Bennett is a book that all students and teachers of the Enneagram should have readily available. The lovely and effective metaphor of the seasons of life lends itself perfectly to gaining new insight into the Enneagram as a tool for growth and grace. Rather than stereotyping each Enneagram type and keeping things on the surface, Elisabeth takes a deeper dive into how our types form, respond, and can grow throughout the various stages of life. I found the spring (childhood) chapters particularly revealing and helpful in my own life and in my work as an Enneagram coach. The personal voice and shared experiences make this resource a quick and engaging read, but you had better have a highlighter in hand as you will want to go back again and again to the insights contained in this book.

—*Stacy DeVries*
Fresh Tracks Enneagram Coaching

When my husband Jeff and I first discovered the Enneagram, it wasn't easy finding books written from a Christian worldview. We understood how important gospel-centered Enneagram resources could be, and that inspired us to start our business, Your Enneagram Coach. Since then, we have had the honor and privilege of certifying thousands of Enneagram coaches in more than twenty-five countries. Jeff and I are thankful the Lord has provided more gospel-centered Enneagram coaches like Elisabeth Bennett. No matter what season of life you currently find yourself in, we know that you'll find lasting value in her book. We're praying that God will meet you on these pages, and you will recognize your inherent value as His beloved, uniquely created child.

—*Beth McCord*
YourEnneagramCoach.com
Author, *More Than Your Number*

Applicable to all relationships in each season of life, this comprehensive and practical Enneagram guide is one-of-a-kind and a resource you need! Elisabeth's Enneagram knowledge and ability to offer it to readers in relatable and understandable ways makes it a tool for transformation and a source of enrichment for relationships.

—*Meredith W. Boggs*
The Other Half Blog and Podcast

ENNEAGRAM *Life*

PERSONAL, RELATIONAL, AND BIBLICAL INSIGHTS FOR ALL SEASONS

ELISABETH BENNETT

WHITAKER
HOUSE

All Scripture quotations are taken from *The Holy Bible, English Standard Version,* © 2016, 2001, 2000, 1995 by Crossway Bibles, a division of Good News Publishers. Used by permission. All rights reserved.

Boldface type in the Scripture quotations indicates the author's emphasis.

Photo of Elisabeth Bennett by Jena Stagner of One Beautiful Life Photography.

ENNEAGRAM LIFE
Personal, Relational, and Biblical Insights for All Seasons

www.elisabethbennettenneagram.com
Instagram: @enneagram.life
Facebook.com/enneagramlife

ISBN: 978-1-64123-920-2
eBook ISBN: 978-1-64123-921-9
Printed in the United States of America
© 2022 by Elisabeth Bennett

Whitaker House
1030 Hunt Valley Circle
New Kensington, PA 15068
www.whitakerhouse.com

Library of Congress Control Number: 2022944414

1 2 3 4 5 6 7 8 9 10 11 **ᰛ** 29 28 27 26 25 24 23 22

DEDICATION

To my husband Peter, who makes me feel seen and loved: I still have a crush on you.

And to my best friend and sister, Alison. This work would not exist without your support and encouragement.

CONTENTS

SECTION THREE: ADULTHOOD (HARVESTING/FALL)

SECTION FOUR: ADVANCED ADULTHOOD (RHYTHM/WINTER)

FOREWORD

A good teacher teaches people how to see, not what to see.
—Richard Rohr

My first interaction with the Enneagram came courtesy of a strained relationship, unhelpful counseling, and a trip to Google. I had never heard about it through conversation, as a counseling or discipleship tool, or as a framework to deepen self-reflection and understanding. My introduction to the Enneagram was me, myself, and I, plus my laptop.

All of my subsequent Enneagram learning and discovery came because I sought it out for myself, and I'm so glad that I did. As an Enneagram type One, my movement toward curiosity over judgment and grace over rules has come, in part, because I started to understand how judgment and rules had so carefully and cunningly tainted my vision of this life and my place in it.

I became aware of the ways I had written a compelling but twisted story for myself as a means of protection. I discovered that I didn't have to stay stuck in old stories. Instead, I could choose to reorient toward the sacred truth of who I am created to be. I have a sneaking suspicion that hope for your own discovery is part of what led you to this book.

Now, years after my seemingly coincidental appointment with Google, I look back and a part of me wishes I had been introduced to the Enneagram the way the author Richard Rohr was—through a spiritual director who already knew me well, led me through nonjudgmental self-discovery, and pointed me back to my Creator while reassuring me that I was safe and loved as I was. By a teacher who taught me *how* to see, not just *what* to see when it comes to my spiritual journey.

And yet I also know I found the Enneagram when God knew I needed it. My journey is unique to me, as your journey is to you. Wherever you find yourself right now, I trust that you're where you need to be as you read these pages, and that you'll find what God has for you in this season.

The book you are holding in your hands is a wonderful unfolding of what the Enneagram is—a journey. Elisabeth has laid out a path that has signposts along the way to explain the Enneagram clearly, but she also gives space and breathing room to allow yourself to get lost in the scenery as you discover more about who you are.

Seasons of life are such a beautiful and unique picture of what the Enneagram is and can be in the life of someone seeking to know themselves and how they relate to God on a more personal level. I found as I read through these pages that even after years of learning and teaching about the Enneagram in my own way, I was discovering new things about myself in relation to the childhood, adolescence, and adulthood seasons that I've already lived through.

Elisabeth is that good teacher Richard Rohr talks about. In this book, she offers a new way of seeing ourselves and our life's seasons through the lens of the Enneagram. It is truly a valuable and needed resource for anyone seeking to use the Enneagram in their faith journey.

I am so glad you picked up this book. May it bring insight and appreciation of previous stages of your life, open up new wisdom and understanding in your present season, and provide some hope and clarity as you move forward to the future.

—*Kim Eddy*
Author, *The Enneagram for Beginners*

ACKNOWLEDGMENTS

Gratefulness fills my heart as I reflect on the journey this book has taken to now be in your hands. I am endlessly in awe of God's ability to take a dyslexic and rejected little girl and give her the gift of spreading her words like seed on the earth. May God grow a good work in your heart as a result of the effort He worked through mine. I am forever honored to be a tool God uses in the holy work of growth and transformation.

This book was not a solo effort, and I want to take this space to honor those whose names belong in this book just as much as mine:

My amazing agent Amanda Leudeke, who is equal parts warmth and a force to be reckoned with. I am so grateful God let our paths cross, and that you've been a steady anchor through this exciting and crazy process.

I want to thank everyone at Whitaker House who worked on this book, specifically my editor Peg Fallon and publisher Christine Whitaker.

Enneagram teachers I look up to, whose teaching has influenced this book: Beth and Jeff McCord, Ian Morgan Cron, Suzanne Stabile, Tyler Zach, Christa Hardin, Meredith and Justin Boggs, Amy Wicks, Drew Moser, Kim Eddy, and Brittany Thomas of Enneagram Explained.

I'd like to thank my wonderful coaching clients, who have taught me more than reading a library full of books could ever have, as well as everyone who submitted their own experience for me to quote from @ennea-gram.life. The richness of your words and experiences added so much depth to this book.

To the spiritual mentors in my life, Bubba and Shelly Jennings, Dave and Jacquie Harris, Kristen LaValley, K.J. Ramsey, Phylicia Masonheimer, and

Summer Joy Gross. All of you have lovingly called me out on sin, whether in person or online, and have helped fix my eyes on Jesus. Thank you!

To our Sister Page women who teach me so much about their types and give me honest feedback: Recah Harward, Rachel Jewett, Madeline Smith, Angeline McKinney, Cassandra Rupp, Kellyn Swift, Anna Alvelo, Faith Todd, Katie Albert, Angee Robertson, Molly Wilcox, Nikola Dunkelberg, Danielle Bate, Tracy Mann, and, of course, Alison Bradley. You have all been a wonderful source of encouragement and given me a firsthand education about your type. Thank you for your vulnerability and honesty.

My friends and family: Mom and Dad, thank you for encouraging me and not letting any one thing define me, especially my faults. Seeing my books on display in your kitchen always makes me feel so loved. John and Jan, thank you for asking me how I'm doing and for showing up for our family during writing seasons. It warms my heart to see my kids light up when they see you both. Sarah, thank you for loving my kids and being the best "Aunt Sar-Suh!" You are the best sister I could've asked for, and I love you dearly. Mikayla Larson, thank you for your support and friendship. I am so grateful for how you cheer me on in all of my life, but especially in my writing. I will never forget that you always show up no matter the cost.

Thank you to all of our brothers and their families: John and Haddie, Paul and Emily, Mark and Julie, David and Luke. Thank you for supporting my work and celebrating me here.

And last but not least, those to whom this book was dedicated:

To Alison, who is my most trusted sister and best friend, thank you for your presence and encouragement to me through not only this writing process but also in life. You are my favorite notification. I am so grateful for how God has grown our friendship despite distance, and how He has given me such a gift in you.

To Peter, thank you for being strength, encouragement, and love for me even when I don't deserve it. You believe in me enough for the whole world, and I don't know where I would be without you. I still have a crush on you.

Wellington and Avonlea, Mama loves you so much. Thank you for all of the running hugs, *Peppa Pig* watching, and snuggles I am honored to have with you. You ground me.

INTRODUCTION

In November 2018, Katie was scrolling Instagram when she stumbled across a friend sharing a bingo card that she captioned, "It's crazy how accurate this is!" Curious, Katie tapped on the tagged account. There were nine bingo cards with different traits listed in the boxes. People were sharing the bingo cards they related to the most in their Instagram stories, circling all of the personality traits they believed they had.

Intrigued and feeling a bit left out, Katie started reading the bingo cards. The first one definitely wasn't her, but the second was all things she had said about herself—things like, "I have a hard time saying no," "I love to help people," and "A cozy blanket and coffee is my jam!" Excited, Katie shared this bingo card to her stories and quickly got responses from her friends. "You're a Two! So am I!" or "My sister is a Two!"

Katie felt so understood by this simple share and so connected to several of her followers that she started searching for more about "Enneagram Twos." She stumbled upon websites, other Instagram accounts, and Pinterest boards. Everything deepened how much she related to being a Two—and she was hooked. A mere two weeks later, she was reading a primer on the Enneagram, and she frequently heard phrases like "I'm an Eight" or "Do you know your Enneagram type?" around her college campus.

Now, three years later, Katie is married to Matt, an Enneagram Five, and when she reads about marriages of Twos and Fives, some ideas and concepts click but others don't. She finds herself in a stressful job and her responses are surprising her.

Katie hired an Enneagram coach to help put her mind at ease about truly being a Two. She asked the coach, "How can I truly be a Two if I'm this burnt out on helping?"

Katie's story is one I've heard countless times as an Enneagram coach. One of my initial questions in working with clients like Katie is always, "How did you learn about the Enneagram?" This question gives me a pretty good idea about whether someone may be mistyped and why.

People often think that typing that is confirmed by those who know them the best should be correct, but the problem with hasty or stereotype-fueled typing is that others trust your thoughts about yourself, or at least don't always challenge you to your face. This is good! We should only trust ourselves to know our own motivations. However, when someone is typing themselves based on stereotypes of the Enneagram, without knowledge of the entire personality typology system, there is bound to be some mistyping.

Such was the case with Katie. Throughout our hour-long coaching session, the fog cleared and her true typing as an Enneagram Nine became clear. Katie had the opportunity to fall in love with the Enneagram all over again as she felt more exposed and understood than she ever had before.

Throughout this book, I share some of the stories I have heard firsthand as an Enneagram coach. My clients have taught me more about the Enneagram than any book I've read or any class I've taken.

THE ENNEAGRAM BOOM

Katie didn't know it then, but she was swept into the Enneagram boom of winter 2018. This boom was prompted by Sarajane Case's Enneagram Bingo posts and quickly became something everyone wanted to share. People were learning about the Enneagram out of pure fear of missing out.

Those who had access to the Enneagram before this tended to hold it in high regard and didn't want it to go mainstream because of the very real possibility of rampant misuse and mistyping. Their fears have come true, but we have also seen beautiful fruit from the Enneagram boom, with more people understanding both themselves and others a little better.

There has to be a balance between the Enneagram being *too sacred for mere mortals* and *just a personality quiz*. This is where my teaching style comes in. I felt a need for this book and how our Enneagram type impacts all seasons and practical moments of our lives.

As we encounter the Enneagram for the first time, it can be overwhelming to say the least. Numbers? Arrows? Wings? And what's with that funky symbol? It's true that the Enneagram is not like most other personality tests. Right when you think you've got the Enneagram figured out, you discover another facet of information that brings you a level of deeper understanding. Personally, I have been studying and teaching the Enneagram for years and yet I'm still learning new things all the time.

I find that many people can either quickly feel overwhelmed by all the information that is *the Enneagram*, or they try to deconstruct it to the point of oversimplified stereotypes and wide sweeping platitudes. The Enneagram *is* complicated, but it is within its complicated depths that we find its beauty and helpfulness. No matter how complex the Enneagram may be, it's not too complicated to be practical.

● ● ●

NO MATTER HOW COMPLEX THE ENNEAGRAM MAY BE, IT'S NOT TOO COMPLICATED TO BE PRACTICAL.

● ● ●

Learning about the nuances of the Enneagram takes time, so I want to warn you upfront that this book is not an Enneagram 101 resource. If you're unfamiliar with the Enneagram, I'd encourage you to read some of my book recommendations for beginners before you continue. However, if you are familiar with the nine types and know or suspect your Enneagram number, this book is for you.

As we find ourselves fascinated with the Enneagram, learning all we can find out about our own type and growing in self-awareness, we can hit a wall of questions like, "How do I apply this? How do I grow and change? Am I doomed to repeat all my worst moments over and over for the rest of my life?" These questions are on our hearts, and we yearn for answers when we think of growing as an Enneagram type. However, most of what we find online consists of cutesy sayings and fun-yet-unhelpful memes.

It may be interesting to know which Disney princess represents each type, but how much does this actually impact our day-to-day lives and relationships? A fall color palette that accurately represents our aesthetic may be fun to share, but how is this information actually changing us? In short, can we transition from simply being aware of Enneagram types, caricatures, and their relevance to our lives to actually seeing our lives and our relationships transformed by our growing understanding of ourselves and the people around us?

MORE THAN JUST A TEST

Well, friends, as an Enneagram coach, it's my job to guide people through using the Enneagram as more than just a personality test. With a greater understanding of the Enneagram comes a greater appreciation for how personality both hinders and helps all areas of our lives. The practical application that comes with further study of the Enneagram is astounding, both in how we think about ourselves and how we interact with others. This is where the Enneagram starts changing your life.

As I talk with clients who are in all stages of life, I have seen so many patterns of hurt, joy, disappointment, misunderstanding, and a longing to be truly known and understood.

My understanding of the Enneagram and how it impacts the seasons of our life is a combination of my personal research done within my coaching practice and extensive research others have undertaken. Traditional Enneagram theories and my clients' experiences intersected so that all of these patterns began to take shape and make sense. Recognition of these nine individual patterns can expose blind spots, correct mistyping, help you forgive others, and give you permission to move on from the parts of yourself that you might not have otherwise understood or even realized were there. Life is hard enough without the added mess of not understanding our own proclivities and reactions, especially when we are faced with intense situations, hard seasons, and uncharted waters.

● ● ●

LIFE IS HARD ENOUGH WITHOUT THE ADDED MESS OF NOT UNDERSTANDING OUR OWN PROCLIVITIES AND REACTIONS.

● ● ●

In different seasons of life—childhood, adolescence, adulthood, and advanced adulthood—there are certain players who are typically taking the field, while others might be on the bench. In this book, we will explore different topics within each season of life; however, this doesn't mean that topic is only in play during that particular season. Rather, that season is one in which that particular topic may have taken form or has a lot of playing time.

Things like birth order, gender roles, culture, and love languages are all things that make more sense when seen through the lens of the Enneagram. It's my hope that by combining these practical realities with the understanding of the Enneagram, you will be able to look at your life with a little more understanding, grace, and hope for breaking any destructive patterns you may have.

WHAT ARE THE SEASONS OF LIFE?

It is clear in Scripture and creation that God fashioned us to go through seasons. (See Ecclesiastes 3:1–8.) We see seasons in nature, in relationships, and in our lives in general. This being the case, I have linked different stages of life to different seasons of the year to help us understand their role as well as their fleeting nature.

Childhood is our spring, when we grow the fastest physically, our personality blooms, and we require care and nourishment from others.

Adolescence is our summer. These are the intense years of our quickest and most formative season. Things that happen in our summer years will greatly impact our fall and winter years. Just as a farmer who plants in summer will reap his harvest in the fall, so will we reap the rewards of good choices and growth from our adolescence as adults.

Adulthood is our fall, a time in which we prune off what we don't want in our life, do the work to reap a harvest, and prepare for the winter ahead.

Fall is by far the longest season of our life and holds the most life-altering decisions.

Advanced adulthood is our winter. If everything falls into place, this is the season in which you reap the rewards of hard work and get to rest. However, winter is not without its high highs and low lows. Grief is a big theme of our winter, knowing it is our last season and typically begins with the death of our own parents. But the winter is also the time of our greatest maturity and comfort in the relationships we have built over the years.

In the coming chapters, we will look at these seasons and the factors that are forming or loudest at those times. I would encourage you not to skip over any of these chapters, as the factors explored might be ones you have hit prematurely or are just now processing. All of these chapters are talking about either who you have been, who you are, or who you have yet to become. Taking the time to explore all the facets of yourself and the seasons of your life will lead to accelerated growth and more balance as you process your current circumstances with your whole story in mind.

SECTION ONE:

CHILDHOOD (FORMATION/SPRING)

Childhood represents the spring of your lifetime. A season of much growth and celebrations, it sets the stage for a healthy summer and fall. There was an opportunity in your springtime for the soil of your heart to be prepared for planting in the summer (adolescence) in order to achieve a bountiful harvest in the fall (adulthood). Like pansies popping up amid the snow, some seeds sown by those who tenderly cared for you during your childhood may appear in this season, which is why the people in your life are so significant. The springtime growth is ultimately the responsibility of the gardeners tending to the life that is blooming. These gardeners are the adults who were charged with overseeing your mental, emotional, and physical growth.

Springtime is a time of innocence, rapid growth, and blooming, a time when we are fragile, observant, and in a constant state of discovery. Childhood is the second shortest period of life, but it also tends to provide us with the most vivid memories.

Thinking back to childhood can give us many hints about the person we became. Some may be clear as day, while others may be complicated. Whatever the case may be, there is so much rich information about childhood in the Enneagram. While different teachers may disagree about how personality is formed, we all agree that childhood is the cornerstone upon which all other seasons of our life are built.

1

HOW OUR TYPES ARE FORMED

> One of the most important gifts a parent can give a child is the
> gift of accepting that child's uniqueness.
> —*Fred Rogers*

I was born in mid-June, the same day an earthquake shook Aigio, Greece, resulting in several deaths and significant damage to many buildings. It was the same year that O.J. Simpson's murder trial began. The number-one song in the US was "Have You Ever Really Loved a Woman" by Bryan Adams. I was a second-born child and the firstborn daughter, almost named Rachel during the height of *Friends'* fame on TV.

The world was rotating the sun just like it is now, but everything looked a little different. There were no iPhones, no Instagram, and no Zoom calls. Things I use every day, things that help me earn a living, didn't even exist. It's odd to be so marked by a year I will never remember. I have no memories of 1995, my birth year, but it defines me.

Think of the day you were born. What month was it? Can you imagine what the weather might have been like? Who was waiting for your arrival? Can you imagine what they might have been feeling?

All of these things impact you and flavor your personality in ways that we may never be able to fully know. However, throughout my research of the Enneagram, I have come to believe that you were born your Enneagram type. Looking at personality from a biblical worldview, we see God giving

His people unique skills and gifts. Some of these are fruits of the Holy Spirit that are manifested after we are saved, but many are strengths that our personality possesses. When we are walking in Christlikeness, we can use these gifts for God's glory.

Proverbs 20:11 says, *"Even a child makes himself known by his acts."* Children are not all the same, but are known by how their personality manifests even from a young age. As I have studied the Enneagram and the deep motivations of the soul, it has become impossible not to worship our souls' Creator. God created us, even down to the quirks of our personalities. He was not blind to every aspect of who you are when He created you in your mother's womb. Personality is not beyond His control and design.

● ● ●

GOD KNEW EVERY ASPECT OF WHO YOU ARE WHEN HE CREATED YOU IN YOUR MOTHER'S WOMB. PERSONALITY IS NOT BEYOND HIS CONTROL AND DESIGN.

● ● ●

Some may say that we are born a blank slate and receive our personality due to specific wounding messages in our childhood. But if that were true, wouldn't all siblings who received the same wounding messages have the same personality? Obviously, we all react to even the same wounds and trauma very differently, so personality must already be formed before these occur.

Our situations, traumas, and the nurturing we receive all impact us in different ways, but when it comes to your Enneagram type, it's more like shifting the hue of your base color. You may have been nurtured to become a little more of a deeper purple—say plum rather than lilac—but at the end of the day, you're still purple. This is kind of how Enneagram types work. You are born a specific core type but your circumstances will change how that looks to others.

Some well-known Enneagram teachers favor the soul child theory, which says that we are born our growth number and *descend* to our current Enneagram type as a way of coping with the world. But if this were true, why would we see personality show up in children two or three years old and remain constant into adulthood? Would some of us descend into our current number, while others are born and remain their growth number? Other Enneagram teachers say the specific wound you receive will determine your chief motivation in life and hence your type. But if this were the case, wouldn't children who all went through the same traumatic event or received the same parenting be the same Enneagram type?

What I have seen in patterns during coaching sessions is that we are born with a leaning toward one Enneagram number. Often we can reflect on our lives and recall going to our core stress number at an early age or even drawing toward our growth number.

If we were born our Enneagram type, this would make a lot of sense. And since we are seeing the world through those specific Enneagram type's eyes, we are most sensitive to the messages that form that number's wounds. We perceive the world from that vantage point and only severe trauma can drastically change the personality that was set at birth.

A Three may react to a harsh dad by thinking, *I must change who I am to be liked. Maybe if I were successful, I would be worthy of love.* At the same time, their type One sibling thinks, *I must not be good enough to be loved. I must do everything perfectly and not make mistakes in order to receive affection and praise.* Meanwhile, the youngest child, a Four, is thinking, *There must be something wrong with me that I am not making Daddy happy. I'm just not lovable.*

All three children had the same dad with the same expectations, but reacted to his harshness in different ways. On the outside, it may have appeared that each one was thinking, "*I must change myself to please Dad.*" However, their individual thought processes resulted in divergent long-term consequences. This suggests an inherent and very young formation of our base personality.

DO NOT TYPE CHILDREN

If you're a parent, you may wholeheartedly agree with children being born their Enneagram type as you watch your little daredevil who would try anything and your shy younger child who wants you to cut the tags off their clothes. You can see personality and differences clear as day even when they're infants or toddlers. However, I am going to implore you not to hold too tightly to what you may perceive as your child's Enneagram type. Here's why:

CHILDREN CHANGE

I know this sounds like I'm contradicting my theory that we are born our type, but different Enneagram types can adapt to parents and environments in different ways during childhood. Their motivation may be the same as another child of their same Enneagram type, but their behaviors can be drastically different—and you should not presume to know your child's motivations before they can communicate them to you.

Behaviors may be a symptom of motivation, but any motivation can produce almost any behavior if the circumstances are right. Usually we see personality solidify between ages twelve and eighteen. At that point, the child may be ready to learn about the Enneagram. Keep in mind, however, that each child takes their own amount of time to become fully comfortable with their personality or tries to hide it.

TYPING CAN DO MORE HARM THAN GOOD

Hearing something like, "You're such an Eight!" while growing up can make a child either feel boxed in because of your perceptions about them, or cause them to form their reactions around your expectations. Either scenario can cause them to present as the wrong Enneagram type, or give them permission to act out in the more unhealthy characteristics of their personality. Meanwhile, you would wrongly assume that's just who they are.

IT ROBS THEM OF A JOURNEY TO SELF-AWARENESS

I know this point may sound a little silly, but there is so much gold in learning about yourself *by yourself* and not from other people. First, they could be wrong, and second, we tend to cling to the negatives we hear and not the positives.

God willing, you are going to have a long-term relationship with your children, and most of the time you spend together will occur when they themselves are adults. You'll be able to ask them how they see their personality and learn *about them from them* one day! How sweet will it be to let them discover their Enneagram type for themselves and then teach you what they've learned?

2

CHILDHOOD MESSAGES

The world is not always a kind place. That's something all
children learn for themselves, whether we want them to or not,
but it's something they really need our help to understand.
—*Fred Rogers*

A perfect childhood does not exist. Those of us who think we had a perfect childhood are often only comparing ours to childhood horror stories we've heard. However, all of our experiences are relative. Even if you didn't suffer trauma with a capital T, small slights, mistakes, and bad days impacted you, giving you a front-row seat to sin and its effects. We know from Genesis that we were not created to live in a world with sin, separated from God and suffering. The pure realization of being born into a world you were not meant to live in is enough to leave you with wounds. This wounding is inescapable.

In this chapter, we will discuss and examine the childhood wounds of each Enneagram type. Whether or not you're aware of these wounds, there is a good chance they are affecting your everyday life even now. Your specific Enneagram type gives us a good idea of what specific wound you may have suffered and what you're trying to do to cope with its damaging impact.

● ● ●

*YOUR ENNEAGRAM TYPE GIVES US A GOOD IDEA OF WHAT
WOUND YOU MAY HAVE SUFFERED AND WHAT YOU'RE
TRYING TO DO TO COPE WITH ITS DAMAGING IMPACT.*

● ● ●

There is a moment in all of our lives when we realize that the world isn't a safe place and doesn't openly accept us as we are. Perhaps you even vividly remember that moment. Whatever happened, the message was deep-seated into your subconscious and likely has been confirmed over and over again ever since. What was that message for you? Your Enneagram type gives us an idea.

ENNEAGRAM ONE

IT'S NOT OKAY TO MAKE MISTAKES

As a child, Enneagram Ones hear or think they're hearing the wounding message, "It is not okay to make mistakes," or "You're only as good as your behavior."

This impacts them for the rest of their lives by creating an *inner critic* that chastises them anytime they make a mistake or do something wrong. Enneagram Ones, even as children, try hard to be good, so their inner critic starts collecting *rules* to follow so they don't make mistakes or behave badly. The list of rules becomes too long for the One to remember on their own so the critic takes over, reminding them if they mess up.

These rules can be as silly as not wearing white if you're going to drink grape juice or wearing only matching socks, or as serious as not driving drunk or not stealing. These rules make Ones feel safe; if they know what *not* to do, then they can avoid being bad. But they will never foresee all possible rules, and mistakes happen.

A One might've heard this wounding message if a parent or guardian punished them harshly for a mistake, punished them for something they didn't do, had unrealistic expectations for their age or disposition, or otherwise communicated that mistakes resulted in the One being seen as a "bad" child.

I think being praised when I did things the "right" way or for following the rules reinforced my hardwired tendency toward perfectionism. I took scolding or correction very personally so I tried hard to avoid that uncomfortable feeling.—*Callie, Enneagram One*

As Callie points out, praise can complicate matters for young Ones. They know how to get praise, and they thrive off of it as confirmation that they are good. So when they don't receive praise or are being corrected, it becomes devastating.

Ones report that being praised more for who they were instead of what they did right would've helped them deal with correction in a better way. Remarks like, "Good job getting an A+!" can make a B- feel like failure, but hearing, "I really admire how hard you try at school, no matter what your grade is" will help a One tone down their inner critic if their grade fluctuates.

ENNEAGRAM TWO

YOUR NEEDS ARE A BURDEN

As a child, Enneagram Twos hear or think they're hearing, "It is not okay to have your own needs," or "Don't be a burden."

These children often feel like their own needs are selfish, and they are only truly loved when they are helping others. This leads to a life of frantically putting the needs of others before their own and becoming increasingly frustrated when they realize their own unmet needs.

Enneagram Twos' motivation is to receive love. Twos learn early that those who are sacrificial, helpful, and focused on others are adored. Who doesn't like a helper? So Twos set out to make this their identity. They will be selfless, even if it kills them. And it does. Twos burn out, feel underappreciated, and struggle to name what they need to thrive more than most other types. This is all because of their wounding message, "Don't be a burden!"

A Two could've heard this message when a parent or guardian said something like, "Be a good boy (or girl) and help me," "You're so selfish," "You need to put others before yourself," "You need to help your mom— she needs you," or "You're so thoughtful! I just love how helpful you are." Only getting positive attention when they "help" can also be damaging.

I felt really guilty all the time. My needs were never a priority.
—Troy, Enneagram Two

Your needs are selfish. Think about how what you did affects the family. You're always thinking about yourself? Do you ever think about how your decisions affect others? —*Payton, Enneagram Two*

As children, Twos tend to *play the parent* to their siblings and friends. Helping Mom with the other kids and keeping the other children in line brings them favor and love from adults.

Adults must have clear boundaries with their child about their role *as a child* and the adults' role as adults. Twos are not responsible for other children; that's the parents' role. Twos are loved even when they don't feel like helping, and they are loved even if they need something that disrupts your day. These are invaluable messages for Twos to hear.

ENNEAGRAM THREE

YOU NEED TO BE WHAT I WANT YOU TO BE

As a child, Enneagram Threes hear or think they hear, "It is not okay to have your own identity and feelings," or "Your emotions and true self aren't wanted here."

Threes grew up thinking their worth and identity was found in their achievements, that any identity that didn't gain the praise and attention of those they were trying to impress was worthless. Threes are extremely socially aware, even as children, so they look for what the adult wants to see. What impresses them? And they form that into who they are. They think:

Are you impressed by athletes? Fine, I'll be the best.

You want me to be a straight-A student? I'll kill myself making that happen.

You always wish you could've been a cheerleader in high school? Fine, fulfill your dreams through me.

If a Three grew up in a family that highly valued sports, but they themselves weren't athletic or interested in sports, you would never know the Three's true feelings. They would participate in sports because that was their family's version of success.

When a Three learns that success is a high priority in their family, their own feelings are selfish or wrong, or their home environment is chaotic, they cling to hard work because success brings stability and validation.

ENNEAGRAM FOUR

YOU'RE TOO MUCH OR NOT ENOUGH

As a child, Enneagram Fours hear or think they hear the wounding message, "It is not okay to be too much or not enough," or "You need to change to fit in."

This message comes through when the Four child hears, "Why are you always so emotional?" or "Stop being a drama queen," or "Why can't you be more like your brother?"

> I didn't hear those exact words, but the message was loud anyway from a parent who went silent and withdrew when I was brokenhearted or showed big emotions. I learned to shut them off and vent in my journals. I constantly had an inner world of conversation and emotion that I lived in. I was sure no one truly understood me and felt at school like I was never unique, amazing, or outstanding enough to catch my teacher's attention. I was jealous of the kids who were praised or somehow managed to be popular and well liked. I experienced so much angst and longing to be seen and loved for who I was. I sabotaged my friendships with the assumption that I was unlikable and too much, so I withdrew periodically.
> —*Kyle, Enneagram Four*

Enneagram Fours are often intuitive and creative children who are easily bored. This can make them appear to be attention-seeking, hyper, or ungrateful. The reaction most adults have to hyperactive children who need more stimulus than they are willing to provide is to subconsciously dismiss the child as in the wrong. They think the child is "just too much" and wonder why they can't be "more like so-and-so."

The net result is that Fours become filled with internal paradoxes such as push-pull relationship tendencies, the imposter syndrome, shame, longing for community yet looking for rejection, and a host of other internal heartaches. Fours long to be understood and accepted for their authentic self, someone they dream is acceptable to others.

ENNEAGRAM FIVE

YOU DON'T HAVE WHAT IT TAKES

As a child, Enneagram Fives hear or think they're hearing, "Do not be comfortable in the world," or "You don't have enough (*fill in the blank*) to make it here."

The reality of how much the world would ask from the Five—emotionally, physically, and mentally—was made clear to them as children who either had withdrawn or overly involved parents. In either case, the Five child may build walls around themselves and retreat into their minds.

Fives subconsciously started hoarding information as a way to find security in the world. If they could understand something then maybe they could face it.

A Five could've heard this message if a parent or guardian consistently required more from the Five than the Five could deliver by saying things like, "I'm just helping you prepare for real life," "You're going to have to go places and socialize when you're an adult," "You're just not smart (or athletic enough) to do that," "You can't stay home," "You're just being lazy," or "The world doesn't revolve around you."

> I don't remember hearing those specific words, but to this day, I adapt very well to changes or something not going my way because I'm used to it. I'm used to being uncomfortable.
>
> —*Shantel, Enneagram Five*

> That wasn't really the message for me. For me, it was more so that I didn't know what I was talking about, so I would research. The wounding message was that I wasn't worth listening to.
>
> —*Eric, Enneagram Five*

ENNEAGRAM SIX

IT'S NOT OKAY TO TRUST YOURSELF

As a child, Enneagram Sixes hear or think they are hearing, "It's not okay to trust yourself," or "Your gut isn't trustworthy; turn to others for security."

As a result, Sixes experience internal anxiety over making decisions and second-guessing their internal compass. Thinking it's wrong to trust themselves leads Sixes to either overly depend on those in authority over them (phobic) or demonize these authority figures (counterphobic). Trust is huge for Sixes, and if the people they trusted in childhood exhibited an inability to foresee danger, the Six may end up distrusting themselves.

Sixes look for security in others whom they trust so that they don't have to trust themselves.

A Six child might hear this message if a parent or guardian tells them, "No, let me do that," "You need to ask me first," "You're so stupid," "You can't do anything right," or "The world isn't fair or safe."

> I remember being told that the things I thought were wrong and selfish.   —*Leo, Enneagram Six*

ENNEAGRAM SEVEN

YOU'RE ON YOUR OWN

As a child, Enneagram Sevens hear or think they're hearing, "It's not okay to depend on anyone for anything," or "No one is going to take care of you."

Sevens learn early on to go into their minds as a sort of safe play space to find distractions from their fear and pain. Sevens crave nurturing and often need a gentle and protective touch far longer than most children.

A Seven child might have heard this message if a guardian or authority figure said, "You're on your own," "I can't help you right now," or "You need to learn to do things for yourself," or was otherwise unavailable. Even though the parent or guardian may have been neglectful, often they withdrew affection simply to help the Seven mature or because they had to care for a sibling.

> I didn't hear those specific words but I had a brother who was eighteen months older and demanded more attention from our parents than I did. My grandmother apparently told my mom on several occasions that she couldn't just leave me in the crib all day even though I was content and her hands were full with my brother. My parents have story after story of me trying to do things on my own and not letting anyone help me and insisting on feeding myself long before I was ready to do so. —*Bethany, Enneagram Seven*

ENNEAGRAM EIGHT

YOU CAN'T TRUST ANYONE

As a child, Enneagram Eights hear or think they are hearing, "It is not okay to be vulnerable or to trust anyone," or "You can only trust yourself."

This message causes Eights to take their security into their own hands and fight off— sometimes literally—anything or anyone who may want to control them. Eights become exceptionally protective of both themselves and the ones they love. They trust only a few people, and even with those few, they may find it hard to be vulnerable.

An Eight might've heard this message if their parent or guardian failed in some big way, making the child feel betrayed or scared, or if they were told, "You can only trust yourself," "The world is a scary place," or "Never trust a man (or a woman)! You'll only get hurt."

> Still to this day, I never admit my vulnerabilities, and I find people weak who do admit their vulnerabilities.
>
> —*Claire, Enneagram Eight*

> Thankfully, no one ever told me those things because I already struggle with being vulnerable enough. —*Lilly, Enneagram Eight*

> My abusive alcoholic father and emotionally absent mother who mocked me conditioned me to not trust anyone.
>
> —*Bill, Enneagram Eight*

ENNEAGRAM NINE

IT'S NOT OKAY TO ASSERT YOURSELF

As a child, Enneagram Nines hear or think they hear, "It is not okay to assert yourself," or "Your wants or needs don't matter as much as everyone else's."

This makes any assertion of their own feelings or desires feel selfish and wrong, so Nines learn to step back and view others as more significant, more worthy of having their needs heard. This may feel a lot like a Two's wounding message, and you're right. However, instead of turning this message into actively serving others, Nines start on a more passive road of accommodating and merging.

A Nine might've heard this message if their parent or an authority figure had a strong personality that overshadowed the Nine, or if they otherwise said, "No, you need to let them go first," "Stop whining," "Stop talking," "What you want just isn't important right now," "You need to be good," or "Can't you tell I'm busy?"

> Through my parents' divorce when I was eight, there was a lot happening. My dad was really upset, my mom was flying off the handle, my sister was sad, my brother was angry, so I didn't feel like I could be any of those things. I had to be the calm one. I didn't express myself because everyone else was being too intense. I think growing up in that constant conflict formed the need for peace in my life.
> —*Charity, Enneagram Nine*

> I was the youngest of six. My parents were starting a business and I was left with my siblings a lot. They called me the baby of the family and treated me as the baby. My input was never sought. I always felt like I was too young to have an opinion.
> —*Boyd, Enneagram Nine*

> I had a childhood best friend who would get upset with me, crying or making me feel guilty, if I disagreed with her or didn't want to do something she wanted to do. I wasn't allowed to have any other friends besides her because she would get upset. I wasn't allowed

to assert myself in our friendship and we were best friends from kindergarten until seventh grade.   —*Kayla, Enneagram Nine*

● ● ● ● ● ● ● ●

These exact words might not have been spoken to you, but you were born predisposed to finding them in the things that made you feel unsafe, uncomfortable, unfairly treated, or shamed. Often these wounding messages aren't the only ones you receive, but they do tend to be the ones that still sting the most.

● ● ●

WE SEE THESE WOUNDS OPERATING IN OUR EVERYDAY LIFE BECAUSE OUR MOTIVATION SEEMS TO "FIX" THEIR EFFECTS.

● ● ●

We see these wounds operating in our everyday life because our motivation seems to "fix" their effects. The wound was a problem, and your main motivation was the solution. You may not think of your childhood wound much, but it affects every part of your life.

If a One's wound is, "It's not okay to make mistakes," then their subconscious says, "Well, then, I'll just be good enough that I won't make mistakes." The Enneagram One's main motivation is to be good, right, or perfect. This motivation makes sure that their wound won't be triggered, and they won't need to bear the shame that comes with doing something wrong, even by accident.

If a Two's wound is, "Your needs are a burden," then their subconscious starts to focus on the needs of others. Give love and you will receive it, right? The Enneagram Two's main motivation is love—both the giving of love and receiving it. They fear they cannot be loved if they are a burden, so they distract themselves from their own needs by fulfilling the needs of others.

If a Three's wound is, "You need to be what I want you to be," then their subconscious will start to find their worth in pleasing whoever is laying down the expectations and trying to exceed them. The Enneagram Three's main motivation is self-worth. However, the wound of needing to "perform" and not fully being seen can only be solved by finding their self-worth in who they are in Christ, not in what others think of them.

If a Four's wound is, "You're too much or not enough," then their subconscious will aim for radical authenticity as a way of finding acceptance. Fours have this suspicion that the person hiding deep within them, their very being, can't be too much or not enough. They just need to find out who they are and live out their glorious purpose. The Four's main motivation is authenticity.

If a Five's wound is, "You don't have what it takes," then their subconscious will start searching for things that make them feel competent and capable. They latch onto these nuggets of knowledge to help them cope and survive. The Enneagram Five's main motivation is competency, which they believe will keep them afloat when their energy and resources fail them.

If a Six's wound is, "It's not okay to trust yourself," then their subconscious will find their security in authority, telling them what to do, or rebel against authority and question everything. Their trust is tethered to an anchor that's planted on a couple of things that have proven trustworthy. An Enneagram Six's main motivation is security so they don't have to rely on themselves.

If a Seven's wound is, "You're on your own," then they subconsciously parent themselves, being either hard on themselves or giving themselves fun, adventure, and indulgences. There can also be a mixture of both. An Enneagram Seven's main motivation is finding satisfaction. They plant their gaze on the future and continuously tell themselves, "Tomorrow will be better. I'll find what I'm looking for—I'll take care of myself."

If an Eight's wound is, "You can't trust anyone," then their subconscious decided to never let anyone else be in control of them or those they love. An Enneagram Eight's main motivation is to be autonomous and in control of their own life. If they are the ones in control, they don't need to trust anyone else.

If a Nine's wound is, "It's not okay to assert yourself," then their subconscious will focus on keeping the peace, so they won't need to assert themselves. An Enneagram Nine's main motivation is peace, and they hope that finding peace will allow them to have a gentle, drama-free life.

As a Four myself, I felt that I was "too much" as a child. I was too loud, too dramatic, and too wild—but I was also not enough. My brother was calm and easy. Why wasn't I like that? I was corrected constantly for not being polite enough; I couldn't live up to the expectations put on me. My impulses were louder than the rules, and I wouldn't even remember all the rules anyway. I was *too much*, and because of that, I was also *not enough*... at the very same time.

No one ever told me, "Elisabeth, you're too much and not enough," but that's the message I received when I was called wild and crazy while also being compared to my cautious, calm brother. Somewhere in my subconscious, my Four-ness decided that if I was authentic enough, if people only understood the real me, then they couldn't possibly find me to be too much or not enough. If I was authentic, a perfect representation of my inner-world, then I could make others understand me and accept me.

You may resonate fully with the sentences written about your type to the point that it's painful to read, or you might be shaking your head, unsure if it truly fits. If the latter, I would encourage you to keep those phrases in mind and do a little digging. What are the moments of your childhood that still hurt? What message did they instill in you? What is your motivation, and what is it trying to fix?

If you still resonate more with another type's wound, it wouldn't be ridiculous to start researching that type more. What are their wings, arrows, and subtype behaviors? Do those resonate with you too?

Although you can be a Nine and not resonate with, "It's not okay to assert yourself," it's still good to ask yourself some questions regarding your absence of pain here. Why doesn't that sentence ring true for you? Did you have wonderfully healthy parents? Do you have an Eight wing? What happened in your life that might have reversed the effects of that message? Information about yourself and your personality are meant to be reflected upon and explored. The questioning, hesitation, and surprise are all part of the self-awareness journey.

3

LOST CHILDHOOD MESSAGES

With each wounding experience that left you vulnerable and wondering if you would be accepted in the world, there was an opportunity for a different message to be spoken to you.

This lost childhood message encompasses the truth you need to hear about yourself and your relationship with God. It contains the words that can heal your wounds. It may even be the message you are still striving to hear from those in your life today.

The problem is, we are all sinful people, and only God can give us the truthful messages we long to hear. Anyone can say anything; even as children, we know how to compare words and actions. It doesn't matter what adults say; we are smart enough not to believe them.

For example, an Enneagram Eight needs to hear, "You won't be betrayed," but when I tell them this in coaching sessions, their response is often, "Even if I had heard that from someone, I wouldn't have believed them." This is an astute observation because they're right. We know people make mistakes, they can lie, and they can change. We don't trust people to say something and mean it forever.

●　●　●

GOD IS THE ONE WHO ULTIMATELY SPEAKS HEALING MESSAGES TO YOUR SOUL, GIVING YOU HIS STRENGTH, PERFECTION, AND WISDOM.

●　●　●

But God is the One who ultimately speaks these healing messages to your soul, giving you His strength, perfection, and wisdom. He will not betray you, He understands you, and He will never leave you.

> *Be strong and courageous. Do not fear or be in dread of them, for it is **the LORD your God who goes with you. He will not leave you or forsake you.***   (Deuteronomy 31:6)

When we look at the lost messages and reframe them into the way we receive them from Christ, we gain a better understanding of our Savior. We also learn how to point our own children toward the messages and the Savior who will not only accelerate their growth but save their souls. It may be too late to go back and educate your own parents about the messages you needed to hear, but it's not too late to let God speak them to your soul and guide your children toward the same.

ENNEAGRAM ONE

YOU ARE ALREADY GOOD BECAUSE YOU'RE IN CHRIST

For by grace you have been saved through faith. And this is not your own doing; it is the gift of God, not a result of works, so that no one may boast.   (Ephesians 2:8–9)

The lost childhood message Ones long to hear is, "You are already good." These words take the weight of being good off the One's shoulders. As Christians, we believe Christ was the only truly good and perfect human who ever lived, and through His death in our place, God now sees us through Christ's clean record. Enneagram Ones are right to have this sinking suspicion that they are not good, but when they put their faith in Christ, their identity is goodness, righteousness, and perfection achieved by Jesus's life.

I never felt like I was good enough to please my father.
—*Curtis, Enneagram One*

For many years, Curtis desperately tried to please his dad, only to end up disappointed and feeling like a failure.

As a parent to young Ones, it's of utmost importance that you believe that your own goodness comes from Christ's spotless record and not your own lack of mistakes. The kinder you are on yourself, the more kindness your children will be able to give themselves when they err. If you believe you are good enough in Christ, then your children won't have to struggle as much to reach that conclusion on their own.

ENNEAGRAM TWO

YOU ARE WANTED AND YOUR NEEDS ARE SEEN BY GOD

Beloved, I pray that all may go well with you and that you may be in good health, as it goes well with your soul. (3 John 1:2)

The lost message Twos long to hear is, "You are wanted." Even if you have needs, even if you don't help, or even if someone else has to step up to the plate, you're fully wanted and loved by Christ. Not only that, but you're fully wanted and loved even when you say "no" and even when you ask for your needs to be met. You're not too needy for His love.

> The wounding message for Twos was not spoken but it was assumed. It seemed to me that it would be better to have one less voice in the mix of a family of six. Being the oldest, I was told I had more responsibility. —*Brooke, Enneagram Two*

As children, Twos are quick to assume responsibility and look for where their own needs can be put on the backburner for the greater good. The hard part about parenting an Enneagram Two is that, as parents, it feels easy. It's hard to deal with emotions and needs that are blaringly loud (and inconvenient) in our children, but Enneagram Twos need to know that it's fine to have their own needs. They are just children, after all, and all children need parenting. That is not a defect.

If you believe it is acceptable for you as a parent to have needs, rest, and prioritize self-care, it will be easier for your Two child to learn from your example. You may also need to expressly tell them that they are not the parent, and it's appropriate for them to need parenting.

ENNEAGRAM THREE

YOU ARE LOVED FOR YOU AND HAVE THE FREEDOM TO BE WHO GOD MADE YOU

So if the Son sets you free, you will be free indeed. (John 8:36)

The lost message Threes long to hear is, "You are loved for who you are." If they fail, lose everything, can't succeed in whatever they're trying to do, or need a break, God's love for them won't change. His love does not depend on success or achievements. He literally cannot love us any more than He does at this moment.

> As a child, I would do things and act in certain ways that weren't like me to gain validation from someone who would never accept me for who I was.   —*Kate, Enneagram Three*

This sort of behavior will look different for each Enneagram Three child. They may try to rid themselves of an accent, put stuffing in their bra, or pretend they've seen movies they haven't seen.

As a parent, it's vital to not only praise the Enneagram Three for what they have achieved, but also for who they are, created by God and made with purpose. Their prerogative is not to please man, but to glorify God. They need to hear things like, "I love being with you; you're so kind!" instead of "Good job at soccer practice today; you're getting better." It's not that the latter is wrong, but it feeds into the mentality of being better or having success that attracts Threes. They need to know they are loved even if they don't fit in or make mistakes.

ENNEAGRAM FOUR

YOU ARE SEEN AND LOVED FOR WHO YOU ARE; YOU'RE ENOUGH IN CHRIST

Let not your hearts be troubled. Believe in God; believe also in me. In my Father's house are many rooms. If it were not so, would I have told you that I go to prepare a place for you? And if I go and prepare a place for you, I will come again and will take you to myself, that where

I am you may be also. And you know the way to where I am going.

(John 14:1–4)

The lost childhood message Fours long to hear is, "You're seen (and loved) for who you are." When Fours rest in the fact that Jesus both fully sees them and loves them, they can silence their shame, live as accepted instead of rejected, and pursue community in confidence.

> As a child, I was always too emotional and sensitive. My parents constantly told me they didn't know how to deal with me. I assume that meant my emotions. —*Ryan, Enneagram Four*

This can be such a painful acknowledgement from a parent for an Enneagram Four. They do not find the parent lacking, but hear loud and clear that there is something wrong with them.

If you are the parent of a Four, you need to validate that you love them just as they are. They are not broken, wrong, or "too much." Fours need a lathering of love, affection, and words of affirmation from their caregivers.

ENNEAGRAM FIVE

YOUR NEEDS ARE NOT A PROBLEM; EVEN JESUS HAD NEEDS, AND HE WAS WITHOUT FAULT

> *Now when Jesus heard this, he withdrew from there in a boat to a desolate place by himself.* (Matthew 14:13)

The message Fives long to hear is, "Your needs are not a problem." If a Five child is confident that their needs will be met, they won't need to hoard resources or feel like they must make it on their own. Even Jesus had needs, and He tells us not to be anxious about our lives but to rest in His care for us. (See Matthew 11:28.) When you have Jesus, you don't have to worry about being enough or having enough because you're not left to your own devices and you have nothing to prove. You don't have to live on edge because the Lord cares for you.

> To this day, I adapt very well to changes or something not going my way because I'm used to it. I'm used to being uncomfortable. —*Shantel, Enneagram Five*

If you're the parent of an Enneagram Five, it may feel confusing to read about their lost childhood message. Fives are so independent, it almost feels like they are out to prove that they don't have any needs. So listen carefully, don't overreact or underreact in the times when they do express a need, and try to be endlessly curious about who they are. Assume they are just as needy as any other child.

ENNEAGRAM SIX

YOU ARE SAFE BECAUSE GOD IS WITH YOU

The name of the LORD is a strong tower; the righteous man runs into it and is safe. (Proverbs 18:10)

The message Sixes long to hear is, "You're safe"—and in Christ, they are. The Bible tells us that *nothing* can separate us from the love of Christ, nor can any person or anything in the world do anything to us that is of eternal significance. (See Romans 8:31–39.) You're eternally held in Christ's hands, and you are safe there.

> As a Six, I was brought up being taught that I should always check things back with my parents because I might be doing wrong, hence the decrease in trust within myself growing up.
> —*Trish, Enneagram Six*

As a parent to an Enneagram Six, you will be walking the tightrope of reassurance and encouraging independence. Sixes need to know that they are safe, you're not going to leave them, and you're keeping watch. They also need to learn to trust their own judgment and see their decision work out. So ask them questions when they come to you. Show them that you believe they can find the answer, but don't refuse to tell them what you think too.

ENNEAGRAM SEVEN

YOU WILL BE TAKEN CARE OF BECAUSE GOD WILL NOT FAIL YOU

And my God will supply every need of yours according to his riches in glory in Christ Jesus. (Philippians 4:19)

The message Sevens long to hear is, "You will be taken care of." This message takes the weight of responsibility off the Seven and gives it to Jesus, where it belongs. He will take care of His children. With Jesus, Sevens don't need to fear pain, boredom, or abandonment. He has a plan for them that is far greater than anything they could devise themselves, and that plan includes Him taking care of them, which is of the utmost comfort.

> My parents are also extremely independent people so I think they expected me to need less nurturing. Consequently, I didn't learn to deal with deep emotion until I was in my late teens.
> —*Patrick, Enneagram Seven*

Sevens need more nurturing as children than other Enneagram types. (For more on this, see chapter 5 on Parental Orientations.) However, we are conditioned to want our children to be fully independent from us around age five. For Sevens, this stretching to independence can feel like being told that they are now on their own.

As a parent, nurturing your Seven means letting them know, "I am here to take care of you." This might mean cuddling on the couch and packing lunches for them or helping them with this well into middle school. But don't worry; you're not damaging your Seven. They need this kind of gentleness growing up because adulthood tends to feel disappointing to them. Let them be a kid while they are still a kid!

ENNEAGRAM EIGHT

YOU WILL NOT BE BETRAYED BY YOUR GOD, AND HE WILL SUSTAIN YOU IF OTHERS FAIL

*Know therefore that the L*ORD *your God is God, the faithful God who keeps covenant and steadfast love with those who love him and keep his commandments, to a thousand generations.*   (Deuteronomy 7:9)

The lost message Eights long to hear is, "You will not be betrayed." Only God can speak these words to our souls and have them be true—and He does, assuring us that He will never leave or forsake us. (See Deuteronomy

31:6.) We have a God who is 100 percent trustworthy, even when everyone else might not be. When we trust Him, He helps us trust others as well.

> As a child, I learned, "Don't trust anyone! Do it yourself, and it will get done." —*Ben, Enneagram Eight*

Betrayal for young Eights can definitely look like saying you'll do something and not doing it.

As a parent to an Eight, it's important to weigh your words and be quick to apologize when you're wrong. However, what is of utmost importance is that you point them to God, who is the only One who will truly never betray them.

ENNEAGRAM NINE

YOUR PRESENCE MATTERS; GOD MADE YOU WITH VALUE AND PURPOSE

Fear not, therefore; you are of more value than many sparrows.
(Matthew 10:31)

The lost message Nines long to hear is, "Your presence matters." And it does! God made us, and He cares about all of our needs, even when we try to brush them off, as Nines are prone to do. We can trust Him to take care of us and love us. Nines especially need to know that they have value, that their presence matters.

> My parents taught me that it was not okay for children to "disrespect" adults by disagreeing with them or stirring the pot with our own opinions. We weren't allowed to share how we felt without being labeled dramatic or trying to cause a scene.
> —*Paul, Enneagram Nine*

The wounding message of Nines is the epitome of, "Children should be seen and not heard." As a parent to a Nine, you can counteract this message by asking them to share their opinion and valuing them as an added voice to your household.

Their presence does matter, so make sure you're telling them this. Nines need to know that they are precious to you, but more than this, they need to be pointed to the God who made them and set them apart.

4

BIRTH ORDER

During my childhood, birth order was often a topic of discussion. I was the second child of two firstborn parents. I lived as the youngest for six years, a true middle child for three years, and one of the two "oldest" children for the rest of my childhood. Looking at the psychology of birth order, I've always identified most with the only child, which is odd for someone who has four siblings.

However, when we look at the Enneagram, this makes sense. My feelings of being alone, misunderstood, and longing for parental approval can all be seen in Enneagram Fours. I also had a responsible and self-righteous streak for much of my childhood. I felt secure and was dipping into my One growth arrow.

My mother, an Enneagram Three, has always expressed her distaste for the birth order theory because she felt like it excused a lot of her two siblings' behaviors. The middle child was, of course, a little rebellious, and the youngest was never blamed or held accountable. As the oldest, she was always held to a high standard. No wonder Mom disliked the theory!

When we read about the characteristics that are assigned to each child in birth order, we can see stereotypical Enneagram trends.

OLDEST CHILD

RESPONSIBLE, HIGH STANDARDS, SUCCESS DRIVEN, THOUGHTFUL

This would lead some to believe that oldest children are most likely to be Enneagram Ones, Twos, Threes, and Eights. All of these types share a sense of responsibility, grow up quickly, and tend to be good leaders. They are debaters, delegators, and teachers.

MIDDLE CHILD

SOCIAL, CAN BE REBELLIOUS, INDEPENDENT, WANTS TO PAVE OWN WAY

These characteristics can lead us to believe that most middle children must be Enneagram Fours, counterphobic Sixes (see chapter 11 on Subtypes), Sevens, or Eights, all of whom share a sense of challenging the rules and wanting to lead the life that is best for them. They are freedom seekers. They ask questions and are adverse to the status quo.

YOUNGEST CHILD

CHARMING, SELF-FOCUSED, LOVES TO HAVE A GOOD TIME, EASY-GOING

Why is it that the youngest child sounds like a mix of Enneagram Two, Three, Four, Seven, and maybe some Nine? Some of these types have charm and an easygoing nature (Two, Three, Nine), while the others are up for a good time and more self-focused (Four, Seven). However, we would call all of these types resourceful at getting what they want.

ONLY CHILD

MATURE, MAY FEEL LIKE AN OUTSIDER, RESPONSIBLE, CONSCIENTIOUS

These characteristics are like a firstborn amplified with some Four/Six notes. The feeling that they don't fit in is common for Fours and Sixes, as they ask the hard questions and challenge the status quo. We would call both of these types "reactive seekers."

ENNEAGRAM VS. BIRTH ORDER

In every survey done on birth order and the Enneagram, we see that one does not naturally indicate the other, which fits in with our theory of personality being born and not formed. You may naturally pick up some of the pressures of your birth order along the way, but you can absolutely be any Enneagram type no matter whether you were the oldest, youngest, or middle child, or an only child.

● ● ●

YOU MAY NATURALLY PICK UP SOME OF THE PRESSURES OF YOUR BIRTH ORDER, BUT YOU CAN ABSOLUTELY BE ANY ENNEAGRAM TYPE.

● ● ●

We see a lot of children who are in the supporting role for their parents—typically oldest daughters and only children—mistype as Twos. They are helpful and have learned to look out for others' needs, behaviors that earn them praise while they are growing up. The characteristics that people speak into your life will be the easiest for you to recall when asked, "What are your strengths?" or "What do you bring to a team?" or "How do others describe you?"

If something like "helpful" has been a word that your parents used about you often, it'll act as a trigger descriptor for you going forward. So when you read anything about being helpful on an online quiz, your automatic assumption is, "That's me," which can lead to inaccurate Enneagram test results.

- Ones: oldest children, only children
- Twos: oldest daughters, middle children, only sons
- Threes: oldest daughters, youngest sons, only children
- Fours: middle children, only children
- Fives: oldest children, only children, only sons
- Sixes: middle children, oldest daughters, youngest sons
- Sevens: oldest sons, youngest children
- Eights: oldest children, youngest sons
- Nines: oldest daughters, middle children

If you are a little thrown by this information and believe your birth order is indicative of your personality type, I'd encourage you to research arrows, which you will find in chapter 7, Seasons of Stress and Growth.

Any type could present like almost any other type if the situation is right. However, your stress and growth behaviors will also help to clarify the Enneagram type from which you are actually operating.

Can birth order impact how your personality presents? Yes! However, your birth order does not dictate what your Enneagram number will be. Just like culture, birth order can change what is expected from you, so you may lean into the number that most fits that perception, depending on whether you have an arrow or wing that can help you with that.

But you are born who you are. If you're the youngest, you can still be an Enneagram Three. If you're the oldest child, you can still be an Enneagram Seven who pulls from stress arrow One and wing Eight to be the responsible, dutiful child the family is expecting. Yet you would still be motivated by satisfaction and would always be an Enneagram Seven at your core.

5

PARENTAL ORIENTATIONS

Have you ever noticed that you and your siblings don't relate to your parents in the same way? Your older brother may think Mom is overbearing, difficult, and pushy, while your biggest pain point is her caring too much, and you have the utmost patience for her. You may have a sibling who could care less about having a relationship with either of your parents, for no real reason that you can discern, which leaves you frustrated and picking up the relational slack.

The dynamics within a family can vary due to cultural pressures, traumatic events, and even the size of the family, but one of the biggest and most unpredictable variables is personality.

I often say that my parents may have wanted a baby, maybe they even wanted a girl, but they did not cherry-pick my personality.

The parental orientations theory provides helpful insights into how you might interact with your parents given your specific Enneagram type. Think of it as a kind of attachment theory meets Enneagram type. It centers around us each being connected, disconnected, or ambivalent (apathetic) toward one or both of our parents. Learning about your orientation toward your parents can explain a lot of your struggles in childhood as well as your current relationship with them.

● ● ●

LEARNING ABOUT YOUR ORIENTATION TOWARD YOUR PARENTS CAN EXPLAIN A LOT ABOUT YOUR CHILDHOOD STRUGGLES AS WELL AS YOUR CURRENT RELATIONSHIP WITH THEM.

● ● ●

Now before we jump into what this theory tells us about your Enneagram type, I have a couple disclaimers.

First, I've seen this theory to be accurate about 85 percent of the time. If you don't relate to what is written about your Enneagram type *at all* that should not make you doubt your type. You may be among the 15 percent that this theory can't explain.

Second, when talking about parental figures, we will use the terms *nurturing figure* and *protective figure*. A lot of people did not have a mom who was nurturing or a dad who was protective.

NURTURER VS. PROTECTOR

NURTURER

To figure out which parent or figure in your life was your nurturer or protector, ask yourself, "Who did I go to when I got hurt as a child? Who would hold me, get a bandage for me, and reassure me that I was going to be fine?" This person was your nurturer.

If you can't think of anyone who was this person for you, then the role will default to your mother, or the closest adult female in your life. If you did not trust those people in this way, then you probably have a nurturing figure wound.

PROTECTOR

Now ask yourself, "Who would I tell if some injustice happened to me, and I wanted an offending party to be put in their place? Who did I trust to protect me if a robber broke into my house?" This person was your protective figure.

If you can't think of someone in your childhood who you trusted in this way, then the role defaults to your father, or the closest adult male in your life. If you did not trust those people in this way, then you probably have a protective figure wound.

FIXED POINTS IN CHILDHOOD

The nurturer or protector can be male or female, much older than you or almost your same age. We make this person a fixed point in our life usually between the ages of five and eight.

Sometimes we have one figure who is both our nurturer and protector, and this will work differently for each Enneagram type. The types whose connection or disconnection is only indicated toward one figure—Ones, Twos, Threes, Sixes, Sevens, and Eights—may be connected toward the more nurturing or protective parts of this figure or disconnected to those parts. Being the only nurturing/protective figure for a child means you get the best of connection and the worst of disconnection because you are bearing the weight of all parenting.

Those types who lean toward one figure often wonder how they relate to the other figure who is not mentioned. Since that relationship is not fixed, it can be almost anything. Sometimes I see patterns, such as Twos and Eights gravitating toward one parent because the relationship with their other parent fluctuates.

The parental orientations theory is not impacted by your Enneagram wing so it can be useful in initial discovery of someone's core type. For example, it would be impossible for a One wing Nine to be both "disconnected from the protective figure" and "connected to both parents."

ENNEAGRAM ONE

DISCONNECTED FROM PROTECTIVE FIGURE

For Enneagram Ones, the protective figure often felt like a rule-giver and an extension of their inner critic. Because of this disconnection, Enneagram Ones set out to prove themselves to their protective figures. They can be good enough! If the protective figure is not impressed, then the

Enneagram One is left heartbroken. If the protective figure is loving and kind, their approval can help heal this disconnection and help their little Enneagram One's inner critic to have a quieter voice in their life.

Jane never had a bad relationship with her father, but he was often absent. Jane believed that if she was good enough in school, housecleaning, and sports, maybe she would win his approval and he would in turn be more present in their family.

No amount of striving and being good on Jane's part changed her father. He never said, "Good job" or "I'm proud of you." Jane is now in her late thirties, and her protective figure wound has caused her to set higher and higher expectations for herself in her life. Perfectionism cripples her every decision, as she still strives to hear "Good job!" from those who represent a protective figure to her.

Father God is our ultimate protective figure, and He can be a healing balm to the soul of an Enneagram One who did not have compassionate, protective figures here on earth.

Ones tend to approach God with either abundant awe for a protective figure who loves them as they are, or as a firm overseer who's waiting for them to mess up. We know from Scripture that the latter simply is not true.

God is abundant in love, patience, and faithfulness. He is the only perfect protective figure, and He is the true healer of our wounds.

> But when the goodness and loving kindness of God our Savior appeared, he saved us, not because of works done by us in righteousness, but according to his own mercy, by the washing of regeneration and renewal of the Holy Spirit, whom he poured out on us richly through Jesus Christ our Savior, so that being justified by his grace we might become heirs according to the hope of eternal life.　　(Titus 3:4–7)

ENNEAGRAM TWO

AMBIVALENT TO PROTECTIVE FIGURE

When I ask most Enneagram Twos about their dads or protective figures, they respond with ambivalence, saying this person wasn't of much use. Twos tend to emulate their nurturing figures, as they themselves are gifted nurturers, so they didn't find much need for protection or a harsher presence.

However, when Twos dig deeper, we usually find that their mixed feelings about their protective figure are hiding something much darker. An Enneagram Two's go-to defense mechanism is repression. They push down unpleasant emotions and cover them up with acceptable emotions in order to not be a burden to others. They typically cover up bitterness and frustration with ambivalence.

You see, Enneagram Twos don't merely emulate their nurturers; many of them fall into the role of protector and support for the nurturing parent. Since this is not a natural or healthy position for a child, the young Enneagram Two child becomes embittered toward the person who should be fulfilling this role for their nurturer—the protective figure. Whether this protective figure was truly absent, neglectful, horrible, or just unaware, the Enneagram Two saw the needs of their nurturer clearly and believed the protective parent was not meeting those needs.

Paul was the oldest of three boys. He doesn't remember a time where he wasn't acutely aware of how his mother was doing and how he could help her. She lavished Paul with praise, even telling him, "I couldn't do this without you!" All of this made Paul feel purposeful and needed, while his frustration toward his dad only grew. As he scrubbed the dishes, he would think, *Doesn't he see how overwhelmed she is? How can he just watch football and not help her?*

In his adult life, Paul is close to his mom, but his dad is an afterthought. His bitterness is covered with a kind of stony ambivalence. If he never saw his father again, his life would not be much altered.

Like Enneagram Ones, Twos' wounds are inflicted by their protector. They may either run to God as a good protector or stand back and give God the side-eye, as if He's just someone else who offers no real support and leaves them to pick up the pieces.

Enneagram Twos can find healing when they discover that God is not only a kind, loving protective figure but also attentive to the needs of His children.

Consider the ravens: they neither sow nor reap, they have neither store-house nor barn, and yet God feeds them. Of how much more value are you than the birds! (Luke 12:24)

ENNEAGRAM THREE

CONNECTED TO NURTURING FIGURE

Enneagram Threes are considered to be connected to their nurturing figure. This makes a lot of sense considering the high standards Threes set for themselves and how independent they are. Quite often, nurture is the only need they cannot supply for themselves. They want someone who will look after their needs, make them take breaks, bring them a hot drink in the middle of studying, want to have long conversations with them, and cheer them on.

This is the ideal nurturing relationship for a Three. When they do have a nurturing figure who fulfills this very role for them, it can be hard for the Three to ever see their nurturer in a negative light. Instead, they will easily shift blame to another party when their nurturer is found wanting.

But some Threes don't have a healthy, loving nurturer, which leaves this longing exposed. Threes will try to make a relationship with their nurturer work and will constantly search for nurturers in their romantic relationships or friendships.

Malia did not have healthy parents growing up, but she did have Aunt Beth, who came to all of her soccer games, sewed her prom dress, and was there to listen when Malia called her to cry about some boy. In many ways, Aunt Beth was Malia's favorite person.

Malia's own mother was an alcoholic and often absent. She still longs for her mother to make the right decisions and want to take care of her, but that longing is quieter because of the surrogate nurturer Malia has found in Aunt Beth.

It can be helpful for Enneagram Threes to see God as a nurturer, a friend who can provide them with support rather than a God who is impossible to please. God is not confined to our traditional male stereotypes. In Scripture, He says He is nurturing, loving, and gentle.

As one whom his mother comforts, so I will comfort you.

(Isaiah 66:13)

ENNEAGRAM FOUR

DISCONNECTED FROM BOTH PARENTS

Fours are considered to be disconnected from both parents. However, this does not mean they have no relationship with their parents or a bad one.

Being disconnected for Fours means that even if the relationship is a good one, their parents are not their main source of nurture and protection. In early adolescence, Fours usually feel like their parents don't understand them, so they start idealizing a "savior" who would be the perfect nurturer and protector. They don't often verbalize this, but this strong need for perfect, deep, protective love is evident in their relationships.

Being disconnected can also mean that Fours long for their parents to be connected to them and may try to make that relationship something it's not. I typically hear two different stories from Fours.

Kyle had absent and dysfunctional parents. He always felt like he should be seen and not heard and anything he tried to do was never good enough. He was discouraged and misunderstood. To this day, his relationship with his parents is less than ideal. He'd drop anything for them and craves their affection, but their interactions leave him feeling like they don't understand him and also think that he's "too much."

Lexi had connected and healthy parents who tried hard to understand her and nurture her creativity. Although they weren't perfect in doing this, Lexi felt close to her parents. Digging deep, however, we see that their relationship is more akin to friendship. She doesn't call her mom when her heart is breaking, and she doesn't bother her dad when something needs to be fixed. Instead, she turns to friends, mentors, and romantic relationships, looking for the ideal nurturing and protective love, someone who will truly understand and choose her.

Fours are acutely aware that their parents didn't choose them. They may have chosen to have or adopt a baby, but their protective and nurturing figures did not cherry-pick their specific personality. Fours grow up feeling like they are fatally flawed and aren't accepted for who they are, creating a complex of push-pull relationship behaviors and a huge drive to please yet be fiercely independent.

The Savior that Fours are longing for is Jesus. No romantic figure, mentor, friend, or perfect parents can truly lift the weight of shame that Fours carry. That shame was nailed to the cross, and Jesus is the only person who can ever protect and nurture us perfectly.

> So we have come to know and to believe the love that God has for us. God is love, and whoever abides in love abides in God, and God abides in him...We love because he first loved us.   (1 John 4:16, 19)

ENNEAGRAM FIVE

AMBIVALENT TO BOTH PARENTS

Enneagram Fives are considered to be ambivalent toward their parents. This is neither disdain nor deep affection. This is something that doesn't have emotion tied to it. Fives enjoy having a relationship with their parents if it's good, and if it's not...then they could care less. They are apathetic toward the need to be protected and nurtured.

Fives are independent creatures, even from an early age. To young Fives, parents tend to feel either too overbearing or too detached. Each of these postures creates a need for the Five to function without being nurtured or protected. They learn this out of necessity, and they perfect it in adolescence.

It's hard for adult Fives to express how much they truly don't care whether they have a relationship with their family. This disposition is birthed out of independence rather than emotions. However, almost every other Enneagram type cannot fathom that this is not connected to the Five's feelings, so this stance can feel hurtful to them.

Melissa had an overbearing mom who had her hand on every aspect of her life. Her mom was trying to protect and care for her, but Melissa just felt pressure and a lack of independence. Melissa learned to be quiet, read, and cherish her alone time, making her mom feel rejected and angry.

Melissa's dad, on the other hand, was in the military, and when he was home, he never really tried to have a relationship with her.

As an adult, Melissa doesn't think of her parents often. She honestly admits that she does not enjoy their company when she sees them a couple times a year. After a falling-out over how much her parents were expecting from their relationship with her, Melissa broke off contact with them, and she doesn't feel sad about it.

A Five's independent stance can make the need for protection and nurture feel irrelevant. Thus, the Five's relationship with God and faith can be a bumpy ride in the beginning. However, once an Enneagram Five is sold on God, it's hard to shake their resolve.

Fives are comforted when they see God as a protective and nurturing figure. This viewpoint helps them work through their wounding childhood message, "You don't have enough." They learn to trust that even if *they* don't have enough, God does.

> God is in the midst of her; she shall not be moved; God will help her when morning dawns. (Psalm 46:5)

ENNEAGRAM SIX

CONNECTED TO PROTECTIVE FIGURE

Enneagram Sixes are considered to be connected to their protective parent. They tend to have more grace for this person and long for a good relationship with them more so than they do with their nurturing figure.

Because Sixes' motivation is security, they are on the lookout for what will keep them and those they love safe. The Six thinks that the protective figure is strong, while the nurturing figure is just nice and soft.

Kat's parents had a messy divorce when she was only five, but even at that young age, she picked her dad's side without hesitation. In her mind, Dad was the victim in all of this, and she resented the weekends she had to spend with her mom. Her siblings all saw the situation from the opposite perspective, so Kat took the role of Dad's advocate.

As an adult, Kat doesn't see her mom much but lives only two minutes away from her dad. He never remarried, and Kat has had to help him out financially. Her siblings think their father takes advantage of Kat, and she gets angry when they suggest this. She doesn't understand why they can't see that their dad isn't to blame for his situation and why they don't resent their mom like she does.

Sixes' connection to the protective figure can have a lifelong impact that affects them in three ways:

+ A codependent figure: I overly trust authority and don't trust my own judgment

+ A healthy figure: I can trust my inner compass and use discernment in trusting others

+ An harsh or absent figure: I cannot trust authority and others don't have my best interests at heart

Because Sixes' very health can be tied up in their relationship with a protective figure, we tend to see this type finding a lot of healing in their faith. Letting your earthly protective figure off the hook and putting your identity, hope, and trust in God is the only way you won't be hurt, wounded, or disappointed.

I will say to the LORD, "My refuge and my fortress, my God, in whom I trust." (Psalm 91:2)

ENNEAGRAM SEVEN

DISCONNECTED FROM NURTURING FIGURE

Enneagram Sevens are considered to be disconnected from their nurturing figures, but this rarely looks like the relationship on the surface. It's difficult for Sevens to disconnect from their mothers or nurturing figures, but they also may feel a lot of pain in this relationship.

To many Sevens, their nurturing figure abandoned them and caused a lot of harm in their life, even if they were a good mother or guardian. This disconnection almost makes the Seven cling tighter to the nurturer. They want to be loved and nurtured *so much* by this person that they will often turn a blind eye to all sorts of dysfunction in order to be close.

There is often a big event—such as exposed abuse or a meaningful new relationship for either of them—that exposes the Seven's bitterness and anger toward the nurturer. Sevens are experts at avoiding pain, so this exposure may take a lifetime.

Sevens don't like conflict in general, but they *hate* conflict with their nurturer. It's like being abandoned all over again. Facing the fact that their nurturer wasn't everything they needed is usually painful for both of them.

Oliver was the youngest child of seven, his mom's "baby." They had a close relationship growing up, and he even slept in her bed until he was almost ten. However, around that time, his older sister got sick, and his mom rearranged her life to get the sister the treatment she needed. This was the right decision, but it left Oliver feeling abandoned. Mom was gone, sometimes for days at a time, and he retreated into his own internal fantasy world in order to feel safe.

Now in adulthood, Oliver will drop anything for his mom in an effort to restore the closeness he once felt. He's lost romantic relationships and turned down job opportunities, yet still he feels like he can never do enough.

It's helpful for Enneagram Sevens to see God in the light of a nurturer. They need to see Him as close, caring, and approachable in order to heal their wounds.

> *Can a woman forget her nursing child, that she should have no compassion on the son of her womb? Even these may forget, yet I will not forget you.* (Isaiah 49:15)

ENNEAGRAM EIGHT

AMBIVALENT TO NURTURING FIGURE

Enneagram Eights are considered to be ambivalent toward their nurturing figure. For most Eights, this looks like a strong allegiance to the strong parent and an apathy toward the one they perceive as the weak parent.

Eights value strength in both themselves and others. This starts at an early age, and they are experts at sniffing out weakness. They will respect the protective parent, although they may not feel like they themselves need protection. However, the nurturing parent may almost feel like an annoyance to an Eight—someone to carefully navigate around to avoid hurting their feelings, someone who can't stand up for themselves. The Eight may tolerate the nurturer, but there's nothing about the "weaker" parent that they want to emulate.

And yet it's indispensable for Eights to connect to nurturing in order to grow in vulnerability. It's no coincidence that the biggest strength of the Two, their growth number, is nurturing. A lot of Eights grow in this way as they age, have their own children, or when everything they use stops working. This can be a painful process for most Eights. They need to let go of the idea that nurturing is a weakness. A mother who holds her child and patiently tends to their wounds while they are wailing loudly is exhibiting strength.

Jesus is a perfect example of someone who was strong but tender, someone who spoke with authority and was respected yet nurtured those around Him who needed it.

> And they were bringing children to him that he might touch them, and the disciples rebuked them. But when Jesus saw it, he was indignant and said to them, "Let the children come to me; do not hinder them, for to such belongs the kingdom of God. Truly, I say to you, whoever does not receive the kingdom of God like a child shall not enter it." And he took them in his arms and blessed them, laying his hands on them.
>
> (Mark 10:13–16)

In these verses, Jesus tells the disciples that children—in their innocence, weakness, and vulnerability—are truly deserving in God's sight. Their weakness does not disqualify them, and neither does yours. In fact, weakness makes you strong, and humility makes you great. These are the great paradoxes we grapple with as Christians.

> But he said to me, "My grace is sufficient for you, for my power is made perfect in weakness." Therefore I will boast all the more gladly of my weaknesses, so that the power of Christ may rest upon me.
>
> (2 Corinthians 12:9)

ENNEAGRAM NINE

CONNECTED TO BOTH PARENTS

Enneagram Nines are considered to be connected to their parents. It doesn't matter if their parents are wonderful or horrible people, Nines still long to have a relationship with them.

Nines feel a lot of responsibility for making this relationship a good one. They will spend a lot of their life turning a blind eye to any dysfunction that is affecting their parents.

Nines are one of the only Enneagram types for which this applies almost specifically to their biological parents. Even if they have never met them, they still long for a relationship and may hold onto the feeling that it's their fault that there is no relationship.

If they were raised by anyone but their biological parents, they will still want to have a good relationship with the people who raised them, but it may not hold as much weight as wanting to be close to their biological parents.

Nines experience a lot of growth when they are able to separate from their parents and gain objectivity about their relationship. This requires an end to any subtle overstepping of boundaries. Nines grow when they can see their own worth and know that their presence matters. They don't have to be the only one making sacrifices to ensure the relationship is a good one; their parents need to do their part.

When an Enneagram Nine has had a particularly bad relationship with their parents, a couple things may occur:

1. They project a need for protection onto their own children. Feeling any sense of separation or apathy may feel like they are being abandoned by their own parents all over again.

2. They mistype as an Enneagram Four. They may adopt a sense of "something is wrong with me" or find comfort in melancholy that is quite Four-like. However, it tends to be wrapped up in their relationship with their parents. Nines will blame themselves for the absence of relationship with their parents, whereas Fours blame the parents.

We see in the Bible that God tells us to cut off relationships with people who are hurting us or our faith. It doesn't matter if those people are related to us or not. No one has earned the right to abuse you, use you, or disrespect you by trampling on your boundaries at every turn. You may have had a wonderful relationship with wonderful parents, but Nines grow when they uphold their own image and needs above the comfort of having a relationship with someone who is harmful. This goes for all areas of life.

Now we command you, brothers, in the name of our Lord Jesus Christ, that you keep away from any brother who is walking in idleness and not in accord with the tradition that you received from us.

(2 Thessalonians 3:6)

●●●●●●●●●

As children are growing up, it can be confusing to both them and their parents if one party seeks to relate to the other differently or seems to want a different relationship. Healthy parents are curious about what appears to be their children's connection, disconnection, or ambivalence toward them and work hard not to take these observations personally.

I can tell you as an Enneagram Four, someone who is considered to be disconnected from both of my parents, that this has no impact on how much I love them. Just because I don't need them as my protector or nurturer has little to do with how much I need them as people in my life whom I love. Your children will feel the same way, even if it's hard for you to understand how that could be true.

6

OUR PARENTS'
ENNEAGRAM TYPES

As we parent our children, our own childhood wounds tend to become particularly loud. We try not to inflict what we experienced onto our children, but at the same time, we might find ourselves reverting back to doing what we know.

In chapter 14 on Parenting, we will dive into how each Enneagram type functions as a parent, with their specific strengths and weaknesses. But while we are talking about childhood, we cannot ignore how much our parents' personalities impact us.

I don't find it odd that the first time I took an Enneagram test, I tested as my mother's type. The second time, I appeared to be my father's type. My similarities with both parents were highlighted and buried my actual core personality. I didn't identify with common Enneagram Four descriptors because those weren't typically named in me, and the traits that were more Three-ish or Five-ish were. When it comes to Enneagram typing, we tend to name what we recognize or admire, not what we don't understand.

• • •

WHEN IT COMES TO ENNEAGRAM TYPING, WE TEND TO NAME WHAT WE RECOGNIZE OR ADMIRE, NOT WHAT WE DON'T UNDERSTAND.

• • •

Now my situation is interesting because my parents' Enneagram types are my wing types. I have access to the energies and behaviors of both of their numbers, so the pressure to push into those was not hard for me to achieve. I also see this with my sister, whose wing is my father's type and whose stress number is my mother's type.

We all are impacted by other Enneagram types. For most of us, the fears and motivations of our parents influence our lives far beyond our childhood.

ENNEAGRAM ONE PARENT

A child of an Enneagram One will be exceedingly aware of rules—or at least the rules their parent cares about—and either become a rule follower or rebel, depending on their own Enneagram number and the health of their Enneagram One parent.

If you had a healthy One parent, you may have actually been blessed by how well they exhibited grace, both for themselves and others. They would've spoken kindly and apologized when they were wrong. Their fire for goodness would've given you a jump start toward integrity. Healthy traits we pick up from our Enneagram One parents are a deep sense of justice, moral integrity, responsibility, discipline, and a desire for truth and consistency, just to name a few.

> My Enneagram One mom was super present with us, and I knew
> my siblings and I were her top priority.   —Rachel

Many children of Enneagram Ones report feeling sad for their parents and how little grace they had for themselves. They could hear the weight of the One parent's inner critic because they were so hard on themselves. However, these children also felt frustration at how much was expected of them.

> I felt very controlled in my childhood. My mom had a lot of big
> responses to my mistakes, which made me feel like mistakes were
> the ultimate sin. That is definitely a feeling I still fight in adult-
> hood, even though I am not a One myself.   —Amanda

Wounds we may carry from an Enneagram One parent can be a fear of making mistakes and invoking anger, paralyzing self-consciousness, an inability to express anger in a healthy way, holding ourselves and others to an impossible standard, and fear of *doing wrong* unknowingly.

If you were raised by an Enneagram One, you might find yourself identifying with aspects of this type that your parent imparted to you. We observe and emulate our parents so much in childhood that in a sense, we try on their personality. Perhaps we pick up a couple traits here and there that worked for us. Keeping this in mind while reading about healthy growth practices for Ones may be helpful for you in your own journey.

ENNEAGRAM TWO PARENT

A child of an Enneagram Two might be cognizant of what is expected of them socially and what they need to do to help. This feeling can turn into a wonderful gift...or can be a huge burden, depending on their own Enneagram number and the health of their Enneagram Two parent.

If you had a healthy Enneagram Two parent, you would have found a wonderful, inspirational example in their emotional awareness and how hard they had to work to choose to take care of themselves. You would have felt tenderly loved but also free to be your own person with your own feelings. You wouldn't be afraid that your Two parent would keel over in exhaustion just to help you when you asked.

Healthy traits we can pick up from our Enneagram Two parents include a positive outlook on life, a generous heart, awareness of others and how we impact them, a warmth toward the needy and hurting, a willingness to sacrificially love others, and a wide vocabulary of *loving* words, just to name a few.

My Enneagram Two mom was always there for me. I never doubted that.   —*Ben*

Children of Enneagram Twos report that they were expected to help their parents' own helpful pursuits. The importance of duty or servanthood was stressed during their childhood. They served at church or local events and helped their parents prepare to host gatherings at their house. They may have also watched other people's children at such events.

> I felt like I was walking on eggshells with my mom growing up. She wouldn't clearly state her intentions or expectations, but was so sensitive to us making her feel unappreciated that we lived scared of setting her off. Our relationship got much better once I moved out, but I still have to work hard to have boundaries with her. —*Lauren*

Wounds we can carry from our Enneagram Two parents include a pressure to put our needs last, people pleasing, fear of manipulation, anxiety around forgetting social rules such as sending thank-you cards, and a deep sense of shame for never being able to love, serve, or be generous enough.

In Western culture, females are pressured to present like Enneagram Twos. So whether or not your own parents were Twos, if you are a female, especially firstborn, wrestling with growth points of Enneagram Twos can be helpful, in particular the sense of shame for *not being enough* and not doing enough.

If one of your parents was an Enneagram Two, be careful that you do not let their expectations become your own personal inner critic. Your parents are not your conscious, and the expectations they have for themselves is not your birthright. You are free to make your own path, find your own strengths, and pursue loving others in different ways.

ENNEAGRAM THREE PARENT

A child of an Enneagram Three might be acutely aware of how others perceive them and what they need to do to correct mistaken impressions. They also might be mindful of their parents' expectations for their career, behavior, clothing choices, or other aspects of living. They might not have heard their parent verbalize these pressures often, but they feel the weight of them.

If you had a healthy Enneagram Three parent, then you had a powerhouse of an encouraging cheerleader on your team. You would've felt inspired to pursue what you loved without fear of failure or what others thought, and your parents would've gone out of their way to make sure you knew how much you were worth. Healthy traits we may pick up from our Enneagram Three parents include the ability to see the big picture, being comfortable in social settings, the art of small talk, feeling free to pursue passion and success without shame, the ability to break down big tasks into smaller chunks, and being generally organized.

> My dad's an Enneagram Three and his focus was on efficiency, so the rules and expectations were super clear for me.　　　—*Lucy*

Children of Enneagram Threes may bear the burden of their parents' missed opportunities or feel pressure to enjoy the same sports, hobbies, and academics that their parents did.

> My Enneagram Three parents deny their own emotions and minimize those of others. I feel like I'm only seen by them if I'm doing well, and they don't want to know when I'm not.　　　—*Max*

Wounds we can carry from Enneagram Three parents include being super self-conscious about how others see us physically, intellectually, or socially, never feeling good enough or successful enough, struggling to give value to our emotions or process them in a healthy way, and a sensation of drowning under the weight of expectations.

If you had an Enneagram Three parent, it can be helpful to unpack the image they may have created for you. What are you holding onto that may never be you? What has helped you become who you are today?

In Western culture, Threes are almost a standard to which we aspire. High energy, social efficiency, success, and drive are all things that are praised and expected. Even if neither of your parents was a Three, you have probably been influenced by *Three culture* somewhere along the way. While none of these traits are bad in and of themselves, they can leave little room for the differences that we all possess. This pressure and expectation is not from God; you are free to take the good and leave behind the things that make you feel ashamed or defeated.

ENNEAGRAM FOUR PARENT

The child of an Enneagram Four might feel a lot of pressure to want more out of life than what they might desire. They might feel judged by their parents for wanting a regular nine-to-five, Monday through Friday job, or for wanting to fit in. The Four parent might inadvertently pressure them to stand out, be unique, and not go with the flow.

If you had a healthy Enneagram Four as a parent, you would've felt wholly loved and accepted for who you are, no matter how dissimilar you were to them. You wouldn't feel judged for your emotions but also not expected to display them. Your parents would've been curious about who you were and championed your individuality. Healthy traits we can pick up from Enneagram Four parents include the ability to express emotion without shame, the appreciation of the simple and the beautiful, being unafraid of the harder emotions in life, feeling freedom to be uniquely you, and gentleness when processing hard things.

> My mom always wanted to talk about how we were feeling and how things impacted us. This gave me a lot of room to actually process things instead of just stuffing them down.   —*Grace*

Children of Enneagram Fours report not knowing what to expect from their parents emotionally and being exhausted by the roller coaster of emotions their parents were constantly riding. They felt pressure to feel more than they did and pressure to open up about what they were feeling when they didn't want to.

> My Enneagram Four parent struggled with a lot of self-pity and seemed to always want to drag us kids into their emotional spiral. It was honestly exhausting.   —*Alex*

The wounds we can carry from Enneagram Four parents include an inability to handle criticism, feeling easily overwhelmed by others' emotions, fixating on the negative, a dissatisfaction with life and not feeling like you can change it, being too exhausted by others' emotions to even notice what yours are, and feeling like you need to be careful not to set off your parent.

If you had an Enneagram Four as a parent, it was probably pretty obvious, and you may have gone through seasons where it felt like nothing was allowed to matter other than how they were feeling. This type of fixation on emotion as a child can free up some space for you to process big emotions, but it can also put you into a state of emotional exhaustion starting from an early age.

No matter how they made you feel, your parents are solely responsible for their own emotions. Not having space to be around them is a valid reaction. You're also allowed to want the ordinary and boring.

ENNEAGRAM FIVE PARENT

A child of an Enneagram Five might feel corrected or pressured to pursue knowledge in the way the Five does, or they may feel like their parent is aloof.

If you had a healthy Enneagram Five parent, then you would've gained the best of their sacrificial love and objective thinking. They would have been both an active, nonjudgmental presence in your life and the humblest person you know. Healthy traits we can pick up from Enneagram Five parents include objective thinking skills, the ability to enjoy solitude and slowness, a love of learning, an attraction toward the drama-free things of life, focus, and the ability to teach yourself.

> My Enneagram Five mom homeschooled us and passed on an insanely deep love of learning. —*Samantha*

Children of Enneagram Fives report that their parents were either apathetic and distant or an opinionated presence in their life, leaving the children either feeling abandoned or instantly held up to making certain decisions, depending on their Enneagram type and the health of their parents.

> My dad struggles to show emotion, and it was hard to feel close to him emotionally or physically. —*Faith*

Some of the wounds we can carry from Enneagram Five parents include not feeling like there is space for your emotions, feeling like your parent was absent much of your childhood even if they were physically present, never feeling like you know enough or can be educated enough to not be stupid, and feeling like your parent doesn't have an emotional investment in you.

If you have an Enneagram Five parent, it can be helpful to write a list of the ways they show you love that may not have been verbal or physical. Fives are the most traditional in the ways they show love; their affection is often demonstrated quietly and through acts of service or time.

Even if your Enneagram Five parent loved you in reserved ways, you may still feel some sense of disconnection or loneliness in your relationship with them. If that's the case, you may need to fill the gaps of their presence with other nurturing or protective figures in your life. Depending on our own personality, we may crave types of affection, praise, and closeness that we may not be able to get from our biological parents or guardians—and there's nothing wrong with that! Not one person can fulfill every need we have, and the village is full of people who can love you.

ENNEAGRAM SIX PARENT

A child of an Enneagram Six might feel like they are being kept in a bubble—not allowed to get hurt or experience things they might enjoy.

If you had a healthy Enneagram Six parent, then you received the best of both protection and independence. Your parents wanted to prepare you for reality and not just protect you from it. Sixes are ride-or-die loyalists as parents; if you wanted something, they would burn the midnight oil to help you get it. Healthy traits we can pick up from Enneagram Six parents include a high value on responsibility and teamwork, practical life skills, a sense of humor, self-sufficiency with safety and finding answers, and priority on family and loyalty.

> Mom is an Enneagram Six and she was always there for us. I always felt like I didn't have to worry because she was always prepared and provided for us so well. —*Carter*

Children of Enneagram Sixes report knowing exactly what their parents will say before they say it—things like, "Make sure you put on sunscreen," "Let me check the traffic before you go," and "Let's run over the safety procedures one more time." They felt both cared for and annoyed by the constant reminders and sometimes wished there was more trust, both for themselves as the growing kids and for their parents to trust themselves.

> My dad worried about everything, always assumed the worst, and was way too loyal to toxic relatives. —*Lisa*

Wounds we can carry from Enneagram Six parents include a hum of *what ifs* that can feel paralyzing, an inner cautioner, not feeling like you can trust your own judgment, feeling like you need to question everything, not being able to confide in your parent because they are prone to overreact or overthink, and a temptation to control your environment beyond what is actually possible.

Enneagram Sixes appear to be controlling, fearful, and anxious because of their motivation for security. Thus we may all relate to certain aspects of type Sixes whether we were raised by them or not. That being said, it can be helpful to engage in some of the growth practices of Sixes, such as slowing down, scheduling rest, and receiving therapy when it's needed. (See chapter 7, Seasons of Stress and Growth.)

It can be helpful to see the Six parent's cautions, worry, and fear as the love that it is. Sixes worry only about those they fiercely love. This doesn't mean that it's easy to grow up with an unhealthy Six, but nobody is all bad or all good.

ENNEAGRAM SEVEN PARENT

A child of an Enneagram Seven will grow up with big, glittering memories of fun, adventure, and spontaneity. Whether or not they enjoyed all of this will depend on their own personality, but for the most part, the highlight reel from a child of Enneagram Sevens seems like a blast!

If you had a healthy Enneagram Seven parent, then you had the best of playmates and loving parents rolled into one. You laughed, played, and experienced a magical childhood that many people would envy. Your parent was fun, but you knew where the line was. Healthy traits we can pick up from Enneagram Sevens include the ability to laugh at ourselves and be spontaneous, a positive outlook on life, a willingness to try new things, and a variety of experiences that can help in many facets of life.

> Both of my parents are Sevens and we were always doing something. I have tons of memories of traveling, hosting parties, and laughing till my sides hurt. —*Crista*

Children of Enneagram Sevens report feeling a little exhausted by their parents. Being constantly on the go is only fun for so long, and it's followed by a restlessness. The Seven always wants more. Right now is never good enough. Sevens move on quickly from one experience to the next, and kids often need downtime to process things.

> My dad is a Seven and it *kills* me that we can't talk about hard things. —*Meg*

Wounds we can carry from Enneagram Seven parents include the urge to run away from hard things, not feeling satisfied in the present, a nagging sense that you need more, not knowing how to handle difficult emotions, feeling like it's only acceptable to be positive, and a lack of self-control around food, shopping, entertainment, or anything else that attracts us.

Having an Enneagram Seven parent can jump-start your life experiences and give you a positive outlook on life, but it can also stunt your emotional development if they aren't healthy. If you think this may be the case with you, therapy or confiding in a close friend, mentor, or spiritual adviser may be helpful.

It's fine to look at your parents and appreciate the good while also acknowledging the hard. We learn from both equally.

ENNEAGRAM EIGHT PARENT

The child of an Enneagram Eight is likely to view strength as the ultimate virtue and emotion as something to move through quickly, if at all. They may be encouraged to toughen-up and handle things on their own while also knowing that they have a fierce protector in their corner when needed.

If you had a healthy Eight parent, then you received the best of toughness and tenderness. This balancing act can be hard to find, but healthy Eights exhibit this ultimate paradox. They are good listeners, action oriented, thoughtful in speech, and quick to defend. The traits we can pick up from Enneagram Eight parents include a great work ethic, no shame putting up boundaries, a priority on independence, life skills, an awareness of the marginalized and social justice issues, and a feeling that you can take on anything you set your mind to.

My dad was an Eight, and the way he was untouchable was so cool to me. He could go from unfazed to guard dog in a matter of seconds, and I always felt so protected by him. —Jane

Children of Eights report that their parents show love by defending them from all the threats and unfairness of the world. They weren't very affectionate in words or touch, but the Eight parent's protection was indicative of their love. Some of the negatives they dealt with included harshness, controlling tendencies, and unpredictability.

My Enneagram Eight parent yelled a lot and could never be wrong. —Haden

Some of the wounds we carry from Enneagram Eight parents can include an inability to trust anyone but yourself, repressed emotion, feeling worthless unless you are able to contribute, shame for being too sensitive, a barrier to showing vulnerability in relationships, and impulse control issues, especially around anger.

If you had an Enneagram Eight parent, learning about Eights can help you gain a better understanding of their paradoxical nature. You will see how being part of the gut triad brings up a lot of anger, how tender Eights can be, and why they are both laid back and refuse to be controlled. It can be a relief to understand them in a way they may not be vulnerable enough to express.

ENNEAGRAM NINE PARENT

The child of an Enneagram Nine will be highly aware of what brings peace to their parent or the family and what things undermine that peace.

Some children take it upon themselves to be the gatekeepers of these things, trying to manage their parents' emotional equanimity as their responsibility, while other children just let it play out day to day.

If you had a healthy Enneagram Nine parent, you had no doubt that you were seen and heard, and you experienced their empathy. They were a calming presence in your home and found their stride with rest and action. You could borrow their calm when you were upset, and you knew they would be quickly repentant if you ever brought a misstep to their attention. Traits we can pick up from Enneagram Nine parents include sensitivity to others, the ability to resolve conflict, being able to live life at an unhurried pace, love of the simple and the beautiful, the art of connection, and patience.

> My Enneagram Nine mom was always approachable and gentle. I always knew she was really listening. —*Katie*

Children of Enneagram Nines report that their parents were soft but sometimes felt apathetic and distant. There were times when the children would've appreciated their parents standing up for them, but instead the Nine avoided the issue or caved in quickly to resolve it. Some say they struggled with their Nine parent's time management and how it impacted them.

> My dad is a Nine, and he never wanted to get in the middle of conflict and avoided hard conversation like the plague. His avoidance still impacts and hurts me as an adult. —*Paula*

Wounds we can carry from Enneagram Nine parents include a fear of causing conflict, anxiety surrounding noises or messy situations, not wanting to cause problems or be a burden, difficulty managing big emotions, lack of experience with conflict or hard conversations, low self-confidence, and feeling responsible for others' emotions.

If you had an Enneagram Nine as a parent, their dysfunction may still be affecting you, as quiet as it might have been. Unpacking the ideas that it's all right for you to be too much, you are not responsible for others' emotions, and conflict is often worth the discomfort can be lifelong work. You're going to have to play catch-up with some conflict resolution skills and being in uncomfortable situations may still feel life-threatening, but the discomfort is worth the growth you will experience.

Being easy is not a virtue and being more difficult is not a flaw. No matter your disposition as a child or an adult, God has called you a blessing. Nothing can take that away. Our human nature as parents makes us gravitate toward ease and comfort. Parenting can be downright inconvenient and uncomfortable, especially to children who are louder about their need for parenting. If you felt like a burden to your Nine parent, that speaks more to the state of their heart than to yours.

●●●●●●●●●

It's both fascinating and sad that children often feel responsible for their parents' emotions, reactions, and maybe even their troubles. As adults, we can see more clearly the circumstances surrounding our childhood and the innocence we possessed in those moments of our greatest shame. However, no matter what your personality type is, if your childhood brings back memories of responsibility and blame, you need to let go of that. You were just a child.

The details of your childhood set the foundation for every other season of your life. Any dysfunction or dysregulation you are dealing with today may have started back then.

As you process how your personality was formed and impacted by your childhood, I hope revelation and understanding can bring healing. The lack of understanding we had as children need not be where we remain as we look back on those years.

As adults, we can hold the tension of a good childhood that wounded us or a bad childhood that nonetheless yielded good memories—and give God glory for the story that has formed us. He can heal any pain that is still in our lives.

SECTION TWO:

ADOLESCENCE (EXPLORING/SUMMER)

Adolescence is a war and none of us comes out unscathed.
—*Harlan Coben*

Adolescence is one of the shortest and most formative times of our lives. For the sake of this book, we'll be referring to the ages of twelve through eighteen as adolescence in general terms, but some professionals believe early adolescence can start as early as age ten, and late adolescence can last well into your early twenties.

During this summer of our life seasons, the tension between childhood and adulthood is palpable, and our self-awareness starts to truly bloom. Like the season of summer itself, adolescence seems to last forever, while simultaneously being over in the blink of an eye.

In our culture, we started to become obsessed with this idea of adolescents or teenagers in the 1950s and '60s—around the time Baby Boomers were reaching this age range. Entertainment, fashion, and even the American mall started to take advantage of this new demographic with its seemingly insatiable desires. Movies like *Rebel Without a Cause*

(1955), *Juvenile Jungle* (1958), *This Rebel Breed* (1960), *Wild Youth* (1961), and *West Side Story* (1961) were the first of their kind to feature this truly angst-ridden period of life in all its glory.

The goody two-shoes, the rebel, the jock, and the nerd all became character types we would know and sometimes emulate or scorn. In 1978, the musical *Grease* truly perfected the genre.

Teenage angst is real, but we all deal with it in unique ways. When it comes to working with the Enneagram, adolescence is the first season of life in which we can actually try to help people type themselves, usually around ages fifteen through eighteen. During this period, our self-awareness and understanding of our motivations can be developed enough to discern which Enneagram type is our core.

● ● ●

DURING ADOLESCENCE, OUR SELF-AWARENESS AND UNDERSTANDING OF OUR MOTIVATIONS CAN BE DEVELOPED ENOUGH TO DISCERN WHICH ENNEAGRAM TYPE IS OUR CORE.

● ● ●

However, we need to take into account how different and challenging this season of life is.

During adolescence, your life is up in the air, and many factors ranging from your home life to your friends can create a false sense of self that contributes to the chaos and disequilibrium of the summer.

So whether you have an adolescent in your life or are currently in this season yourself, we need to hold typing loosely. This way, if the suspected Enneagram typing is incorrect, nobody's vision of that person is destroyed or shaken. We can look forward to another layer of discovery because we never clung to the typing as a fact in the first place.

This is also how I prefer to hold the typing of those who will never be able to confirm nor deny my opinion of their Enneagram type, such as deceased relatives or celebrities, both living and dead. We may have a very good idea of their type, but we should think of it in a way that would not leave us devastated, shaken, or defensive if that proved to be untrue.

If you are younger than twenty-five and your idea of yourself would be shattered if you found out you've mistyped, then you're holding your Enneagram typing too tightly. In reality, I think at any age, we should all only be *at most* 95 percent sure of our typing. This provides us with a bit of mystery and discovery that we can enjoy over the course of our lives.

As we talk about adolescence and the Enneagram, we will be diving into basic Enneagram topics that impact us dramatically during this season of life, such as stress versus growth, introvert versus extrovert, male versus female, subtypes, and friendships.

7

SEASONS OF STRESS AND GROWTH

Looking at life seasonally can enable you to be more positive about the hard seasons, which will pass in due time, and also put more energy into enjoying good seasons. When we look at our current situation as ever-changing, we can be grateful for what is good here and hopeful for the hard things to change.

We see seasonal thinking illustrated in Ecclesiastes 3:1: "*For everything there is a season, and a time for every matter under heaven.*"

We do not get to be both young and old, both married and single, both living here and living there, or both weeping and laughing all at the same time. We have marked seasons in our life—seasons of stress in which we are surviving and seasons of growth in which we are thriving. This is one way to categorize overarching themes we see throughout our lives. We all experience them.

In Enneagram terms, your stress number is the type whose average to unhealthy behaviors you adopt in seasons of stress. We tend to see a lot of these behaviors during our high school years, when social and academic pressures are at a boiling point.

● ● ●

*WE TEND TO SEE A LOT OF UNHEALTHY BEHAVIORS
DURING OUR HIGH SCHOOL YEARS, WHEN SOCIAL
AND ACADEMIC PRESSURES ARE AT A BOILING POINT.*

● ● ●

You don't become your stress number, but that type's negative behaviors do help you cope with stress.

SEASONS OF STRESS

ENNEAGRAM ONE

In stress, the emotional evenness of a One is flipped upside down when they go to type Four. Normally logical, dutiful, and hard to slow down, Ones will become moody, snippy, and almost impossible to cheer up. This can look like a dark cloud hanging over them in seasons of stress, and those around them may even worry that they are experiencing depression.

As Ones feel the toll of a season of stress, they'll start to feel out of control, disappointed, and frustrated. To cope, they'll develop skills to try to process their stress and grief. However, the coping skills they get from going to Four generally have them dwelling in unhealthy emotional extremes rather than processing what's happening.

Ones often feel a profound sense of disappointment both in themselves and others when things aren't ideal. This disappointment is a normal human response and worthy of acknowledgement. However, it becomes skewed when Ones dive headfirst into hopelessness and moodiness. They refuse to be cheered up and cope with emotions by eating or otherwise trying to numb themselves to whatever is bothering them. It's often said that Ones' seasons of stress can look like seasons of depression as they go to Four.

In seasons of stress, Ones need to openly process their disappointment without giving way to hopelessness. They need to let go of any bitterness or blame they are feeling toward themselves or others, forgiving, moving on, and doing what they actually *can* do to control the situation.

ENNEAGRAM TWO

In stress, the normally sweet and giving Twos will become aggressive, argumentative, and even hostile as they react out of the unhealthy side of Eights. It might surprise even the Twos themselves when they lash out and become quite a force to be reckoned with when stressed.

As Twos feel the toll of a season of stress, they'll start to feel out of control and seek coping skills to try to piece their world back together. However, the coping skills they get from going to type Eight for the most part provide a false sense of power or control rather than actually fixing anything.

Twos will start to feel irritable as they sense a loss of control, and they look to relationships to help them feel wanted, loved, and important. However, in stress, they can overreact if they don't feel these things from those closest to them. This leads to arguments, manipulative behaviors, and comments such as, "I guess you just don't love me," or "I just have to do everything myself." The Two may also try other tactics to make their loved ones give them the feelings that will alleviate some of their stress.

In seasons of stress, Twos really need to focus on what they can control and leave the rest to God. This is much easier said than done, of course— and holds true for all of us, no matter what our Enneagram type.

ENNEAGRAM THREE

In stress, a Three will slow down and have little to no motivation as they behave like an unhealthy Nine. A Three in stress will indulge in mind-numbing behaviors, lose track of time, and procrastinate on projects. They may even use passive-aggressive behavior to get your attention.

As Threes feel the toll of a season of stress, they gain coping skills to help them rest and not *feel* everything that's going on during this time. However, the coping skills they get from going to type Nine provide more of a numbing than actual rest. They'll be tempted to shut down and look for rest in unthinking behaviors such as snacking, shopping, binging a TV show, or otherwise going on autopilot. This does help the Three to stop pouring out of their low reserve, but it does very little to fill them back up, keeping them stuck in stress.

What Threes really want is true rest that only God can provide as we trust Him to handle what's weighing us down.

ENNEAGRAM FOUR

In stress, a Four's fixation on what is missing in their life becomes relational as they pick up the unhealthy behaviors of Twos. A stressed Four will dwell on favors, gifts, or acts of kindness that have not been reciprocated. They may even try to bait people they admire into affirming them.

As Fours feel the toll of a season of stress, they gain coping skills to help them feel loved and keep the shame at bay. However, the coping skills they get from going to Two provide more of a momentary affirmation than actual love or lasting relief from shame. They'll be tempted to become clingy at first and then distance themselves to see if you respond. They'll start to fixate on flaws in relationships that make them feel unloved and want to fix the situation. They may also act in attention-getting ways without realizing it until the affirmation doesn't come.

What Fours really want is to feel loved—fully known, understood, and loved despite their idiosyncrasies. A compliment may make your hour, but it can hardly bear the weight of the love that Fours seek.

ENNEAGRAM FIVE

In stress, a normally organized and thoughtful Five will start to behave like an unhealthy Seven. Scattered, noncommittal, and even hyperactive, a stressed-out Five can be easy to spot.

As Fives feel the toll of a season of stress, they gain coping skills to help them find relief from the feelings of anxiety, incompetence, and agitation. However, the coping skills they get from going to Seven provide more of a false comfort than actual, lasting relief. They'll be tempted to become physically lazy or indulge in gluttony; overall, their impulse control toward things that tempt them the most won't be as strong as it normally is.

What Fives really want is to feel relief from the stress that is plaguing their minds. A night spent watching TV or indulging in another form of temporary comfort isn't always wrong, but in long seasons of stress, Fives need to find lasting comfort through healthy activities like a walk in the park or talking to a friend.

ENNEAGRAM SIX

In stress, our normally sweet Six will pick up the worst traits of Threes, becoming arrogant and controlling. A stressed Six may start to behave like a workaholic in order to feel safe and secure about their job.

As Sixes feel the toll of a season of stress, they gain coping skills to help them feel confident in their ability to handle it. However, the coping skills they get from going to Three provide a false sense of security rather than actual confidence. They'll be tempted to overwork, compare themselves to others to boost their sense of pride, and even boast about their knowledge or abilities to make others think they're more confident than they really are.

Sixes want to feel confident that they can handle this season without losing the security they work so hard to keep or create. Unlike many other Enneagram types, Sixes in stress tend to keep busy rather than shut down.

ENNEAGRAM SEVEN

In stress, our happy-go-lucky Sevens start to act out like an unhealthy One. They'll become critical perfectionists who are frustrated with themselves or others in their lives.

As Sevens feel the toll of a season of stress, they gain coping skills to help them find a solution as they go to type One. These "false control" solutions often look like obsessive cleaning, criticizing themselves or others, or otherwise focusing on things to fix.

What Sevens really want is for this season to be solved, over, and finished so they can stop experiencing the negative feelings that are making them angsty and uncomfortable.

ENNEAGRAM EIGHT

In stress, normally energetic Eights will slow down and even withdraw as they act out like unhealthy Fives. Eights will become disengaged, more emotionally unaware, and suspicious of betrayal as they feel the toll of a season of stress. They'll feel more emotionally vulnerable as they feel control slip through their fingers.

Eights develop coping skills to try to keep themselves and others safe. However, the coping skills they gain from going to Five provide more of a run-and-hide approach to the outside world instead of emotional, spiritual, and physical safety.

Stressed-out Eights report feeling quiet and unmotivated. They shut down and shut up while internally, they're feeling a range of emotions about whatever is causing the stress. Being so emotional feels vulnerable to an Eight. They might struggle to keep their walls up, so they retreat to feel safe. If they can't deal with the feelings, they might indulge in mind-numbing behaviors to distract themselves.

In seasons of stress, Eights need to feel safe; instead, they feel vulnerable because nothing's in their control. Leaning on and trusting in the Lord during this time might feel impossibly hard, but He is the only One who is really in control and can keep us safe.

ENNEAGRAM NINE

In stress, normally go-with-the-flow Nines will be anxious and distrusting as they go to Six. Stressed-out Nines experience fear-laced anxiety, difficulty leaning on their own judgment, and suspicion of the people around them.

As Nines feel the toll of a season of stress, their inner peace can feel off-balance. They develop coping skills to try to keep anything else from happening that could tip the balance into unrecoverable emotional, mental, or physical disaster. However, the coping skills they get from going to Six constitute an on-guard anxiety approach to prevent more stress, when what they really need is to walk through what's happening in trust, peace, and hope.

Nines in stress report heightened anxiety, awareness of what could go wrong, trouble sleeping, suspicion of others' motives or intentions, and overpreparing for more trouble. All of these coping measures are designed to prevent additional stress, but they only aggravate the problem.

In seasons of stress, Nines need to respond in a way that will help them endure for the long haul. Anxiety and overpreparation, not to mention loss of sleep, only make this season worse. Nines need to be kind to themselves, acknowledge what they've lost, and openly give the rest of this season into God's loving hands.

SUPPORT FOR EACH TYPE IN HARD SEASONS

A *big* difference in how an adolescent in particular deals with stress is how much support they feel from those around them. This will look different for each Enneagram type. While one type really wants verbal affirmation, another seeks independence. It's essential for both the adolescent and the adults in their life to understand what kind of support they need.

● ● ●

EACH ENNEAGRAM TYPE NEEDS TO FEEL SUPPORT FROM THOSE AROUND THEM, PARTICULARLY WHEN DEALING WITH STRESS AS AN ADOLESCENT.

● ● ●

Here are some examples of what support in adolescent years can look like for each type.

ENNEAGRAM ONE

For Enneagram Ones, support can look like acknowledging how hard they are trying and being purposefully very gentle with them even if they do something wrong. A One told me, "I felt supported when people told me what was going to happen before it happened and gave me the information I needed to respond correctly."

ENNEAGRAM TWO

For Enneagram Twos, support can look like letting them do all the things that are calling their name and encouraging them to do things for themselves every now and then.

ENNEAGRAM THREE

For Enneagram Threes, support looks like showing up and cheering them on, no matter how good or bad they are at whatever they're attempting.

ENNEAGRAM FOUR

For Enneagram Fours, support looks like digging deeper, spending time with them to ask thoughtful questions and truly showing an interest in their inner world.

ENNEAGRAM FIVE

For Enneagram Fives, support can look like giving them space, not forcing them to have friends or seek more, and showing genuine interest in their favorite topics.

ENNEAGRAM SIX

For Enneagram Sixes, support can look like helping them work through their thoughts with compassion and not trying to fix them.

ENNEAGRAM SEVEN

For Enneagram Sevens, support can look like letting them pursue new passions and shift focus without judgment. They'll need to figure it out for themselves. A Seven told me, "I felt supported when people would stay even when things got tough. I needed to feel like I could say how I was feeling and it would be okay."

ENNEAGRAM EIGHT

For Enneagram Eights, support can look like letting them take on adult responsibilities when they feel they are ready. An Eight said, "I felt supported when I was allowed to get a job and drive."

ENNEAGRAM NINE

For Enneagram Nines, support can look like letting them have bad days and not judging them when they are not the same "easy" kid you remember.

SEASONS OF GROWTH

In comparison, our growth number is the Enneagram type whose healthy qualities become easier for us to emulate as we encounter seasons of growth. These are the seasons where life, for the most part, is going well. We have more energy, more capacity, and more focus. Growth behaviors are like seeds that eventually yield an abundant harvest if nurtured properly.

● ● ●

GROWTH BEHAVIORS ARE LIKE SEEDS THAT EVENTUALLY YIELD AN ABUNDANT HARVEST IF NURTURED PROPERLY.

● ● ●

Sometimes, special circumstances prevent people from growing, even very late in their life. Apathy can also hinder seasons of growth.

Yet we learn from Jesus's parable of the talents that we are to steward what God gives us here on earth. (See Matthew 25:14–30.) We are not to let our time, talents, wealth, or relationships wither and die unattended. It is godly work to grow, change, and become the people He wants us to be.

ENNEAGRAM ONE

In growth, put-together Ones will surprise you with how fun they are, as they go to Seven. A normally stoic One will seem happy, playful, and spontaneous when that Seven energy starts to take over. As they grow, they will become less critical of themselves and others and take life a little less seriously.

Ones grow when they prioritize outlets that let them have fun, laugh at themselves, and encourage spontaneity. Fun isn't something we can perfect, and in some ways, that's why it's so helpful for Ones. Obviously, what is fun will vary for each individual One, but if they can prioritize the frivolous, imperfect, and unnecessary elements of life that Sevens are so good at, they find their sweet spot in growing.

ENNEAGRAM TWO

In growth, Twos become more emotionally aware as they start to react to life like a healthy Four. Creative, emotionally honest, and self-nurturing, a growing Two won't need to be fixing someone else's problems to feel fulfilled and worthy.

Twos grow when they get creative, especially if it's for no reason other than to just express themselves. Twos grow when they are honest about how they're feeling and let themselves have needs that could be seen as a burden. Fours are traditionally self-focused, while Twos pride themselves in being selfless. They both have things to learn from each other. But when

Twos choose to enjoy creating, speak truth in love, and are honest about their needs, they become more effective in every other selfless endeavor.

ENNEAGRAM THREE

In growth, a Three will become more in touch with their emotions and less competitive as they pick up the healthy behaviors of a Six. A secure Three will care more about their close friends and family and less about the illusion they need to create to impress others.

Threes grow when they are team-oriented—not just thinking about how a positive team will make them feel or look but caring about the individuals on the team—when they stick things out that aren't popular or successful, and when they grow in humility, which can occur when they experience the Sixes' fear.

Sixes can get a bad rap as being fearful, anxious, and inactive, but they are courageous, balanced, and trustworthy individuals, which can aid those of us who struggle with image consciousness, fear of failure, and going to extremes. When Threes embrace the invisible attributes that make Sixes who they are, they become more well-rounded and humble individuals.

ENNEAGRAM FOUR

In growth, normally emotional Fours gain the logical, organized, and dutiful behaviors of a healthy One. A Four who is growing isn't as likely to withdraw, become overwhelmed by their feelings, or give in to emotional outbursts. Instead, the Ones' energy they have access to in health helps them to logically work through their emotions and feelings of envy and gives them motivation to improve the world with their creative gifts.

Fours grow when they prioritize what *is* right instead of what *feels* right; they grow when they organize, plan, and use discipline to follow through. All of these attributes of type One make Fours' creative gifts and just the gift of their *being* something that the rest of us get to enjoy too.

ENNEAGRAM FIVE

In growth, a Five will start picking up the healthy behaviors of Eights. Normally detached and withdrawn, a growing Five will become more assertive, social, and decisive.

Fives grow when their knowledge turns into action. This passion is something that Eights have in abundance. When Fives give in to the passion that fills them in seasons of growth, they also have opportunities to grow in their confidence, both in their social skills and in their knowledge. Eights are very action-oriented individuals, and when Fives act, the knowledge that they often keep to themselves becomes a gift to the rest of us.

ENNEAGRAM SIX

In growth, Sixes will start to act like a healthy Nine. They'll become less anxious, more even-tempered, and empathetic. Loosening the tight grip they keep on their security, Sixes will be more likely to stop and smell the roses.

Sixes grow when they have the time to respond instead of react. A slower pace in life can be helpful to this type in seasons of growth. Sleep, true rest instead of numbing, long drives alone, and lighting a candle for no reason are all examples of the things, both big and small, that can act as seeds of growth in the lives of Sixes.

ENNEAGRAM SEVEN

In growth, Sevens will start picking up the behaviors of a healthy Five. They'll be focused, better with personal boundaries, and more content, both with what they have and with the mundaneness of everyday life.

Sevens grow when they put away distractions, make time for true solitude, and, in some cases, take up a more minimalist lifestyle. Simplicity is truly a virtuous word for those of us tempted by excess. Sevens can benefit from Fives' contentment with little and ability to focus rather than being led by distractions.

ENNEAGRAM EIGHT

In growth, tough Eights become softer and more personable as they pick up the healthy behaviors of Twos. As Eights feel secure, they're more likely to listen, care for others' needs, and let their emotional side show without fear of losing control or respect.

Eights grow when they choose empathy for those who are not deserving of empathy at first glance, stay present, listen well, and try to assume best intentions. Twos are not pushovers, but they are more trusting than Eights, whose self-protection puts up a barrier against others. When Eights use Twos' warmest traits to lower their shields, we truly get to see their tender hearts.

ENNEAGRAM NINE

In growth, Nines become increasingly bold, decisive, and confident as they go to Three. A secure Nine will stay on task, have more social energy, and be more confident of themselves when they're experiencing the positive side of Threes.

Nines grow when they build their decision-making skills and ability to lead by putting themselves in positions where they get to practice these traits of Threes. Nines are truly humble leaders, which is why leading can be a sweet spot for them. Leading requires action, consistency, decision-making, and energy, all of which can bring Nines outside their comfort zone and into a position of growth.

WATERING SEEDS IN ADOLESCENCE

In adolescence, we see a unique merging of both growth and stress in an interesting way. It's a season of stress because everything is changing—our bodies, our schools, our families, our relationships, our emotions, and even how we think. However, those changes also bring about accelerated growth. In adolescence, we are handed seeds in what is already a volcanic situation. Stress can either drown our seeds or water them.

This is what it looks like to water your growth seeds for each Enneagram type.

ENNEAGRAM ONE

LAUGH AT YOURSELF

Your mistakes are not the end of the world and do not define you. Learning to enjoy the things that make you laugh and feel playful will help you find the Seven-ish energy that helps you grow.

ENNEAGRAM TWO

BE PROUD OF OTHERS FOR NOT NEEDING YOU

Having someone be dependent on you can feel like love to an Enneagram Two. However, it's easy to fall into the traps of codependency and enabling. That yucky feeling you get when you hit someone's boundary or when someone doesn't need your help is an opportunity for you to shift from sadness for yourself to being proud of them.

ENNEAGRAM THREE

LET FAILURE LAUNCH YOU FORWARD

You will fail. There is no escaping that. Failure, in fact, is a vital part of growing as an Enneagram Three. It prompts humility, making you more considerate and more dependent on God. When you feel the burning shame that accompanies failure, let that feeling propel you forward in humility instead of making you hide. Help others not make the same mistakes.

ENNEAGRAM FOUR

ACCEPT THAT YOU CAN BE BOTH MISUNDERSTOOD AND LOVED

Paradoxically, when you're a Four, you both long to be understood and yet firmly plant your identity in being misunderstood. And you can't have both. You can grow in understanding that people don't have to fully understand you to love you well. It's okay! They aren't burning all their "understanding" energy on other people.

ENNEAGRAM FIVE

SHARE WHAT YOU'VE LEARNED

It can be tempting to wait until you are a master at something before you share. You may also feel like you're not smart enough to teach someone else. Growing as a Five does require some action and pushing against your comfort zone, but the confidence you gain from your attempts will propel you toward a fulfilling life.

ENNEAGRAM SIX

PLAN REST

Don't let anxious toil be the story of your youth. There are so many unknowns during these years, and they can make Sixes live in their "work-aholic/adrenal" stress zone. Making time for things that bring you true rest, not just numbing, is a way to steward these years and grow.

ENNEAGRAM SEVEN

DO WITHOUT DISTRACTIONS

It's easy to be entertained, which is why you may choose entertainment when your mind is too tired to choose anything else. However, for Sevens, being focused on some sort of work like practicing a sport or doing home-work is a growth practice that will serve you well throughout your life. You may need to free yourself from music, your phone, or other stimuli to be fully focused, so give that a try. Don't be afraid of silence.

ENNEAGRAM EIGHT

GIVE OTHERS A CHANCE

No one can be fully defined by one choice, one moment, or one circum-stance. Burning bridges too quickly is a protective measure that is second nature to Eights. You don't wait long to let people prove themselves to you. However, being liberal with your second chances is a growth step for you. You don't need to make reckless decisions but opening yourself up to empa-thy and trust will leave you with fewer burned bridges in your adult life.

ENNEAGRAM NINE

DON'T BE AFRAID TO LEAD

Don't let the line "someone else will do it" become your motto! You, dear Nine, are well equipped and natural at leading. It's a work of growth for you to lead, and the confidence that comes with proving to yourself that you're a good leader will help you walk into adulthood with confidence.

Using things we learn from our growth numbers, we can often counter-act some of the stifling pressures of stress and cope with the behaviors that are most tempting in those times. This is how we use our stress to grow.

8

LIVING IN EXCESS
OF YOUR PERSONALITY

One of the most life-changing gifts the Enneagram has given me is the ability to see people as unhealthy instead of bad, evil, or unable to change. Unhealthy people are hurting; they *can* heal and grow. *Bad* people hurt others because that's what they do, but *hurt* people often hurt others by default instead of malice. When we take a moment to focus on someone's unhealthy state and what caused it, we can have some solace in the fact that while they can be difficult, hurtful, or even toxic, there is hope in their condition.

Don Richard Riso and Russ Hudson, the founders of the Enneagram Institute, suggested that there are nine levels of health for each type— three healthy, three average, and three unhealthy. Most of us will live in the average space, but migrate to healthy and unhealthy places of our personality from time to time. This is one of the reasons why most Enneagram teachers focus on each type's average or negative traits. Most people operate out of that average space, so the unhealthier their personality becomes, the more distinct their characteristics. When we are healthy and start to achieve balance, we all start to look alike!

For example, a healthy Enneagram Two and healthy Enneagram Eight will appear to be pretty similar from the outside. It's only when we get to their more negative behaviors and what they've had to overcome to become healthy that we see their true differences.

● ● ●

IN HEALTH, ALL ENNEAGRAM TYPES WILL EXHIBIT MOST OF THE HEALTHY QUALITIES OF THE OTHERS.

● ● ●

This is why you may have struggled to type yourself if you are emotionally healthy. In health, all Enneagram types will exhibit most of the healthy qualities of the others. Health is where we all meet at the center of the Enneagram diagram, with our image of God shining brightest as we trust in His good design for us.

To clarify this concept, healthy versus unhealthy is different from stress versus growth. Stress and growth are seasons, whereas health is more about your overall maturity. You can be a healthy person who is in a season of stress, and you can be an unhealthy person who is in a season of growth. In fact, healthy people deal with their stress season much better than average or unhealthy people. Instead of coping by using the negative behaviors of their stress number, they actually can use that energy to dip into the positive side of that type. However, you have to be pretty healthy in order for that to be your automatic response.

DIFFERENT LEVELS OF HEALTH

Here are some brief explanations of how each type functions when in different levels of health.

ENNEAGRAM ONE

+ *Healthy*: A One's *right or wrong* thinking is mature and much more kindly presented to others. They no longer push people around, stress out, or fixate on their ideals, but can accept that their way may not be the *right way* to do everything. Health most often occurs when the One realizes that their inner critic is a bully, and they become kinder to themselves in their own thought life. Healthy Ones make amazing leaders because they can be trusted to do what is right.

+ *Average*: Ones go through life with a frustrated undertone. Nobody listens to them, everyone else is breaking the rules without consequence, and their pursuit of perfection is exhausting. This causes average Ones to be snippy and impersonal; if confronted about their mood, they're defensive. After all, they're only trying to do the right thing, so if they stepped on your toes, you should not have been in the way.

+ *Unhealthy*: Ones are highly critical of others, obsessive over anything they think they can control, and often workaholics. At their most unhealthy, Ones become mean to rid their life of rule-breakers, their inner critic torments them, and depression starts to sink in. Alone and miserable, these Ones can become plagued with obsessive-compulsive disorder, depressive disorders, and suicidal thoughts.

ENNEAGRAM TWO

+ *Healthy*: Twos can leave a legacy like Mother Teresa. Compassionate, selfless, forgiving, and kind, a healthy Two has learned the art of letting go of expectations and finding their reward in Christ. They are not tempted to bend over backwards for others, but recognize how they can actually help. They have boundaries, know when to say "no," and take breaks, yet they are still generous, warmhearted, and happy.

+ *Average*: Twos can easily fall into the trap of people-pleasing, over-stepping bounds, and meddling—all in the name of love, of course. An average Two will die on the hill of good intentions and has a hard time accepting that their help may not be needed. They can even become hurt if people ask them to step back. These Twos work themselves ragged for other people and often lament how rarely they think of themselves.

+ *Unhealthy*: Twos take on the role of an unappreciated martyr. Having done their part and feeling no return for their efforts, these Twos become manipulative and domineering to get your praise. They may even fake illness, abuse medication or food, or lie to gain your sympathy. They are masters at excusing away any perceived wrongdoing because they themselves are the ultimate victims.

ENNEAGRAM THREE

+ *Healthy*: Healthy Threes *are* the things they believe they are—impactful, generous, and energetic motivators, with a love for people and life. Often speakers, politicians, authors, or ladder climbers, wherever they happen to be, a healthy Three will use their privilege for the glory of God and the good of others. Self-awareness is the biggest hallmark of a healthy Three and results in a much more humble person.

+ *Average*: Threes get stuff done, paying little to no attention to the more emotional side of life. Tasks are clear; feelings are not. This can lead to hurt in relationships, fear of commitment, too much focus on what people can do for them, and workaholism. Highly image conscious, these Threes will often be mistaken for Ones (they want to appear to be perfect) or Sevens (they want everyone to want them around). Average Threes are not very self-aware, so they often struggle to find their Enneagram type.

+ *Unhealthy*: At their most unhealthy, Threes will fall victim to delusions of grandeur, lying so often that they start to believe their own lies. They suffer from delusional jealousy of others' success, which can cause them to maliciously steal opportunities from others, and they can even live double lives. These Threes will literally do whatever it takes to appear to be successful and often leave behind a trail of destruction and hurt.

ENNEAGRAM FOUR

+ *Healthy*: Fours have found the key to respecting emotions without being consumed by them. There is no one more empathetic, understanding, and caring toward people who are hurting than a healthy Four; in fact, Fours are often drawn to hurting people. A healthy Four will still fight the envy, longing, and drama that is associated with their type, but it'll rarely be more than a thought that's quickly dismissed. Their lack of outer drama will make others and even themselves doubt their Fourness, but a healthy Four is self-aware. They dive into their creative gifts and make the world a more beautiful place without being hindered by others' talents.

+ *Average*: Fours will feel strongly, not seeing any choice but to dwell in whatever thoughts and feelings pop up. Protecting themselves from shame, they'll often blame their mood or emotions on outer circumstances, and others may think they're no fun to be around. Average Fours ooze creativity, but there's always something or someone else's talent that stops them from pursuing what they love. They will often do the push/pull game with relationships— testing to see if you truly love them, even with all their missing pieces, and proving themselves unlovable when you leave.

+ *Unhealthy*: Fours give us tragic "they had so much talent, but…" stories. Think of Kurt Cobain, Amy Winehouse, or River Phoenix, for example. When an unhealthy Four experiences the shame of feeling like an imposter, the emotions that say they are fundamentally flawed, and the memories that dare them to think anything could ever get better, the result is often fatal addictions and self-hatred.

ENNEAGRAM FIVE

+ *Healthy*: Fives not only understand and observe the world, but they enrich it with their wisdom. Healthy Fives might still feel the inner panic of the world pulling on their resources, but they don't give in to its demands as much as they normally would. Branching out socially and making friendships helps these Fives continue to narrow their expectations for time alone and expand their desire for company. They will be masters in whatever topic piques their interest and often write books or teach.

+ *Average*: Fives need a lot of time to process and think things through before acting and may experience a fair amount of social anxiety. Average Fives won't view themselves as isolated, but will rarely accept a spontaneous invitation because they tend to hoard their energy. Feeling the need to have strong personal opinions can make average Fives unintentionally argumentative and negative. Sensing others don't put the same amount of thought as they do into any given subject, an average Five will often come off as arrogant.

+ *Unhealthy*: Fives can become a textbook recluse like Ted Kaczynski, the Unabomber. Unhealthy Fives, with only themselves to fact check their thought life, can fall prey to odd or extreme ideas. They'll demonize social structure and purposely push people away by being mean and argumentative. At their most unhealthy, Fives will have a schizophrenic overtone and may even become violent or suicidal.

ENNEAGRAM SIX

+ *Healthy*: This Six might look nothing like the description of Sixes you have in your head. A truly healthy Six is an absolute sweetheart, carefully tending to their relationships and duties. They are fun, easygoing, courageous, and really relational, valuing loyalty over judgment in friendships, which makes them attractive to all types. Their anxieties may continue to ebb and flow like waves, but chances are, only God will hear them spoken aloud. Instead of clinging to authority for security, they'll come to fully grasp that humans will always fail and only God can give us the security we crave.

+ *Average*: Vigilant against threats, Sixes will view you as either a friend (can do no wrong) or a foe (can only do wrong). They become clingy in relationships, counting on the people they admire for guidance and security. These Sixes will look more like the common descriptions of Sixes, which is why healthy Sixes find it hard to type themselves. An average to slightly unhealthy Six may cover up much of their anxiety with sarcasm and humor, or self-sabotage before they can be abandoned by becoming angry and mean.

+ *Unhealthy*: Sixes can become paralyzed and panicky. Seeing danger around every corner and focusing on the negative will often make their fear of losing companionship a self-fulfilling prophecy. Sadly, being one of the addiction-prone types, unhealthy Sixes may turn to drugs or alcohol to numb their anxieties, and many lose their lives to addiction.

ENNEAGRAM SEVEN

+ *Healthy*: Sevens are a bright light and breath of fresh air to our world; other types may only dream about Sevens' experiences. Contentedness is the virtue of a healthy Seven; their already happy disposition is bolstered by the ability to find joy in the present moment. A Seven is always going to be up for an adventure, but a healthy Seven no longer relies on the excitement of what's next to be happy; instead they can rest in the joy that comes from Christ and be happy whether adventure is around the corner or not. A healthy Seven will have forgiven those they felt abandoned by in childhood and processed that deep wound in their own way, finding forgiveness a hard but necessary part of life. This forgiveness only adds to the carefree nature that Sevens possess.

+ *Average*: We love hanging out with our *average to unhealthy* Sevens, but never really count on them in the long run because our instincts tell us that they are unreliable. If you've ever watched the A&E show *Intervention*, you'll have seen many interviews in which a family member describes their loved one as the life of the party, happy, and carefree, so they're baffled when this person becomes a drug addict, thief, or prostitute. Along with Fours and Sixes, Sevens are one of the addictive personalities on the Enneagram. Their impulse control issues, combined with pain avoidance, can create the perfect addiction storm when they're unhealthy. They may be at risk for impulse suicide, according to the Enneagram Institute.

+ *Unhealthy*: Sevens will have impulse-control issues, forget or disregard commitments, sabotage relationships, and overindulge in almost anything that's exciting. These Sevens are nowhere to be found when the rubber hits the road. They often feel frustrated, bored, or disappointed.

ENNEAGRAM EIGHT

+ *Healthy*: Eights are just as confident, energetic, and assertive as ever, but there's a tangible compassion about the way they listen and care for others. These Eights use their strength to protect others and often champion the underdogs in society. At their most healthy, Eights will embrace the emotions they feel and not discount emotions as a weakness in themselves or others.

+ *Average*: Eights will easily intimidate others without even trying. Not wanting to be controlled, they often jump into leadership roles and lose respect for people who don't pull their weight. An average to slightly unhealthy Eight isn't afraid of conflict and will use conflict as a way of determining whether others are worthy of respect, often not understanding how terrifying this is to types prone to withdraw.

+ *Unhealthy*: Eights will lose sight of their own mortality and often have delusions of grandeur. Think of some of the most intimidating gangsters in history like Al Capone and John Dillinger. Flying off the handle when they feel disrespected, these Eights have little patience or compassion for others. The Enneagram Institute has even referred to unhealthy Eights as "murderous."

ENNEAGRAM NINE

+ *Healthy*: Nines are confident enough in themselves and their relationships to engage in healthy conflict without feeling paralyzing fear. Trusting themselves and others, they no longer feel like they need to go along to get along; they focus on the long-term goals instead of momentary peace in their relationships. Feeling self-aware and fulfilled, a healthy Nine can put routines in their life to make sure they stay on task and do what is necessary.

+ *Average*: Nines will often say "yes" before realizing they don't actually mean it and experience clouded judgment when they can sense what the other person wants. Avoiding conflict at all costs, these Nines can be easily bossed around by other types. These Nines become resentful and quietly obstinate when they feel pushed. An average Nine will view merging as how they care for others, without counting the personal cost to themselves. However, God didn't give someone else's life, pain, or opinions to the Nines; they need to be themselves.

+ *Unhealthy*: Nines will become detached and repressed, not wanting to be affected by life. The suppressed anger they've always had will now start to appear more often, causing others to become uneasy around them. These Nines will be unpredictable, neglectful, and numb, making them dangerous to themselves and others.

● ● ● ● ● ● ● ● ●

Living in excess of our personality means that our core characteristics become stronger and more visible. For example, if we tend toward selfishness, we live fully focused on ourselves. If we yearn to please people, we change ourselves completely to fulfill what others want from us. This idea of excess is seen vividly in the season of adolescence and illustrates why many Enneagram teachers think that behavior in our youth may be the key to accurate typing.

One of the ways we misjudge both our own adolescence and those around us going through this season is the false assumption that being immature is being unhealthy. Rather than being unhealthy, most adolescents are exhibiting negative stress coping skills. Don't get me wrong, there are teens out there who fit the unhealthy characteristics of their type to a T, but they are not the vast majority.

● ● ●

WE NEED TO COME ALONGSIDE THOSE WHO ARE IMMATURE AND HELP THEM RATHER THAN WRITING THEM OFF AS INCURABLE, TOXIC, SELFISH, OR TOO HARD.

● ● ●

We would do better as a culture to come alongside those who are immature and help them mature rather than writing them off as incurable, toxic, selfish, or too hard. Those of us who are still growing need support more than anything else; trying to live without it can plummet us into unhealthy behaviors during our early adulthood.

God speaks kindly toward those who are children—not expecting them to be mature, serve in the office of elder, or have a solid doctrine. Instead, they need to be trained, loved, and raised up.

First Corinthians 3:2 tells us, *"I fed you with milk, not solid food, for you were not ready for it. And even now you are not yet ready."* This Scripture informs us that there is a time and a place for immaturity—and immaturity is not wrong as long as it is a stage.

If there are adolescents in your life, I hope this encourages you to support them with patience. If you are in this age group, I hope that knowing adolescence is just a passing season helps you have grace for yourself as you are figuring out life.

INTROVERT VS. EXTROVERT

Most of us are familiar with the idea that people can be introverted or extroverted. It's something we tend to notice about others right away. We might even think we know why some people come across as more bubbly or reserved than others. Like the Enneagram, this concept helps us value our specific strengths and not judge those who are dissimilar. Of course, there are those of us who do continue to judge both ourselves and others based on our differences, but for the most part, discovering whether someone is introverted or extroverted and why benefits all of us, particularly in social situations.

Stereotypically, introverts gain energy from the time they spend alone to recharge—quietly reading a book, for example, or soaking in a hot tub or bubble bath. Extroverts gain their energy from being around people; they love traveling, parties, and adrenaline rushes.

But the concept of introversion and extroversion tends to fall apart when we are talking about the Enneagram. Someone with high energy is typically said to be an extrovert, whereas someone who is reserved is said to be an introvert. These are broad-stroke assumptions that don't take different Enneagram types into account.

For example, most people assume you'd have to be an extrovert to be an Enneagram Seven, or you'd have to be an introvert to be an Enneagram

Five. However, I believe it's more helpful to consider a person's energy level after a social engagement as a deciding factor when thinking of them as introverted or extroverted.

If you go to a dinner party, have a good time, and arrive home late, do you feel so energetic that you struggle to fall asleep, or are you so exhausted that you're out like a light before your head even hits the pillow? Your answer to that question will give me a pretty good idea whether you are an extrovert or an introvert. This is not determined by how much you talked or your particular social prowess. Whether something helps you gain energy or drains you cannot be determined at first glance. We need to see the results. Those who are extroverts get fully charged in social situations, while introverts get depleted. That is what being introverted or extroverted means at its very core.

● ● ●

WHETHER SOMETHING HELPS YOU GAIN ENERGY OR DRAINS YOU CANNOT BE DETERMINED AT FIRST GLANCE. WE NEED TO SEE THE RESULTS.

● ● ●

There are other theories about processing situations as an introvert or extrovert. There are also other labels such as omnivert (someone who is outgoing or reserved depending on the situation) and ambivert (someone who is willing to either talk or listen in any situation). But all of these are rooted in the idea of extroverted or introverted social energy that has most impacted Western culture and stereotyping.

In my own Enneagram coaching practice, I haven't seen any of these theories to be as helpful as the concept of how energy is gained. I want to make sure that you fully understand the basics through and through because too many theories and too much information often make the core less visible.

We will reference different types of energy when we are talking about Enneagram types, but keep in mind that these do not indicate introversion or extroversion in the traditional sense.

We will gain task energy, physical energy, and emotional energy from a variety of places, ranging from eating healthy food to growing in discipline and self-care. You will need to replenish these types of energy regardless of your capacity to gain social energy from other people or from being alone.

Here is a rundown on where we all stand on the energy scale of the Enneagram. Wings can also play a role here. (See chapter 19 on Wings for more information.)

MOST ENERGY

+ *Enneagram Eight*, particularly 8w7 (Eight with a Seven wing), has the most energy on the Enneagram, with a combined big mental, physical, and social capacity. Eights tend to have less emotional energy, so if they are in a particularly emotionally charged social situation, they would start to feel drained before other types.

+ *Enneagram Seven*, 7w8, is almost tied with 8w7 for the most energy because of similar resources and capacity. However, Sevens avoid the more negative aspects of life, which can give them a more limited capacity toward conflict as well as emotionally charged situations.

+ *Enneagram Three*, especially 3w2, will have high social and task energy. Having a big vision for the future and a lot of social aware-ness keeps them going at pedal-to-the-metal speed. However, like their aggressive stance counterparts, they will have a limited capacity toward emotional situations.

MEDIUM ENERGY

+ *Enneagram One* has a lot of energy toward tasks that support their worldview, including their responsibilities, actions that will make life better, and social situations. If a One has a rule in their head regarding a given situation, they have endless energy about follow-ing that rule and doing what needs to be done.

+ *Enneagram Two* has a lot of social energy, especially in anticipation of doing things that will make others feel loved, appreciated, and valued. Twos' minds are preoccupied with relationships, so they tend to have energy for any kind of positive action that nurtures those relationships.

+ *Enneagram Six* types tend to describe themselves as pretty balanced energy-wise. They have access to the wings of both Seven and Five, which are on the top and bottom of the energy spectrum. Sixes have a lot of energy when it comes to precautionary planning or doing things for those to whom they are loyal. For someone outside their group or things that don't make sense to them, the Six will be reluctant to act.

LEAST ENERGY

+ *Enneagram Four*, like Six, has access to wings of both the most and the least energy. However, Fours are part of the withdrawn stance and their tendency to withdraw inward makes them more likely to be introverted rather than extroverted. Fours will have little energy toward anything they don't feel like doing. But they can have endless energy for deep conversations, whatever they are passionate about at the moment, or the spaces that make them feel like they are living out their purpose.

+ *Enneagram Five* tends to have quite a bit of mental and physical energy but limited social and emotional energy. Extroverted Fives need to be around those they are most comfortable with in order to gain energy to be around everyone else.

+ *Enneagram Nine* is known as the type with the least energy overall. Physical, task, mental, future planning, mundane, emotional, and social energy can all be in short supply. Luckily, Nines tend to develop coping skills around preserving their energy, which keeps their inner peace intact. (See chapter 11 on Subtypes for more about self-preservation Nines.) For Nines who struggle with low energy and the need to keep "showing up" in ways that keep relational peace yet drain them, the balance can be hard to develop.

ANY TYPE CAN BE EITHER

Any Enneagram type can be either introverted or extroverted, as the way we gain energy has little to do with our capacity to hold it or utilize it and even less to do with our core motivations in life.

Of course, those types who fall into the "most energy" category have the greatest chance of being traditional extroverts—but they don't have to be. Nor do those in the "least energy" category have to be introverts.

● ● ●

COMING INTO OUR OWN SELF, EITHER INTROVERTED OR EXTROVERTED, IS USUALLY CEMENTED IN OUR ADOLESCENCE.

● ● ●

Coming into our own self, either introverted or extroverted, is usually cemented in our adolescence. Whether you're changing from how you were perceived as a child or continuing along a strong pattern, you're likely aware of how others perceive your energy. Because the years of adolescence are so formative, these observations can become somewhat of a cage that inhibits us our entire lives, whether or not we understand what introversion or extroversion truly mean. We know what people think we are, leaving us either feeling misunderstood or labeled.

I think this is why the "other" categories for energy labeling have become so popular. We have felt misunderstood by traditional introvert and extrovert stereotypes, so new categories like ambivert and omnivert have made us feel understood on a deeper level.

However, I've found that most people who relate to these categories do fit into the traditional introvert/extrovert mold, but not in social situations.

Tina is an Enneagram Five, but others are often surprised to learn this about her. She gives off big-energy vibes in social situations, being anything but a wallflower. She calls herself an ambivert because she enjoys being around people…but she also needs time alone. When she gets home from social events, she is drained in every sense of the word, which means she is a traditional introvert.

Alex is an Enneagram Seven but doesn't like to start conversations. Once someone starts talking to him, however, he turns on and is engaging. Social expectations stress him out because his parents emphasized the importance of first impressions. Once he gets home from a social situation, he is more chatty and energized than he was when he left. He almost needs to get into a social situation before having energy for it, making him a traditional extrovert.

Putting people into categories and boxes is not only second nature, it's oddly comforting. We use labels to help us try to understand others. Obviously, our need to label and stereotype each other as humans is telling; we want to think we can grasp how others think and feel, even on a rudimentary level.

What we are typically observing about people when we want to categorize them as introverted or extroverted is whether they are engaging or reserved. You can be a reserved person and be an extrovert, or be engaging and be an introvert, so observing simple social graces and their effect isn't a great way to understand a person as a whole.

● ● ●

BEING INTROVERTED OR EXTROVERTED FEELS LIMITING WHEN WE GIVE THESE LABELS THE POWER TO EXPLAIN ANYTHING OTHER THAN HOW WE GAIN ENERGY.

● ● ●

Being introverted or extroverted feels limiting when we give these labels the power to explain anything other than how we gain energy. Introversion does not mean you are quiet, any more than being tall ensures that you like basketball. In many ways, stereotypes are limiting, leave us feeling misunderstood and categorized, and can be unkind.

This is why the Enneagram and its nine types cannot be broken down into simple stereotypical explanations of introverted or extroverted—and neither can you. No one is loud and in charge 100 percent of the time, nor is anyone introspective and withdrawn 100 percent of the time. We all have our autopilot, which can be exceedingly loud in adolescence, but we are also capable of using coping behaviors to grow out of autopilot mode if it's keeping us stuck.

10

MALE VS. FEMALE

I remember getting my driver's license and the wonderful feeling of freedom it gave me. I could go to stores, meet someone for coffee, or just drive around with no one supervising me.

However, I quickly learned that the expectations laid out for my brother were decidedly different from what I would be allowed to do. He had a lot more freedom than I did. I was warned that I needed to be cautious not to present myself as being alone in public unless I was in a highly populated area—and even then, my dad would tell me what to do if I was involved in an attempted kidnapping or assault.

My parents were trying to protect me, and I am grateful for that. But those words of advice and warning gave me my first indication of what it was like to be a woman in this world and how different things were for men.

Being male or female impacts every season of your life in numerous ways, but as an adolescent moving into adulthood, these differences and expectations of gender are especially heavy. Gender determines everything from where you are allowed to go to what you're expected to wear and the choices you are permitted to make.

● ● ●

THE DIFFERENCES AND EXPECTATIONS OF GENDER INFLUENCE HOW WE VIEW ENNEAGRAM TYPES.

● ● ●

Gender biases differ from culture to culture, but my experience is fairly typical for Western society. These biases even impact how we view Enneagram types. To give you an example, answer this question:

True or false? Most Twos are female.

Every six months, I release a quiz on Enneagram knowledge for my future coaching students. This quiz is meant to gauge their Enneagram knowledge and discern whether they would make a good Enneagram coach. Every test is a little different, but I keep a couple of core questions the same, including this one about most Twos being female. And one out of every three potential students gets this question wrong.

There is a prevalent misconception that Enneagram types can be gender leaning. People naturally assume that most Twos are female, most Fives are male, and so on.

This bias is often self-confirmed because most of the Twos you know are female and most of the Fives you know are male. All of the posts about Twos on social media are about mothering, hosting, and needing to lean into self-care, while all of the Five posts are about needing to access your emotions, function in a workplace, and let people into your space. Assumptions about gender and the Enneagram are largely based on cultural stereotypes and can lead to mistyping. There is no pattern of facts supporting the idea that gender affects one's Enneagram type.

For example, I see so many women who type their husbands, brothers, and fathers as Threes, Fives, Eights, or Nines. This places masculinity into two basic categories:

1. You can be a loud, aggressive, and impulsive male, like Eights and Threes

2. You can be a quiet, passive, and cerebral male, like Fives and Nines

On the other hand, an overwhelming majority of women test as Twos and Fours, the two most outwardly emotional types on the Enneagram.

It is my understanding that the Enneagram is not gender leaning, but our cultural and personal biases are. When we test for our type, we select the facts about ourselves that have been called out in us. In Western culture especially, women are praised for being helpful, sweet, and nurturing, while men are praised for being strong, smart, and assertive. These compliments impact how we think about ourselves, what we are good at, and *who* we should be much more than we might assume.

● ● ●

GENDER-BIASED COMPLIMENTS CAN IMPACT HOW WE THINK ABOUT OURSELVES AND WHAT WE ARE GOOD AT, WHICH IN TURN CAN AFFECT OUR ASSUMED ENNEAGRAM TYPE.

● ● ●

We know men can be emotional and we know women are just as smart as men, yet we still have these versions of ourselves that are impacted by our cultural biases of what gender should look like. We grow up thinking that boys shouldn't play with dolls and be nurturing, and girls shouldn't want to play with toy weapons and defend their families.

But what happens when children don't fit the stereotypical boxes we have set out for them? I've witnessed worried and panicked parents do a lot of damage to their children even though they mean well.

We know that God made us male and female; He gave us different genetic codes, abilities, and hormone levels. Even the curses after the fall were gender specific. But as is the case with most things that are made by God, we tend to take God's good design to extremes. We try to make gender an all-defining identity that comes with a list of do's and don'ts instead of a specific duty station. Or, at the other end of the spectrum, some think your gender is something you can decide instead of something God decides.

Gender is a physical reality given by our all-sovereign God with specific abilities and responsibilities. But your uterus or lack thereof doesn't impact your personality leanings as much as you might think. Your gender impacts your Enneagram typing only because gender affects how you see yourself and who you are allowed to be.

● ● ●

ENNEAGRAM TYPES ARE BASED ON OUR UNDERLYING MOTIVATIONS,
WHICH HAVE NOTHING TO DO WITH GENDER.

● ● ●

Enneagram types are no more female- or male-oriented than flavors of ice cream. They are based on our underlying motivations, which have nothing to do with gender. However, because gender biases are so ingrained in how we think, it can be hard for us to clearly picture what an Enneagram Five could look like as a female, or what an Enneagram Two could look like as a male. So let me share two scenarios with you.

A MALE ENNEAGRAM TWO

Oliver is the oldest son in a family with three kids. Growing up, he was told he was too sensitive and needed to toughen up. Trying to please his parents, Oliver would join sports teams, go hunting with his dad, and project his needs onto others. He came across as selfless, caring, and deeply protective of those he loved, but Oliver learned early on not to show emotion on the outside because that was "what girls did." The tears only fell when he was alone. Oliver dreamed of being a husband and father. He had so much love to pour into a family of his own, but he wouldn't verbalize his dreams in a romantic way; instead, he would engage in *locker room talk* to mask his deeply romantic heart.

Now married with kids of his own, Oliver pours his love into protecting his family. He is always there for them, goes over safety protocols, and checks in often to make sure everyone is fine and doesn't need anything. Oliver's family mistakenly thinks he's a Six on the Enneagram but in reality, he's a Two.

A FEMALE ENNEAGRAM FIVE

Ashley was a quiet kid who was often called "mature for her age." Raised in a single-parent home, Ashley had to bear the weight of her mom's emotional ups and downs. Growing up, Ashley felt like she was the parent, and it honestly exhausted her—but who else would be there for her mother?

Ashley knew she had deep emotions, but she was always too focused on other people to really reflect on what she herself was feeling. Who had time for that? She knew she was introverted, but if someone needed her, she was there, no questions asked, even if she paid the price for the sacrifice later.

Ashley became a schoolteacher. After she married her high school sweetheart, she settled down in the same town as her mom so she could be close to her.

When Ashley was introduced to the Enneagram, she tested as a Two and didn't give it a second thought. She does often put others first, has intense feelings that shame her, and is passionate about cooking. However, Ashley is actually an Enneagram Five.

GENDER-BASED MISTYPING

Time after time, in coaching session after coaching session, I have heard women say they aren't tough enough to be an Eight, not successful enough to be a Three, or not dispassionate enough to be a Five. So they tend to mistype as these numbers' wing or stress types, identifying with those parts of their core number at least a little bit.

It can be even harder for men to see through all of the expectations put on them and discover their real type. A 2w3 can look a lot like a Three or an Eight if they are male. A Nine can be mistyped as an Eight. A male Four can easily be mistyped as a Seven or a Three.

So taking all of this into account, what do males and females who are trying to fit into the stereotype of their gender look like for each type?

ENNEAGRAM ONE

Male: A male One will more easily embrace the anger and frustration he feels than a female One will. His rules and guidelines for life are held tightly, and it feels disrespectful when people disobey them. Male Ones are more open about their preferences than female Ones because they don't have to worry about being seen as *the B word.*

Female: A female One will often direct her rules toward eating and cleaning. These topics are heavily advertised to women as things over which they have control and should care about doing *the right way.* Female Ones learn early to temper their frustration, pickiness, and options so others will experience them as nice people, not bossy.

ENNEAGRAM TWO (STEREOTYPED AS FEMALE)

Male: A male Two can come across as protective and strong rather than soft and nurturing due to cultural expectations. They're hyper-aware of the needs of others and feel loved when people go to them for advice or help. Going to Eight in stress strengthens this phenomenon and causes a lot of male Twos to mistype as Eights.

Female: A female Two will find it easy to step into the role of mother in almost any situation. Being the shoulder to cry on, the advice giver, and the overall warm, respected, and adored individual is a female Two's happy place. To achieve this, she needs to be available and seen as always willing to help. This leaves the female Two feeling a large weight of guilt whenever she needs to say no.

ENNEAGRAM THREE (STEREOTYPED AS MALE)

Male: A male Three typically uses his social prowess and drive to climb the career ladder. He is seen as driven, competitive, and a gifted schmoozer. The only person not impressed by a male Three is perhaps the Three himself. He thinks he is never good enough, there's never enough time, and things are never perfect. The male Three will go, go, go...until he burns out in a big way.

Female: A female Three tends to fixate on career or relationships. She tends to develop a useful Two wing to help her fit into cultural norms and be seen as a successful woman. Female Threes often struggle to have close nurturing friendships because of a tendency to be the leader who facilitates developing friendships in a group. Female Threes can often be seen as bossy, materialistic, or too competitive—traits that are seen as assets in the male Three.

ENNEAGRAM FOUR (STEREOTYPED AS FEMALE)

Male: Enneagram Four is one of the hardest types to be as a male in our society. Overly sensitive, emotional, and just not tough enough are all things a male Four is likely to hear about himself in his lifetime. Male Fours love beautiful things, a good cry, and romance just as much as female Fours, but it's not as culturally accepted for them to embrace these things fully.

Female: A female Four will often grow up hearing that she is dramatic and should not be so sensitive; in general, she feels misunderstood. Female Fours feel free to be romantic, embrace their aesthetic, and talk about how they cry while watching movies. However, female Fours may still bear the judgment of people thinking their hormones are raging and their emotions are not authentic.

ENNEAGRAM FIVE (STEREOTYPED AS MALE)

Male: No one is surprised when they encounter a male Five. They are quiet, often nerdy, and highly focused on whatever their *thing* is. They thrive in information technology but you can find a few in almost any major field. Male Fives are independent, hardworking, self-controlled, and protective of their energy.

Female: A female Five will feel pressure to express more emotion, to be softer and more social. Sometimes these pressures will work, and the female Five will learn to be social, emotional, and giving in her own way—a pressure male Fives rarely feel. Female Fives tend to lean into their Four wing to find their emotional side and their stress number Seven to find the energy for all that is expected of them. It's not uncommon for a female Five to be mistyped.

ENNEAGRAM SIX

Male: A male Six comes across as steady, dependable, and often funny. They hide their anxiety behind humor, preparedness, and keeping their loved ones close. They are the father bear of the family, even from a young age. They want to be connected and counted on.

Female: A female Six seems to be diligent, skeptical, and cautious. Feeling more comfortable voicing their anxiety than their male counterparts are and sometimes having more to fear in the way of physical safety, female Sixes tend to be labeled as "too careful" or told, "You worry too much." It's easier for them to find their type than it is for male Sixes.

ENNEAGRAM SEVEN (IN HOLLYWOOD, MOSTLY MALE)

Male: A male Seven is upbeat, fun, and easy to talk to. Male Sevens typically have more freedom to act on their impulses than female Sevens do, and their recklessness isn't seen as irresponsible.

Female: A female Seven is bubbly, sweet, and energetic. She will feel more pressure to settle down and express unpleasant emotions than a male Seven would, leading her to sometimes feel out of place when in the company of just females.

ENNEAGRAM EIGHT (STEREOTYPED AS MALE)

Male: A male Eight presents as assertive, protective, and confident. His intimidation factor works to his advantage as it commands a certain amount of respect and a "don't mess with me" vibe.

Female: For females, an Eight is the hardest type to be in our society. They are often pressured to show more emotion, keep their opinions to themselves, not be as assertive, and—my personal eye-roll favorite—smile more. Female Eights either go the route of trying to soften and change to meet cultural norms, often mistyping as Twos, or they fully embrace themselves as strong.

ENNEAGRAM NINE

Male: A male Nine tends to be quiet, thoughtful, and a little flighty. It's easy for him to just ride the waves of the cares and wants of others, and he rarely picks a fight. A male Nine will shove his opinions, wants, and needs aside until he eventually explodes, feeling taken advantage of and unheard, but these episodes are few and far between.

Female: A female Nine is sweet, a good listener, and what many people call "sensitive." Female Nines find themselves in more social situations where help, empathy, and listening are seen as gifts, making them great friends. But they also get taken advantage of more than male Nines. They aren't able to coast through life as quietly as male Nines are because they are typically the ones who decide what's for dinner every night, buy the Christmas gifts, and handle the family's interpersonal dramas.

WE ALL REFLECT GOD

Every type has its own quirks and hardships due to the cultural expectations of gender. Thankfully, although this can impact typing, it has no impact on the strengths you possess as the type you are. Males and females alike reflect God's divine and perfect character, showing aspects of Him to the world around them in their own purposeful way.

● ● ●

ALL OF US REFLECT GOD'S DIVINE AND PERFECT CHARACTER, SHOWING ASPECTS OF HIM TO THE WORLD AROUND US IN OUR OWN PURPOSEFUL WAY.

● ● ●

In adolescence, the negative differences our culture places on each sex become painfully apparent. These differences exist when we are children, but they aren't as loud. It is only when we enter adolescence and experience the push/pull of attraction that our differences become more manifest.

Gender is loud during the adolescent years. We can be tempted to make the pressures of gender all-consuming, either fixating on fighting them or trying to conform to them.

11

SUBTYPES

As humans, we have instincts such as fight or flight, a craving for certain foods, or gut feelings. However, when we talk about Enneagram subtypes, we are talking about relational instincts. These can be helpful variants to consider when you're confused about your type or don't relate to its common descriptions.

We are exploring subtypes in this section on adolescence because this season tends to be the first time your subtype can change. Thus it seems like your personality in general is changing.

The three relational instincts are:

- Self-Preservation (Sp): this subtype values security and is highly aware of their health and safety. Their equilibrium is upset when they don't feel like themselves physically.

- Social (So): this subtype feels a sense of belonging. They are highly aware of the health of their relationships with family and friends. Their equilibrium is upset when relationships are unsettled or there is conflict.

- One-to-One (Sx): this subtype values intimacy and is highly aware of the health of a few intimate relationships. Their equilibrium is upset when they feel rejected or alone. This instinct may be called the sexual subtype—hence the Sx acronym—but I have found that in addition to romantic relationships, this subtype may cling to close friends or a parental figure. One-to-One therefore seems to be the best descriptor.

WHAT ARE SUBTYPES?

As humans, we have instincts (fight or flight for example) but when we talk about Enneagram instincts we are talking about relational instincts.

These can be helpful variants to look at when you're confused about your type or don't relate to the common descriptions of your type.

One-to-One (Sx)   Self-Preservation (Sp)   Social (So)

It is said that an individual will have a dominant subtype and a secondary subtype, with the remaining subtype being their blind spot. This is called stacking.

Your dominant subtype accounts for 51 to 90 percent of your behaviors, while the secondary one accounts for 49 to 10 percent of your behaviors. The blind spot will be where you see insecurities and problem areas. Here are some examples:

+ If you are blind in your self-preservation instinct, you will doubt what your body is telling you. You might not see the doctor when something is wrong, or you might forget to eat or drink enough water to stay hydrated.

+ If you are blind in your social instinct, you will struggle to find your place within a group, whether with family or coworkers, and socialization might feel like pressure to perform.

+ If you are blind in the one-to-one instinct, you may struggle when you are beginning a relationship because you are unable to feel chemistry. You may doubt that people like you or have a hard time noticing if they do.

One of the questions I often hear as an Enneagram coach is, "Do subtypes change?" The answer is yes!

We have a dominant subtype because that is the instinct that is working best to fulfill our needs. If you experience a major change in your life—going off to college, having kids, or changing jobs, for instance—then the subtype that works best to meet your needs can change too.

● ● ●

IF YOU EXPERIENCE A MAJOR CHANGE IN YOUR LIFE, THEN THE SUBTYPE THAT WORKS BEST TO MEET YOUR NEEDS CAN CHANGE TOO.

● ● ●

This is one of the reasons we feel like we can't possibly be one Enneagram type for our whole life. Most of us will see a big shift in personality because of subtype change, wing shifts, or a move to stress or growth.

Typically, I'll see firstborn daughters grow up with a social instinct "for the good of the group." It can make them appear Two-ish no matter what their core number is. Then they'll go off to college, have their first serious boyfriend, and all of a sudden, their "group" is only one person and their one-to-one instinct takes center stage. Later on, when they're married with kids or experiencing a health issue, their self-preservation instinct will become loud as their bodily needs and security are threatened.

Here is a rundown of each type with each instinct:

ENNEAGRAM ONE

THE PERFECTIONIST/SELF-PRESERVATION

Ones who have a dominant self-preservation instinct are true perfectionists. Their inner critic is hard at work on their appearance, finances, eating habits, and other aspects of their lives. These Ones are not as critical of others as they are of themselves. Enneagram teachers around the world say this subtype is "either highly anxious or highly self-controlled."

These Enneagram Ones are not likely to mistype as they fully relate to the title of "the perfectionist."

A Nine wing will subdue this subtype's energy, but it also might make them more focused on the things for which they have rules while procrastinating about everything else. They can be focused, driven, responsible, and dutiful at work, and then crash and procrastinate about responsibilities at home.

A Two wing can make this subtype feel conflicted between serving others and protecting themselves. This may be the very tension their inner critic chooses to nitpick about, and it may lead them to believe they're a Two because their thoughts are extremely relational.

Sometimes people think I'm a Six because of my anxiety! I am a very empathetic and practical person.   —*a One (Sp)*

THE TEACHER/SOCIAL

Ones with a dominant social instinct use their perfectionist angst to teach others. By both being an example and physically teaching others how to do something *the right way*, these Ones focus on their place within social circles and are generally friendlier and more laid back than the other One subtypes. These Ones may mistype as Twos or even Sixes.

A Nine wing will make this subtype more cautious about how they approach the idea of teaching others, knowing it may come off as critical. Being drawn to teaching but overthinking others' reactions can cause a lot of anxiety in this subtype—usually as they watch people do something they wish they were bold enough to teach them to do better. This anxiety can make them mistype as a Six or a stressed Nine.

A Two wing will give this subtype even more charm and sweetness as they lead others into doing things the way they think they should be done. Not only general imperfections but also relationship strife that could've been handled better will stick out to this subtype/wing combo. It is common for a 1w2 to mistype as a 2w1. (See more in chapter 7, Seasons of Stress and Growth.)

THE ZEALOT/ONE-TO-ONE

Ones with a dominant one-to-one instinct exemplify this type's other moniker, "the reformer." This is also the reason some Ones can look like Eights. Feeling secure in their one or two intimate relationships, this One looks outward at boldly improving the world around them. They are more likely to express anger outwardly than the other two subtypes are. Enneagram Ones with this instinct may be mistyped as Eights or Fours.

A Nine wing will temper this One's fire, making them look a lot like a 9w8. This subtype/wing combination may have a lot of inner conflict as they try to be good, keep the peace, and reform the world.

A Two wing will make this One even more focused on the well-being of their one or two close relationships, and they can look even more like an Eight who goes to Two in growth. A Two wing will only add to this subtype's boldness and more extroverted energy.

ENNEAGRAM TWO

THE CHARMING INNOCENT/SELF-PRESERVATION

The self-preservation Two uses their childlike, easygoing, and innocent demeanor to get their needs met. They attract the love and attention they want by being seen as needy without having to demand anything. These Twos are more aware of their physical boundaries and needs than the other Two subtypes. They can often be mistyped as Seven because of their bubbly and carefree nature.

A One wing causes this subtype to have unstated relationship rules, such as always sending a thank-you card and acknowledging their birthday on social media. They may become frustrated when people don't fall in line with these rules. This wing/subtype combo may look a lot like a fun, energetic, extroverted Seven who goes to One in stress. (Read more about arrows in chapter 7, Seasons of Stress and Growth.)

A Three wing will give this subtype even more charm and an infectious energy. They may be more driven, and the combination of being likable and driven tends to bring them accolades.

THE GLUE/SOCIAL

A Social Two is the glue that sticks families, work groups, churches, and organizations together. These Twos feel needed or loved by being at the center of social groups and communities. Assertive, visionary, and passionate, they know how to work a room. They thrive on being the one people come to in crisis or for advice, and they subconsciously avoid asking for advice or help from others. This Two may mistype as an Eight or Three, but it is the subtype that tends to type right most of the time.

A One wing will give this subtype a drive to make sure they're serving the right way and are always above reproach. Criticism can be difficult for this wing/subtype combo to swallow. Because they can have a little more critical "I know the right way" energy, this subtype of Two can mistype as an Eight.

A Three wing will make this subtype energetic and more vocal about their self-sacrifice. They are also even more socially aware than their 2w1 counterpart and respectful of social hierarchies.

THE COMPANION/ONE-TO-ONE

One-to-One subtype Twos are much more focused on helping and being needed by a few intimate relationships than the other Two subtypes. Yes, they'd love to help everyone, but knowing that's not a logical goal, they appease themselves by being available for a few people. These Twos struggle with boundaries and hearing "no" within relationships feels like a personal rejection. This Two can often mistype as a Four because their longing is so strong.

A Two with a One wing will want to be the perfect partner or friend and spend a lot of time thinking about how they can improve their relational connections. A One wing can make this subtype even more easily confused with a Four as they will have some of Four's growth tendencies.

A Three wing will add a more aggressive or competitive edge to this subtype, and they may be more openly bold when they want something. Rejection will be doubly hard for this subtype/wing type, and they may even be tempted to chameleon into whatever they think their friend or significant other wants.

ENNEAGRAM THREE

THE GREAT PROFICIENT/SELF-PRESERVATION

The self-preservation Three is the least likely to boast in their strengths compared to the other Three subtypes. This Three wants to get things done and do them well, making them resemble an Enneagram One. Although they may not like to admit it, their image is relevant to these Threes. They might struggle with anxiety over their image and whether people like them. This is the subtype of Three that is most commonly mistyped as a One.

A Two wing will add warmth and even more social charm to this subtype. A 3w2 Sp is likely to think they're a 2w1, as they may not think the driven and self-promoting nature of Threes describes them at all.

A Four wing will make this subtype even more conflicted and confused about their people-pleasing nature, as it wages war against their authenticity driven wing. A 3w4 Sp will have no limit of creative ideas and may be entrepreneurial. This Three may mistype as a logical and organized Four. They may think their Three-ness is actually going to One in growth.

THE CHAMPION/SOCIAL

The social subtype Three wants to provide for their team or circle of influence by being an effective leader and making them all look good. This Three is competitive and may get defensive in the face of criticism or failure. They can easily read a room and adjust their persona accordingly. This subtype of Three is the least likely to mistype.

A Two wing will make this subtype competitive socially. They may even see friendships and social media engagement as their version of winning. This is the most charming number/wing/subtype combination on the Enneagram.

A Four wing is likely to make this subtype want to achieve at something that is unique to them. They get a thrill out of being good at something no one else in their family has done, but not at the expense of approval from their social group.

THE ULTIMATE HOST/ONE-TO-ONE

This Three's competitive nature is usually aimed at gaining affection or praise from those they love. They want to be the best, but if they don't like you and you aren't close to them, they don't care. This subtype of Three is likely to mistype as a Two because they are extremely social and love being helpful—not because they feel like it's their responsibility but because they like the praise it brings them.

A Two wing can make this subtype even more easily confused with a Two. They are usually more energetic, competitive, and aggressive than your typical Two or 2w3. However, since Threes have a blind spot about their nature, their Two wing tendencies may be louder than their core type's motivations.

A Four wing will make this subtype a little more intense, emotional, and prone to pre-rejection thinking than a 3w2 of this subtype. They may be naturally charming, witty, and likable but they won't see themselves that way. Instead this popular Three may see themselves as misunderstood and not liked for being themselves.

ENNEAGRAM FOUR

THE IDEALIST/SELF-PRESERVATION

Self-preservation Fours still have all of the deep emotions of other Fours, but they don't communicate their emotions. Instead of vocally sharing their misfortunes to gain attention, Sp subtypes take a long-suffering approach to life. They hope that bearing their troubles in silence will make others admire them, but that's not their main goal. These Fours might've learned at an early age that displaying heavy emotions makes others uncomfortable, so they instead put on a stoic or bubbly front for others. This paradox can make them hard to type, especially if they have a Three wing; they often mistype as Sevens or Ones.

It's not a rule, but a Four with a Three wing and dominant self-preservation instinct will usually appear to be cheerful. These Fours are true extroverts and often mistyped as Sevens. Competitive and image-conscious of their own quirks, they cope with their strong emotions by trying to find hope.

A Five wing gives this subtype such an interesting dynamic. These Fours usually identify as ambiverts and struggle with finding their type.

They need alone time, tend to be investigative, and don't outwardly share their emotions except with a trusted few. These Fours display both a bubbly and stoic front to others depending on their internal resources and comfort level.

THE ROMANTIC/SOCIAL

Social subtype Fours most resemble the common descriptions of Fours; as a result, they rarely mistype. Social Fours find comfort in melancholy and suffering. They are less competitive and focus more on their place within social groups. They fear being disconnected and out of the community, but once they're in social situations, they compare themselves to others and assume they're rejected before they are. Social Fours are fixated on being understood and believe being special will make them worth getting to know.

A Three wing will make this subtype more outgoing. Although they may feel rejected in a social group, they know letting that show can be a turnoff to others. These Fours may struggle the most with oversharing and over-exaggerating their struggles.

A Five wing will make this subtype feel mature, quiet, and serious to those who don't know them, but they will go from zero to a hundred quickly when they feel like they can trust you. This Four may struggle the most with pendulum swings, trying not to be too much or not enough. Their thinking side and their feeling side are in a state of constant tension.

THE SENSITIVE ELITIST/ONE-TO-ONE

One-to-one subtype Fours look more like Eights because they're competitive, brave conflict without fear, and tend to subconsciously punish others instead of punishing themselves for their shame. These punishments can include withholding emotions, affection, invitations, or help from those they deem undeserving.

What separates this type from Eights is their deep connection to their feelings, internal shame, and how desperately they want approval from those closest to them.

A Three wing is said to make this subtype *the* most competitive combination on the Enneagram. Not only is this type unafraid of competition, but they *need* to be the best and most unique at whatever they decide to do. They have lots of energy and are much more social than their 4w5 counterpart.

I have heard a lot of one-to-one subtype Fours with a Five wing complain about comments that they "look upset" or "need to smile more." They may not appear to be competitive on the outside, but they definitely won't shy away from conflict, wanting to prove that they are right and competent.

> My go-to emotion is anger. I tend to cry when I'm angry and that just makes me angrier. —*a Four (Sx)*

ENNEAGRAM FIVE

THE RETICENT/SELF-PRESERVATION

Self-preservation Fives are acutely aware of their own boundaries and aren't shy about asking for space, being private by nature. Because they don't often overdo it and tend to save energy, they can actually be happy and talkative in social situations. Illness and anything wrong physically may cause this Five subtype to experience depression. These Fives do not commonly mistype, but if they do, it is likely to be with type Nine.

A Four wing can cause this subtype to have a flair for the creative and appear more outwardly quirky or unique. Most people observing this subtype/wing combo can easily mistake them for a Four.

A Six wing can add an even more cautious or anxious approach to health and safety to this subtype. They are highly loyal to a couple of people, usually childhood friends or family members, who may worry that this 5w6 needs others in their lives. However, the Five (Sp) is content as they are.

THE COMRADE/SOCIAL

The social subtype Five dives feet first into topics of interest and often wants to unload or teach others about what they're learning. They love finding groups of people who are interested in the same things they are and become loyal to *their tribe.* No matter how close they are to others, however, they always maintain some amount of personal ambiguity. This Five might mistype as a One.

A Four wing will cause a lot of tension between the Five's need for independence and depth and their wing's need for closeness and being understood. This can cause a *vulnerability hangover* if the 5w4 feels like they overshared in an effort to gain closeness.

A Six wing can make this subtype more dutiful or exhibit black or white thinking, which is why this subtype can mistype as a One.

THE DEVOTED/ONE-TO-ONE

The one-to-one instinct Five will still appear to be reserved on the outside, only letting one or two people truly see their depth and passion. This Five has strong connections with only a few people and is fully satisfied in those relationships. However, they can become possessive of those few relationships, wanting the same kind of exclusivity in return, so that *their* person can't be wooed away. This Five may mistype as a quiet Four, Six, or Eight.

A Four wing on a Five (Sx) can make this subtype be more romantic and almost dramatic in their relationships. They have a romantic ideal of how they should be as a significant other and find great satisfaction in adhering to that ideal for their spouse or partner.

A Six wing will make this already loyal subtype likely to mistype as a 6w5. A Six wing will make this Five more reactive and suspicious in certain situations, having a protective nature toward those they love.

ENNEAGRAM SIX

THE TRUSTING/SELF-PRESERVATION

A self-preservation Six will be more oriented toward seeing authority figures as protective and safe. This phobic Six focuses their anxiety on who they can trust and how well they are being taken care of. This subtype may resemble a Nine because they're sweet in social situations and unlikely to assert their opinions. This subtype of Six can sometimes mistype as a Two or a Nine.

Add a Five wing and this Six is even more likely to mistype as a Nine. They'll have less energy and need to spend more time recharging. A Seven wing will make this subtype appear to be a Two as they're more socially outgoing and, in some cases, aggressive about getting approval.

THE TRADITIONAL/SOCIAL

The social subtype Six is dutiful and socially aware. They view the world through a lens of right and wrong, which can make them resemble type One. But instead of a One's inner critic, the Six (So) has an inner committee of voices informing them of possible worst-case scenarios. This is the subtype who is in between phobic and counterphobic, depending on the situation and their level of comfort.

A Five wing will make a social Six even more diligent about getting their facts straight. However, unlike a One, a 6w5 is pretty unlikely to say anything when they think you're not doing something *the right way*.

A Seven wing will make a social Six's socially aware behavior become more socially involved. They'll notice the rights and wrongs of social interaction and dutifully become the *best* friend, host, or party-goer ever.

THE QUESTIONING/ONE-TO-ONE

The one-to-one subtype of Six won't look much like a Six at all! In fact, this assertive, anti-authority, and get-it-done subtype will commonly mistype as an Eight. They're counterphobic because they don't trust authority outright and are cautious about trusting anyone. This Six runs toward their fears to deal with them instead of running away.

From a distance, the Five wing of a one-to-one subtype Six might make their assertiveness appear to be judgmental. A quieter version of Eightness, this Six's anti-authority energy takes a lot out of them. They will also want to be kept informed about those in leadership positions. I'm sure we can thank a lot of Sixes with a Five wing and one-to-one subtype for all sorts of sleuthing, like finding old tweets that ruin careers.

A Seven wing makes this Six even more likely to mistype as an Eight because they'll be more vocal, have more energy, and overall be a bigger presence.

ENNEAGRAM SEVEN

THE EXUBERANT/SELF-PRESERVATION

The self-preservation Seven is deeply aware of their own wants and needs and pretty adept at getting what they want, even if that means talking themselves into splurging, running away, or anything else that would ease the discomfort in their lives. This Seven loves having a group of friends to do things with, but the group is almost never ideal, and this Seven can often sabotage a friendship before it falls apart. This subtype of Seven is the least likely to mistype.

An Eight wing will add a bit of a reckless flair to this on-the-go Seven, but they will be much more likely to stand up for themselves and assert their needs than other Sevens.

A Six wing will make this Seven's anxious undertone much louder as part of the head triad with a self-preservation subtype. They may verbally process their anxieties but end up doing what they're anxious about anyway.

THE SERVANT-HEARTED/SOCIAL

The social subtype Seven can take on an almost anti-gluttony stance and instead focus their energy on making those around them comfortable and happy, the opposite of typical descriptions of Sevens. A Seven (So) is most likely to mistype as a Two because of their warmth and the way they articulate wanting to help. Because their deadly sin of gluttony is still knocking at the door, these Sevens have to have a harsh view on anything excessive, even coming across as critical to others when really it's them reigning in themselves.

An Eight wing makes this Seven even more likely to mistype as a Two or Eight because of the arrow connection between those two numbers. (A Two goes to Eight in stress, while an Eight goes to Two in growth.) What you think is your arrows might actually be your wing and subtype behaviors.

A Six wing will make this servant-hearted Seven extremely loyal to their social groups and what they stand for. Not taking commitments lightly, they will feel a firm tension between loyalty and freedom.

THE DAYDREAMER/ONE-TO-ONE

The one-to-one Seven is often confused with a type Four because of their creativity, daydreaming, and deep nature. This Seven likes to keep moving, and their creative nature can come up with a seemingly endless supply of exciting ideas. More assertive than the other two subtypes, this Seven isn't afraid to go after what they want. Relationships are huge to this Seven, and they like to have a partner who is just as excited about the world and its possibilities as they are.

An Eight wing will only intensify the assertive nature of the *dreamer* and add a protective nature over those valued loved ones. Having one of the biggest energy capacities on the entire Enneagram, this type/subtype/wing combo is often an entrepreneur or go-getter.

A Six wing will make the dreamer look even more like a Four as they struggle with an imposter syndrome. They may be more outwardly emotional than their Eight-wing counterparts.

ENNEAGRAM EIGHT

THE NURTURER/SELF-PRESERVATION

The Eight with a dominant self-preservation subtype will be drawn to those who are weak or hurting. They can easily slip into a parental role in many lives. This subtype comes off as strong, confident, and resilient. They don't take any nonsense from others and make difficult decisions without wasting any time. From the outside, this subtype can appear to be cold, but their warm and tender heart is on full display to those they nurture.

A Nine wing will make this Eight quieter, but they won't lack any of the intimidating presence for which Eights are known. They will try to stay out of petty arguments and conflict, but you'll see this wing/subtype combo come to full power when they're defending a loved one.

A Seven wing will make this subtype more energetic, and they may have a tendency to take life at a fast pace. They're likable, but trust very few. They are fun yet guarded. They will likely have many grand ideas for the future, and the audacity to actually make them work.

I am often the mom of my social group, which is just where I want to be. They come to ask me for advice, I get to protect, and I don't have to be overly vulnerable. —*an Eight (Sp)*

THE SACRIFICIAL/SOCIAL

The dominant social Eight will appear much more focused on others than the self-preservation or one-to-one subtypes are. Being the counter-type, this Eight isn't as preoccupied with power or strength. They want to protect, serve, and help those they care about. Usually whole people groups—their culture, workplace, or family—are in this Eight's bracket of those they need to help and protect. They focus a lot of their mental energy on fixing the mistreatment they notice around their people group. This is the Eight subtype that looks the most like a Two.

A Nine wing will give this subtype a more *go with the flow* attitude. As long as their group is happy, they're pretty chill and relaxed—that is, until someone pokes the bear inside them.

A Seven wing will give this subtype a pretty optimistic view on life and an eagerness to help. They'll be fun, often talkative, and appear to have a high social energy.

THE VENTURESOME/ONE-TO-ONE

The one-to-one subtype Eight could be best described as a rebel. At some point, they found the truth to be contrary to what most people passively believe, and they think that if they are open and loud in their rebellion, people will notice and change. This Eight can look a lot like a Four because their passion is intense. They may come across as highly emotional.

A Nine wing makes the Eight (Sx) a walking contradiction. They are both reckless and careful, passionate and reserved, in your face and apologetic. This subtype/wing combo feels a great inner tension. They're typically ambiverts and might assume they're a Four because they feel so misunderstood by the world.

A Seven wing causes this subtype to have the highest energy on the Enneagram. They want adventure, justice, control of their own life, and an endless supply of exciting stimuli. When they're unhealthy, they can act like a wrecking ball, but when this energy is pointed in the right direction, this wing/subtype can change the world.

ENNEAGRAM NINE

THE INTROSPECTIVE/SELF-PRESERVATION

The self-preservation Nine has figured out that to remain at peace, they must put a high priority on things like sleep, time alone, hobbies that they love, and general rest. This subtype is responsible for the stereotype that Nines like to nap. Without relaxation and downtime, the Nine (Sp) tank runs low, and they feel fragile. This priority on self-care can be seen as selfish and demanding to the outside world, so this Nine also struggles with the conflict of needing a full tank and keeping their world peaceful. This Nine is likely to mistype as a Five but sometimes can mistype as a One.

A One wing can make this Nine even more picky and rigid about their schedule and what gives them peace. They may mistype as a 1w9 because they can be organized, clean, and outspoken about their rules. However, their motivation is to keep their peace, not to appease an inner critic or be *good*.

An Eight wing can oddly make this Nine mistype as a Five. They'll be blunt and unapologetic, with strong opinions that their Eight wing tends to voice, causing their Nine-ness to backpedal to fix the conflict.

THE COLLABORATIVE/SOCIAL

The social Nine is considered the countertype. Rather than withdrawing and preserving energy, this subtype engages with the group and sacrifices themselves for its good. Often mistyped as a Two, this Nine's version of peacekeeping looks like running around like a chicken with its head cut off! They are fulfilling the needs of everyone in their group to keep everyone happy, so they can have peace. This type can burn out and quickly turn resentful when their needs are brushed off and they feel unnoticed.

A One wing can cause this subtype to be more perfectionist in their helping, and they may take unneeded steps for the sake of doing things right. They research how to do things right, worry about doing so, and often mistype as a 6w5.

An Eight wing makes this subtype even more likely to be mistyped as a Two. They're bolder and more assertive about making their opinions known or insisting on helping, saying things like, "No, I insist. Thanksgiving will be at my house, and you won't be lifting a finger."

THE INTERTWINED/ONE-TO-ONE

This Nine is fully merged with one or two other people to fuel their need for security and identity. They may even mistype as their partner's or best friend's Enneagram number! This Nine seems happy to go along with whatever *their person* wants because they think it's what they themselves want. This Nine finds less conflict in merging with the opinions and choices of that person so they are never directly responsible for anything that causes strife. Subconsciously they're distracting themselves from their own inner conflict and pain.

A One wing will make this subtype more introverted and aware of their energy levels. They may believe that being *good* means making their partner happy, and they may feel like their partner's preferences are rules.

An Eight wing may make this subtype appear more energetic and outgoing when they're in their comfort zone. Instead of making their partner's preferences their rules, they're more likely to protect and be fiercely protective of their people. They don't let others criticize their person, and the 9w8 tends to view their person in an optimistic light. This subtype/wing combo of Nine is very hard to type, as they have more energy than is typical for a Nine and only they know of their inner battle for peace.

> I'm very passionate, especially about things that are important to me, although sometimes I don't show it out of fear of conflict.
>
> —a Nine (Sx)

● ● ● ● ● ● ● ● ●

As we traverse our later adolescence and transition into adulthood, one of the biggest changes in our personality can be a subtype shift. What gave us a sense of security, belonging, and love during our childhood and early adolescence often stops working as we become independent. This can occur during any number of milestones, such as learning to drive, getting a car, experiencing the first serious relationship, starting a job, or going away to college. All of these typically happen during these tender adolescent years.

● ● ●

ONE OF THE BIGGEST CHANGES IN OUR PERSONALITY CAN BE A SUBTYPE SHIFT, WHICH CAN OCCUR DURING ANY NUMBER OF MILESTONES IN ADOLESCENCE.

● ● ●

It can be unsettling to have your need for belonging be tied so strongly to your family and have that suddenly change. Even if these milestones leave you feeling more excited than anxious, the people in your life may react adversely to them.

It can be hard to feel more like yourself than ever before and listen to other people tell you that you're not acting like yourself at all. As humans, we like certainty and predictability; we want to feel like we know our children, our family, and our friends indefinitely. Change can feel threatening and lonely.

If you are the one who is changing, it's appropriate to have those hard conversations and let your family know what's going on. If they love you and are in growth states themselves, they will champion your own growth.

12

FRIENDSHIPS

Do you think that I shall ever have a bosom friend...
an intimate friend, you know—a really kindred spirit to whom I
can confide my inmost soul.
—*L. M. Montgomery,* Anne of Green Gables

The friendships in my life have been filled with high-highs and low-lows. I was homeschooled, so I did not experience the natural friendships that come with peers at school. I met most of my friends at church and had pretty tumultuous friendships with my cousins and brother. Even so, I pretty much always had a best friend, and I wrote letters and had long phone calls with those friends for most of my childhood.

My personality showed bright in even my earliest friendships. I had expectations of exclusivity in friendships at an early age. I remember birthday parties feeling semi-horrifying to me because I would see all the other friendships that my best friend had. I would feel so inferior and forgotten. At age seven, I promised certain friends that they would be bridesmaids at my wedding. I loved being creative in play and got along best with the friends who would let me lead our imaginary scenarios.

Being a Four in friendships can be tricky. We are surprisingly loyal, but we also have this push-pull instinct that can burn bridges when we were only meaning to test their strength. There is a lot of shame that can come with that; you can believe that you are not a good friend or deserving of friendships. Fours also place high value on being understood, but they don't often find understanding. I think this is what Anne from *Anne of Green Gables*, a true Four in her own right, was looking for in a bosom friend: someone who understood her, wasn't surprised by her, or judgmental. Someone who would be loyal in return and endlessly impressed with their friend's special qualities.

• • •

A TRUE BOSOM FRIEND IS FULL OF SUPPORTING LOVE, WHICH IS SOMETHING THAT WE NEED IN ORDER TO THRIVE IN ADOLESCENCE.

• • •

Being fully known and fully loved creates the feelings of belonging and affection. Our friends choose us every day, even though they are not our family and have made no vows to us. A true bosom friend is full of supporting love, and as we have learned about the season of adolescence, support is something that we need in order to thrive.

When we look at the Enneagram and friendship, we see certain patterns, although just like anything else, if two people are healthy, they won't have any issue being good friends to each other. However, there are certain types that seem to gravitate toward each other.

As always, we have to expect a percentage of mistyping. This is one of the reasons why I think we see type Two pop up so much.

+ Ones are likely to be friends with Nines, Sevens, Fours, and Fives
+ Twos are likely to be friends with Sixes, Nines, Eights, and Fours
+ Threes are likely to be friends with Fives, Sevens, Eights, and Twos
+ Fours are likely to be friends with Fours, Eights, Fives, and Twos
+ Fives are likely to be friends with Nines, Eights, Threes, and Fours
+ Sixes are likely to be friends with Twos, Nines, Ones, and Threes
+ Sevens are likely to be friends with Ones, Twos, Nines, and Threes
+ Eights are likely to be friends with Twos, Fives, Sevens, and Nines
+ Nines are likely to be friends with Eights, Fours, Fives, and Nines

Rather than using the Enneagram as a tool for picking your friends, it's a greater aid to help you love your current friends better and become a better friend yourself. As fun as seeing the patterns may be, they do not indicate incompatibility with other types, so please don't think that's the takeaway.

● ● ●

RATHER THAN USING THE ENNEAGRAM AS A TOOL FOR PICKING YOUR FRIENDS, IT'S A GREATER AID TO HELP YOU LOVE YOUR CURRENT FRIENDS BETTER.

● ● ●

Do you know what makes you a good friend? Do you know the common pitfalls that occur with your friendships? This is the kind of self-awareness that the Enneagram can give us, especially in our most formative friendships, which often form in adolescence.

ENNEAGRAM ONE

As friends, Enneagram Ones tend to be the responsible people who keep everyone else in line, but at the flip of a coin, they can let loose and be rowdy with the best of them. Having a growth arrow to Seven is likely the cause of this, but Ones need to feel pretty comfortable first. (See chapter 7, Seasons of Stress and Growth.) This can create a delightful paradox: the party friend who is also deeply dependable.

Ones can take a joke, but they also want friends who appreciate how much they try to follow the rules and how good they are at being good. They like friends who can appreciate this part of their personality yet help them loosen up every now and then.

However, an Enneagram One who is unhealthy or in high stress can become a killjoy; their high standards can feel nearly impossible to achieve as a friend. Ones carry a bit of frustration and anxiety that can be disconcerting to some other types because it can feel like judgment, anger, and arrogance. But once people get to know Ones, this arrogance melts into what is truly below the surface—the harsh inner critic that is often only judging the One and no one else.

My best friend is a One, and she is the best at planning parties, events, and Bible studies. It's like she thinks of all the problems that could arise and fixes them before they can even happen! She is the most thoughtful person I know.   —*Britt, an Enneagram Two*

ENNEAGRAM TWO

Enneagram Twos are born nurturers and thrive in friendships where they can be your cheerleaders. They are wonderful gift givers and will show up for you no matter what. However, when the Two is unhealthy or in high stress, their giving might come with the pressure of reciprocation and their expectations can feel suffocating.

As much as Enneagram Twos enjoy being givers, in friendships, they want someone to foresee their needs and be generous with them when they need it. If your Two friends are having an especially stressful week, they would appreciate an offer to accompany them grocery shopping or bring them dinner. Even buying them a coffee or sending a kind note would help. It doesn't have to be crazy to be thoughtful. As much as Twos would like you to think otherwise, the only person they are not well-equipped to care for is themselves.

When the Enneagram Two is unhealthy, their friendship can feel like a lot of pressure. They don't openly ask you to do things for them, but they keep record when you don't show up like they imagined you would. The expectations of a Two align with what they expect of themselves, but other Enneagram types are not as well equipped to foresee needs as Twos are.

My friend is an Enneagram Two, and she is the only person I trust with my life! She is responsible, servant-hearted, and exudes thankfulness. I love being around her and her life-giving presence.   —*Pamela, an Enneagram One*

ENNEAGRAM THREE

Enneagram Threes make impressive, encouraging, and larger-than-life friends. It may be hard to keep up with them, but they are also easy to be around. Conversation flows naturally, they match what you need, and they are anything but boring. However, when they are unhealthy or in high stress, Enneagram Threes may not be the most attentive of friends. Their world is moving fast, and it may be hard for you to keep up if you are not a part of whatever they are doing at the moment.

Threes don't need you to be impressive or compete with what they are doing—they'd actually prefer it if you didn't—but they want their friends to tackle their own problems and pursue their own potential. They want to cheer you on, encourage you, and watch you bloom in your own way!

When Threes are unhealthy, they are the quintessential fair-weather friend. They don't want to be bogged down with your hard times and emotions, which they don't know how to handle anyway, so they will move on to the next friend who they can build up and have fun with.

> My friend Kat, an Enneagram Three, is everything I am not. I am endlessly impressed by her drive, skill set, and how she encourages me to be a better person.   —*Lilly, an Enneagram Nine*

ENNEAGRAM FOUR

Enneagram Fours are great listeners, vulnerable, and are generally interesting conversationalists. They won't judge you for having a bad day, month, or year; they will champion your processing and emotional vulnerability without needing to fix it. However, when they are unhealthy or in high stress, Fours can become self-focused and may start to feel clingy and needy, seeking a lot of emotional support and becoming offended if you don't pursue their friendship.

Fours want friends who are willing to go deep with them. They don't only want to talk about your job and your car; they want in-depth conversations about things like childhood wounds. For friends, Enneagram Fours appreciate those who see what is special in them and encourage it into action.

As mentioned earlier, Fours' push-pull tendencies are often their fatal flaw in friendships. This is most active when they are unhealthy, but it can show up in all Fours. They don't believe you'll stick around if you truly see them as they are, so they'll disappear in the hopes you'll reach out or share something deep with them. When you don't run away from the friendship, they will buy gifts for you, shower you with praise, and pull you back in. This cycle is toxic and does not achieve the type of relationships Fours truly desire.

> My best friend is also an Enneagram Four. I feel closer to him than to the people who have known me my whole life. We communicate at the same depth, and truly can let each other have our moods without feeling all rejected or abandoned about it.
>
> —*Oliver, an Enneagram Four*

ENNEAGRAM FIVE

Enneagram Fives are stable and endlessly interesting friends. They're objective and give great advice. When a Five says they'll do something, it's done. However, they are not overly attentive, vulnerable, or available as friends. Their energy stores are shallow and especially in times of stress, you may not hear from them for weeks or months at a time. A lot of Fives are also pretty private. You may be their best friend and not even know that they've been dating someone for six months. This is nothing personal; they're just good at compartmentalizing their relationships.

Fives want friends who are willing to hang out without making a big deal out of it. They want someone who wants to do something with them and talk about subjects that fascinate them. Fives appreciate humor, independence, and down-to-earth characteristics in their friends. When Fives are unhealthy, they can come across as arrogant and unavailable. At their worst, they ignore their friends, but this should not be taken personally.

> My best friend since childhood is an Enneagram Five. We have a great friendship because we are both so independent and can go months without speaking then just pick up from where we left off. We are always laughing together and go on a lot of hikes. I know she'll be there for me no matter what.
>
> —*Elaine, an Enneagram Eight*

ENNEAGRAM SIX

Enneagram Sixes are often called the loyalists, and what will cement their loyalty to you will vary from Six to Six. However, when you have a Six on your side, they are endlessly supportive, kind, and nonjudgmental. A Six can be one of your most treasured friends.

However, when Sixes are unhealthy or in high stress, their anxiety and fear can make them a bit much to be around. You may feel like you're on reassurance duty; depending on your own personality, this can get old fast. Sixes also are known to draw loyalty lines. If someone crosses you, the Six will become their enemy. This might sound good, but it can become problematic if the person happens to be another friend.

Sixes want friends who are open and honest with them. Ghosting a Six is probably one of the worst things you could do. Other than that, Sixes adapt well to all types of friends. Just don't take their loyalty for granted!

My brother is an Enneagram Six, and I consider him my best friend. We are both in our forties now, and through all the ups and downs of life, he has been a constant. I love how realistic he is, endlessly giving, and he's not high maintenance by any definition.
—Chris, an Enneagram One

ENNEAGRAM SEVEN

Enneagram Sevens don't typically hurt for friends because they are easy to talk to, open to spontaneous adventure, and generally have a good time. People tend to gravitate toward Sevens in a social group, but Sevens don't always feel connected or valued as friends. They crave deep, vulnerable friendships, but those can be rare for them.

Sevens want friends who enjoy them and the fun they bring to this world, but they also want friends who feel safe, who aren't surprised when they have a bad day and want to share their opinions and thoughts. Sevens enjoy people who aren't clingy and understand that a forgotten text doesn't mean relational devastation.

When Sevens are unhealthy or in high stress, they may self-sabotage in friendships instead of asserting boundaries and risking rejection. Sevens are not fans of conflict—or any negative emotion for that matter—so they may take a lot of slights and even abuse in a relationship before finally leaving.

> My friend who's an Enneagram Seven is one of the funniest, most creative, and fun people I know! I don't want to throw a party she won't be at, but at the same time, she is so good at those deep conversations. Truly a lovely paradox in her own right.
> —*Petra, an Enneagram Three*

ENNEAGRAM EIGHT

Enneagram Eights make for loyal, protective, and honest friends. They don't hint around about their intentions, so if they enjoy being with you, you'll know it. If you are in trouble or experience any injustice, it's likely you will go to your Eight friend for help. Not only are they reliable, but when you need someone on your team, they are already suited up and on the field before you say "go."

Eights want a friend who is not easily offended, clingy, or needlessly emotional. They appreciate people who can keep up with them at least intellectually, if not physically, and value them for their many strengths. Eights don't need gushy words or gifts. Showing up when they need you and remaining trustworthy means the world to them.

When Eights are unhealthy or in high stress, they can be harsh, mocking, or even withdrawn for long periods of time, making their friends feel abandoned because there's been little to no communication.

> My friend Riley happens to be an Eight, and she is truly the person I enjoy being around the most. I find her bluntness and perspective fascinating. She has a great sense of humor, and I know I can 100 percent trust her.   —*Melissa, an Enneagram Five*

ENNEAGRAM NINE

Out of all the Enneagram types, Nines are among the easiest to talk to and the most approachable. They're empathetic, sweet, and relatively low drama. Befriending them can be effortless, but the Nine's tendency to merge can make it hard to know them on a deep level. You'll have to spend some time really listening and digging to get to the heart of a Nine because it can be hard for them to know themselves much less introduce that true self to you.

The kind of friendship that benefits Nines best are friends who *want* to know what the Nine actually wants, but aren't pushy about them making a decision if they are not ready to do so. Friends who remember the little things about their Nine friend will go a long way in making them feel loved. Nines need friends who respect boundaries and are not demanding, domineering, or overly offended by boundaries in general. Nines need friends who listen as much as they talk and are willing to offer the same level of empathy and understanding that Nines do.

Because Nines can struggle with conflict avoidance, it is possible for people to think they have found a perfect friend when they begin a relationship with a Nine. However, the Nine is not really speaking their own thoughts and opinions but mirroring their new friend's. This may result in uneven expectations of the friendship. An unhealthy Nine may ghost the friendship altogether.

> My best friend is a Nine, and I am so grateful for her thoughtful, wise, and calm presence. She has truly done some of the most internal work I've ever encountered in a friend, and she is a wealth of compassion. She supports me in all my various endeavors with such grace and enthusiasm that is unmatched. She is truly a rare and wonderful friend. —*Elisabeth, an Enneagram Four*

● ● ● ● ● ● ● ●

Friendships tend to be front and center during adolescence, as we are grouped with our peers and see each other often. We may be told to *be* a good friend, but are rarely taught how to find a good friend. Most of our friendships will occur because the other person is close by—a neighbor, the kid who sat next to you in band class, or the only girl your age at church.

● ● ●

AS ADOLESCENTS, WE ARE TOLD TO BE A GOOD FRIEND, BUT ARE RARELY TAUGHT HOW TO FIND ONE. WE BECOME FRIENDS WITH THOSE WHO ARE IN CLOSE PROXIMITY TO US.

● ● ●

When you're little, friendships are uncomplicated and mostly dictated by your parents. The children of their friends become your friends. But when you enter adolescence, you move into a more independent role with your friendships and are able to select your own friends. However, the act of starting that relationship might be more complicated than it was before. Personality can play a role here, as being quiet or loud, studious or adventurous, or a rule follower or a rule breaker all make a big difference in how well you'll support each other as friends.

In adolescence, we have to learn to value ourselves enough not to settle for bad friends. We have to understand how it dishonors God to change who we are in order to feel a sense of belonging.

Friendship is a gift, but it's not a gift worth the sacrifice of our morals, self-worth, or relationship with God. A good friend is worth waiting for, and the years of loneliness within a crowd can be years of deep watering within our souls.

SECTION THREE:

ADULTHOOD (HARVESTING/FALL)

> The day the child realizes that all adults are imperfect he
> becomes an adolescent; the day he forgives them, he becomes an
> adult; the day he forgives himself he becomes wise.
> —*Alden Nowlan*

Adulthood is anticipated with bated breath, and yet it sneaks up on us without warning. Each of us had a different moment when we knew we had hit that coveted finish line of adulthood. Maybe you can think of a couple of them.

I felt different levels of adulthood on my first day of my first job, on my wedding day, and when we signed the papers for our first apartment, but nothing made me realize "I am the adult here" like sitting in a hospital waiting room while my twelve-day-old son was undergoing emergency surgery.

There was a tiny person whose life was hanging in the balance; my husband and I were the adults, signing papers and making decisions for him. Not even our own parents had more say over our son's care than I did. It was a sobering feeling, one you know you'll never recover from. We had been playing the adulthood game…until all of a sudden, the game was over, and the stakes were real.

Adulthood is the fall season of our life. It's the time when all the seeds planted in your childhood become seeds again themselves, ready for you to plant into others. It's a time for preparing for winter, a time when life and survival feel very real. The days are long, the air is crisp, and winter is coming.

Adulthood is the longest season of our life and can be the one filled with the most stress. This is a season with big decisions, big transitions, and constant learning curves. There is a lot of pressure to get things done, find your purpose, have a family, and set up your future self well.

MARRIAGE

*A good marriage isn't something you find; it's something you
make and you have to keep on making it.*
—*Gary Thomas*

Over 80 percent of the population will be married at some time in their lives. Our selection of a spouse contributes to some of the greatest happiness and biggest stress of our adult years.

Before you get your hopes up that I'm about to tell you that your Enneagram type and your spouse's type are perfect for each other, or confirm your nagging suspicions that there is a better choice out there, please be advised that I'm not going to do either of those things.

There may be patterns and trends of certain Enneagram types that tend to gravitate toward each other, *but* this does not mean they work better together than other type couplings.

There is no perfect Enneagram type for you to marry. Your emotional health and your spouse's health have a greater influence on your marriage than your personalities. If two Enneagram types are unhealthy, they will have a contentious, hard, and nearly impossible relationship. If one spouse is healthy and the other unhealthy, chances are the relationship will include some level of abuse. However, two healthy spouses—or even spouses committed to growing in their health through the power and work of the Holy Spirit—will have a relationship that is built on solid ground.

Marriage is hard work, and the work of understanding your differences is key to accurate expectations within your marriage. Unmet expectations contribute to a lot of strife within relationships, but especially within marriage.

● ● ●

THE ENNEAGRAM CAN GIVE YOU INSIGHTS THAT HELP YOU UNDERSTAND YOUR SPOUSE AND IMPROVE YOUR COMMUNICATION, EXPECTATIONS, AND OVERALL JOY.

● ● ●

Committing to your own relationship with God and growing as an individual is the best way to support your marriage. However, the Enneagram can give you insights that help you understand your spouse and improve communication, expectations, and overall joy within your marriage.

Here are some of the facets of each type, particularly as they relate to marriage and other close relationships:

ENNEAGRAM ONE

A One's motivation to be good makes them strive to do relationships "in the right way," however this happens to be defined by their culture or individual morals. Ones also hold those in relationships with them to high standards, and any failure of their spouse can feel like their own failure. Ones report that they know this feeling is misplaced, and they often struggle with being angry at themselves for directing anger at their spouse.

Your Enneagram One spouse will need lots of grace for their mistakes and respect for the frustration they feel all day, every day. Most types are sensitive to One's rules and might feel controlled, but a One can't help their desire to improve life, themselves, and others. They are usually just trying to help.

Their home is one place where you can help Ones feel at ease by letting things be the way they want whenever it's reasonable. They put a lot of thought into the way they do things and are more than willing to explain their reasoning if you ask. In the same vein, if something feels too out of reach or doesn't work for your family, talk to your One spouse about it. Ones do well when you give them all of your *whys* about why a rule might need to be changed or a compromise is in order.

To best love a One, respect their rules as long as they aren't unreasonable, give criticism sparingly, communicate expectations clearly, and articulate how they improve your world. When they're stressed, don't try to fix it. Instead, let them cool down alone or suggest something fun and distracting.

ENNEAGRAM TWO

Twos are motivated by love and while this motivation might be seen as uninspired, it is the reason why Twos' lives revolve around relationships—in essence, the giving and receiving of love. Twos are strong-willed and confident; at their worst, they are master manipulators. But when it comes to relationships, they give us far too much power. Twos fear they're unlovable and any withdrawal of affection can be felt as devastating. This includes saying "no" to their good intentions, having personal boundaries, wanting independence, and withdrawing behaviors that have nothing to do with your love for the Two.

If you're in a relationship with a Two, it'll be helpful for you to say "I love you for you" and express the idea that your love does not depend on the Two meeting your needs. You can do this verbally, in writing, or in as creative a manner as you can think of, but you will need to express this more often than you might suspect.

Twos need this affirmation because they are highly sensitive to rejection. Even dismissing a suggestion, a gift from them that's not a perfect fit, or a dinner they have prepared that you do not like can feel like rejection to a Two. Average to healthy Twos recognize this in themselves and don't want to feel this way. You can help them in this pursuit by softening your comments. For example, you can say, "It shows how much you love me by the time you took making this meal. Thank you! I might just prefer your original spaghetti recipe to it though. That one brings back fond memories of our newlywed years." Or if the Two gives you a gift, you could say, "Thank you for bringing a gift, but you really don't have to. Your being here is a gift enough."

Loving a Two usually requires some sort of action and attention to their needs, which isn't always easy since Twos have a hard time expressing what they want. They think you won't love them if they're too needy, and they value everyone else's needs over their own. How they downplay their own needs will vary from Two to Two, but don't take "I'm fine" at face value if something seems amiss. With Twos, you may have to press a little harder and dig a little deeper.

ENNEAGRAM THREE

A Three's inner motivation of worth and value is often played out by their belief that "I am loved for what I do, not who I am." This puts the power of their worth in the Three's own hands and gives them something to do about the way they're seen.

Threes will work hard to keep their relationships free from strife. They want to have fun, be active, and move forward; they genuinely want their relationships to be successful, however that is defined by their culture or morals. Even hiding behind different personas is a way that Threes try to love you and give you what they believe you want most from them.

Praise may be the main love language of your spouse who's a Three, so make sure to be generous with your words. This could differ when wings are at play, so always ask your spouse what feels the most loving to them.

When negative emotions arise, a Three's reaction is to brush off, reframe, fix, or run from the problem. A healthy Three needs to learn to ask questions of themselves and others and get all of the necessary information before setting up a response.

As a Three's spouse, you can help them to stop and ask questions before reacting or running. This will be a huge gift to your marriage, and you will take down more molehills before they turn into mountains.

At one point or another, your Three will fail and may go through somewhat of an identity crisis. It is helpful for you to point them to Christ in these times and assure them that their true worth is beyond their own doing and is safely resting in Christ's work for them.

Love to a Three sounds something like, "I see you outside of what you're trying to achieve, and I don't care if you fail or make mistakes." Don't get me wrong, Threes will want your full support in their endeavors, but your support should ultimately be for them as a person and not the praise, money, or fame their endeavors may bring in.

ENNEAGRAM FOUR

Fours are complicated when it comes to relationships. As a Four myself, I still struggle to put into words the paradox that Fours feel inside and how it affects others.

Unlike most other types, Fours don't have anywhere to put their emotions. There's no back room, no bottle, and no basement. A Four's emotions are front and center, demanding attention at the slightest trigger. Healthy Fours *can* ignore these feelings if they're not based in reality, but they still feel them nonetheless. Average Fours feel like ignoring these emotions would be akin to ignoring their true selves, which is a no-no when your main motivation is authenticity.

A Four spouse is on a constant hunt for your depth. They want to know you intimately—how you feel and think, why you do what you do— and usually, they glean this information with little to no judgment. When they can tell you're being truthful and trusting them with your fully honest answers, they feel safe and close to you. Fours likewise want you to value them as a unique person who brings depth to your world. Fours are highly sensitive to feelings of abandonment, so they'll want a lot of reassurance.

Perhaps the only thing more exhausting than being a Four is being in close relationship with one. I think all Fours can laugh and cry reading that truth. Fours have a propensity to feel a sense of longing. When you are with them, they might long for you to be different or better, and when you're gone, they long for all the good things you bring to their life. It's a confusing paradox for even the Fours who are experiencing it.

Fearing abandonment, Fours become faithful and committed spouses once they feel like they know you and can trust you. They'll always have projects or ideals that they are striving to meet for which you can be a sounding board, and they're usually highly entertaining and creative individuals. You can help your Four spouse by speaking logic to their spiraling emotions when needed. Fours also thrive under unconditional love, and you'll do well to point them to the true source of that love, Jesus, instead of putting that burden onto your own shoulders.

ENNEAGRAM FIVE

Fives are naturally solitary creatures, but every Five I've ever met is married. This is not odd once you understand Fives. They want to be loved and have companionship, fun, and a life where solitude isn't their only option. A Five's motivation is competency, not solitude, as solitude is only something they figure out is helpful to their mental health, not their main motivator.

If you are married to a Five, you may need to come to grips with the fact that they typically are not naturally romantic or giving of themselves emotionally. In fact, sometimes they literally can't give you the attention you may crave, attend an event with you, or want to hear about your day. And it's not because they don't love you. Being married to a Five means you need to be confident of their love, dedication, and desire to be present even when they can't express any of this. It means letting go of cultural expectations. Coming to terms with this reality and not expecting your Five to change is one way you can love them deeply.

If you're married to a Five, it's helpful if you say, "Can we talk about (fill in the blank) tonight?" This gives them time to think about the matter beforehand. It's also useful if you give them *specific* ways to love you, especially for holidays. For example, you could leave a sticky note somewhere your Five will see it that reads, "I would love a single red rose, a surprise dinner out, or a chocolate cake sometime around Valentine's Day." Let your Five do the rest.

ENNEAGRAM SIX

A Six's motivation for security might lead you to believe they're all about relationships, and to some extent that's true. Sixes look for security in authority/protective figures and dependable systems of thought, but when it comes to love—well, what's less certain than love?

The beginnings of a relationship are especially hard for a Six. They tend to see early romantic gestures as manipulative and fear they're falling for a trap instead of falling for a genuine person.

In the end, they're still the most loyal number on the Enneagram. When they fall for someone, they fall hard but it takes dedication for the other person to help them get there.

A Six as a spouse will be supportive, trustworthy, and pessimistic at times, but day to day, they're a pretty low-maintenance partner. This is why a lot of spouses are surprised when they learn their partner is a Six on the Enneagram. They say, "But anxiety isn't a huge thing for you?" This is especially true of a Six with a Five wing, who might not be as vocal about their anxieties as a 6w7. The Enneagram is a great tool to help you understand your Six spouse because it'll help you see into their inner life and what they believe is a normal thought life.

A Six spouse will have seasons when they need *lots* of reassurance. It's as if they are thinking, *Are you going to change your mind about me?* If your spouse is in one of these seasons right now, it will pass. Sixes' security anxiety can be triggered by a lot of outside sources, and it probably has very little to do with you. Make sure you verbalize your dedication and love for them, saying, "I love you and would never leave you," "You're the only one I love," "You're my rock," or "You can trust me because I long to be obedient to Christ."

ENNEAGRAM SEVEN

A Seven's motivation for freedom might make them seem noncommittal, but this isn't true for the vast majority of Sevens. Their fun energy and deep thinking can make a relationship with them seem like the best of times—and also, briefly, the worst of times. There's no question that Sevens are incredibly fun spouses and will ensure you'll have no end of laughter and adventure.

However, no matter how much Sevens try to avoid it, pain and hard times are a part of life. Help your Seven verbally process this and don't get miffed when they aren't their happy-go-lucky self. After all, life is not perfect all of the time. Work with them to identify the cause of their stress. If it's beyond the control of both of you to fix matters, help your Seven stop fixating on it by planning something fun for both of you to do.

Loving a Seven means understanding that they deeply want to be appreciated for the fun and lightheartedness they bring to any environment, but can become distant if they begin to feel used or unseen. Sevens want you to have fun with them, but they also want you to seek their opinion and have deep conversations with them. Long talks about the future, wants, desires, and who you really are will touch a Seven's heart.

ENNEAGRAM EIGHT

Eights are motivated by autonomy, independence, and freedom; overall, they do not want to be controlled by others. In relationships, they are straightforward, independent, and highly protective. Eights fear being betrayed, so they hesitate to enter into a relationship where the revelation of secrets can lead to catastrophic consequences. This fear of betrayal also causes Eights to detach when they feel rejected or lied to even if they are just suspicious that this is a possibility.

If you're married to an Eight, you know that they like to show you that they love you rather than being gushy with their words. Protection is the Eight's preferred mode of affection, but those they dearly love also get to see their tenderness at times.

Loving an Eight looks a lot like standing up for yourself, telling the truth, and holding on for the ride. Eights value their spouse's independence and integrity. If you're married to an Eight, rest assured you have been vetted and found to be exceptional.

It can be tricky to deal with an Eight spouse if you like a lot of affection and vulnerability in your relationship. It helps to remember that they can't read your mind. Although they won't change to suit you, being upfront about your expectations can produce positive results.

There's not much guesswork with an Eight spouse. If they're angry, you will know it. If they want something, they'll tell you. If they need space, they'll be silent. And all they want in return is for you to do the same.

ENNEAGRAM NINE

A Nine's desire for peace can't help but affect those closest to them. Nines avoid rocking the boat, making them a pleasant partner indeed. To prevent any conflict that would disrupt their peace, a Nine will merge with the thoughts and feelings of others, often forgetting or avoiding what they themselves actually want or feel.

This is especially common among married couples because the person you sleep next to might just have the most power over your sense of stability and peace. This phenomenon is confusing to most other types, who have no idea what it feels like to forget what you personally want, feel, or think. This is one of the many reasons why the Enneagram is a great resource in your marriage for giving language to your inner world.

It can be hard to tell, even for Nines themselves, if they actually agree with you or are merging. Nines have this trick of repeating what you say back to you in an affirming way without actually expressing their agreement. The Nine's propensity to merge is neither good nor bad, and its nature is really determined by the health of your Nine. Unhealthy Nines tend to merge in unhealthy ways. Try not to demonize or glorify their merging in general; instead start trying to notice when your Nine says nothing at all, or doesn't openly agree with what you're saying.

To best love a Nine, you need to encourage them to *know their own mind* and not take advantage of their conflict avoidance. You can do this practically by encouraging your Nine to be alone so that they are away from the thoughts and feelings of others when they need to make a decision. Respect the decisions and feelings they do express, listen to them, let them know that their very presence is valuable to you, and do not take their slothfulness personally.

Nines can be stubborn when they feel they are being taken advantage of, used, or pushed. You can take passive-aggressive behavior as a warning that there is something deeper going on.

Nines are known as the sweethearts of the Enneagram, and you discover why if you have a Nine spouse. But you'll be doing yourself and your relationship a favor by championing your spouse to become more confident.

DIFFERENT ENNEAGRAM COUPLES

Now that we have explored what it's like to have each Enneagram type as a spouse, let's turn to the possible ramifications of specific couplings.

ONE/ONE, THE EFFICIENT COUPLE

You may think that two Ones together would make a *perfect* couple since they are both motivated by being good and doing things right. But because each One's rules are different, their rules and how they view *right* can really clash with each other. The good news is, Ones are usually open to learning a *new right way* if you can convince them it makes sense, so this One/One couple has a lot of room to compromise and learn.

With wings, subtypes, and levels of health taken into account, these two Ones will look different from each other, and those differences will help balance out the other's weaknesses. Like any couple, communication and grace are key ingredients for a harmonious marriage.

ONE/TWO, THE WARMTH AND RULES COUPLE

Ones and Twos can complement each other well and have a lot of understanding for each other, particularly if each has the other's Enneagram type as a wing. However, they do not have the same demeanor. Ones are logical, often more introverted, and rigid, while Twos are feeling, relational, and tend to be overly involved. These traits can be well balanced in a relationship when these two work to appreciate their significant other's giftings and differences.

This couple can experience tension if the One becomes frustrated and views the Two's advice as judgment. The Two likewise may feel controlled and enslaved to their spouse's rules and how they need things to be, causing bitterness and the feeling of not being seen in the relationship.

ONE/THREE, THE PRODUCTIVE COUPLE

One and Threes can share a similar energy to get things done and can even mistype as each other. Self-preservation Threes looks a lot like Ones. It is common for Ones and Threes to bond over similar goals and work ethics. Ones respect Threes for their clear communication, ambition, and social poise, while Threes respect Ones' consistency and integrity.

Tensions can rise when the Three's fixation on the end goal might lead to cutting corners and breaking a few rules, horrifying their rule-following spouse. The Three can become frustrated when the One fixates on doing something perfectly rather than just doing it. This couple has to work hard on communicating not just facts and plans, but also feelings and fears. Vulnerability will strengthen their bond.

ONE/FOUR, THE KITE AND STRING COUPLE

Fours and Ones share a line on the Enneagram diagram: Fours go to One in growth, and Ones go to Four in stress. This marriage can be endlessly helpful to the Four, especially if their One spouse is healthier and exhibits healthy One traits, and the Four is humble enough to accept their guidance. Fours are creative, inconsistent, and fascinating, while Ones are great supporters, encouragers, and champions to their Fours. Their life can be both joyous and firmly tethered to reality when the Four is the proverbial kite while the One holds the string.

However, Ones and Fours are both idealists, and sometimes those ideals clash. Fours' ideals tend to revolve around how they want to feel emotionally, while Ones' ideals are about everything working together logically and practically.

The marriage can become volatile if the Four feels judged, criticized, and condemned by the One, which only confirms the brokenness they feel inside. In turn, the One can feel like a living, breathing version of their inner critic, walking on eggshells around their Four spouse, feeling like no matter what they do, it's wrong. This makes the One angry because it's not something they can compute.

Overall, this is not a couple that works on autopilot or in an unhealthy state. But when they work together for understanding and extend grace to each other, they will complement each other beautifully.

ONE/FIVE, THE INDEPENDENT COUPLE

Ones and Fives may often mistype as each other, but it's not often that you find a One/Five romantic couple. Both types are independent and can be stuck in their ways for different reasons. Ones want *a lot* of communication, but Fives only want to stick to what's necessary, which can be tricky when you live together.

The Fives and Ones who make it work find a lot of freedom in how independent their spouse is. They also can trust that their spouse is going to be 100 percent honest with them. They are both steady and loyal types, so when they give each other grace, they can have a sublime and happy marriage.

ONE/SIX, THE STEADFAST COUPLE

Both Ones and Sixes have a similar energy when they see something being done *wrong*, and this passion about rule-breaking and recklessness can attract these two numbers to each other.

They both share qualities of being loyal, steady, and consistent. For Sixes, this is more evident in relationships, while Ones exhibit these qualities in work environments.

But the One/Six couple can get stuck in negative thinking, especially when the One is stressed. They have to take care to stay away from dwelling in the doom and gloom of the world and work hard to encourage each other in faith and hope. Together, they can have a delightful and vibrant relationship.

ONE/SEVEN, THE TWO SIDES OF A COIN COUPLE

Enneagram Sevens and Ones tend to be drawn to each other. The epitome of the idea that opposites attract, Sevens give Ones permission to have fun, be less uptight, and grow, whereas Ones provide stability and grounding to their Seven's go-go-go nature.

This couple shares a growth/stress arrow, with Ones going to Seven in growth and Sevens going to One in stress. The Seven spouse will be instrumental in the growth of their partner, giving them permission to let loose, an example to follow, and a path toward growth. It can also be encouraging to the Seven to see their One learn to have fun.

However, the Enneagram One is not automatically helpful to the Seven when they're in stress. All of the One's natural instincts to deal with stress only fall into the negative coping mechanisms Sevens have. The One's attitude is, "Go clean it, fix it, do more!" Sevens in stress need Five-ish behaviors. They need time alone to think, obtain more information about the problem, and plan a solution. Their One's impulse to act first often only feeds into the Seven's angst. The One must learn to leave their Seven spouse alone when they are stressed. Unless they ask the One for help, they can better handle the problem on their own.

For a Seven and a One in a marriage, it's critical for both parties to fully encourage the other and remember that their differences can work well together. Every gas pedal needs a brake pedal. You both don't need to be the same to support each other and strive for understanding and love.

ONE/EIGHT, THE JUSTICE COUPLE

When a One and an Eight get together, you can be guaranteed of two things: they're going to be a force to be reckoned with when it comes to productivity, and they're going to bring out anger in each other. At first glance, these two types can look a lot alike. After all, they both think they're right, both have action-oriented energy, and both are in the gut triad, with its defining emotion of anger.

However, their motivations are like night and day. Ones think they're right because their passion to be good has led them to the correct conclusions. Eights think they're right because they have challenged the status quo and aren't afraid of the truth. Romantically speaking, this couple is drawn to each other by their differences. Ones are typically disciplined and responsible, but Eights pride themselves on being rebels.

ONE/NINE, THE RULES OF PEACE COUPLE

Ones and Nines are both repressive types in the gut triad, and with corresponding wings, they can look a lot alike. Ones are attracted to the Nine's unargumentative nature, and Nines are attracted to the One's clear direction and leadership. The Nine in the relationship can often begin to merge with their One spouse's opinions and rules. If the Nine has a One wing, they can appear to be just like a One themselves in some cases.

This couple may struggle to make quick decisions—the One because they are afraid of error, and the Nine because they are afraid of conflict. This couple may wait out situations in order to forego decision-making altogether. The Nine must be on guard against the opinionated One exerting too much control and assuming the Nine's silence is agreement. Unless they learn to speak up, the Nine will end up feeling angry and resentful.

TWO/TWO, THE CARING COUPLE

Twos are not often married to fellow Twos because when you are a helper, you look for someone to help, not someone who might be better at helping than you are. However, with wings and subtypes taken into account, it does happen. Usually, one of the Twos, perhaps with a Three wing, will take on the role of inspirational leader in the relationship, and the other Two will fit in comfortably as the supporter or helper.

Otherwise, both Twos may be frustrated when their spouse doesn't take the lead or let the other spouse aid them. Tempers can rise as they both feel purposeless in the relationship.

TWO/THREE, THE HOSPITALITY COUPLE

Twos and Threes share a similar energy toward people—they love to love and be loved by people! Their social draw often brings them together, and they will continue as a social power couple all throughout their relationship.

Threes adore Twos' giving energy, and Twos really admire Threes' ambitious nature. They both can seem similar, especially if they have a wing of the other, but the Two's energy is more relational whereas the Three's is more task oriented.

Feelings can get hurt when the Three becomes preoccupied with their pursuits and doesn't pay much attention to the Two's needs. Meanwhile, the Three can get frustrated when the Two's response to being ignored is to try to manipulate them to regain their attention.

Twos and Threes are on different wavelengths when it comes to expressing emotions, which can also cause some strife. In the long run, when this couple makes the effort to communicate and understand each other, their relationship will be full of love, various hospitable pursuits, and lots of people.

TWO/FOUR, THE EMOTIONAL COUPLE

A Two and a Four make for an emotionally intelligent couple. They both want romance and connection, they both fear abandonment, and they both seek fulfillment from relationships. Since Two goes to type Four in growth and Four goes to type Two in stress, they will see parts of themselves in their spouse. A Two will practically see the Four's emotional honesty as permission to ask for their own wants and needs to be met as well. This is one of the helpful parts of being married to your growth number. The Four's desire for connection can be facilitated by the Two's ease with other people, so the Four doesn't have to be the one seeking out the relationship.

Tensions can arise when the Four feels like they are not enough; the Two's needs outside the relationship feels like abandonment to them. Meanwhile, the Two can feel like their helping is never enough to make the Four truly happy.

TWO/FIVE, THE PARADOX COUPLE

Twos and Fives share no connection in Enneagram terms, so their strengths and weaknesses are polar opposites. This can either build contention between them or work out like an exquisite dance, depending on the emotional health of each spouse.

Twos are natural caretakers and nurturers, which works out well in this marriage because Fives often need some caretaking. Twos can also have a lot of emotional ups and downs, which can make having a steady and faithful Five as a partner feel grounding and safe.

Twos need a lot of reassurance, and although Fives aren't very well-versed in providing verbal reassurance, their steady presence speaks volumes to a Two's anxious heart. Fives need someone who will keep life going socially, push them out of their comfort zone, and be easy to talk to—and Twos fit this bill nicely.

TWO/SIX, THE RELATIONAL COUPLE

Twos have the tendency to come off too strong for Sixes in the beginning of a relationship. Sixes can have a healthy suspicion about people who seem *too nice* or *too romantic* before they truly know them. However, once the Two has won the Six over with their genuine loveliness, they can become inseparable.

If the Six has a goal or cause they support, their partner will be their number one cheerleader and give them a pep talk whenever they need it. This makes the Sixes feel secure and particularly loved. The Two will not take the Six's loyalty toward them lightly and will work hard to help their spouse truly rest.

Troubles can emerge when the Six feels manipulated or used by the Two who is trying to fulfill their need for love and admiration. If called out, a Two can become defensive; fearing anger, the Six will mostly shut down. Twos can also become personally hurt over their seeming inability to cheer up their Six and can be drained by their pessimism.

TWO/SEVEN, THE JOYFUL COUPLE

Sevens and Twos are both optimistic and people-oriented, so this pair is quite the fun couple to hang out with. They also complement each other well as a Two will often help a Seven follow through on their dreams and plans.

A pain point between this pair happens when the Two strives to do something nice for the Seven. Although the Seven is thrilled in the moment, they often move on to the next thing without thinking of reciprocating, making the Two feel hurt and unappreciated. Sevens, likewise, can feel like their Two spouse desires a level of closeness that doesn't allow for much freedom.

TWO/EIGHT, THE STRONG COUPLE

The difference between Eights and Twos is often what brings them together. Twos are warm, giving, and focused on others, while Eights will push against people in order to gain independence, have a hard time showing a softer side, and are radically stubborn. Marriage to a Two can soften the Eight's hard exterior, while the Eight can help the Two become more aware of their own needs and work on their backbone. This couple is connected by an arrow on the Enneagram, with the Eight becoming more giving and softer in growth as they go to Two, and the Two challenging their spouse's own anger when they go to Eight in stress.

This couple can hit hard times if the Eight gets frustrated with the Two's giving nature, which the Eight may view as almost groveling for attention, causing them to argue or moodily withdraw. If this happens, the Two will feel the withdrawal as devastating and go into hyper-attention mode toward their spouse. The Two's need for attention and reassurance can be a common pain point for their Eight spouse.

TWO/NINE, THE CALM WATERS COUPLE

Twos and Nines are often mistyped as each other because of their other focus/merging nature although they do this for different reasons—Twos to people please and Nines to avoid conflict. However, they are both emotional and take conflict hard. They might be tempted to sweep issues under the rug, but they'll need to learn to have healthy conflict if they want the relationship to last.

This pair will understand each other very well and enjoy each other's company on both the good days and the bad ones. Although their amount of energy can vary drastically, they both like people and are easy to talk to, making them many people's favorite couple.

THREE/THREE, THE TROPHY ROOM COUPLE

Two Threes together are a force to be reckoned with. They both want to be successful, and they know what it takes to achieve where they want to be and how they want to look. They appreciate their spouse's similar drive and high social energy.

The tension can come when their competitive undertones turn hurtful and harmful to their relationship. This couple also does not like unproductive emotion, so they may repress their feelings until they avalanche.

THREE/FOUR, THE BIG PURPOSE COUPLE

Despite being opposites internally, Threes and Fours present an evenly matched front to everyone else. Both types are image conscious, so they help each other excel on social media and in social gatherings. Threes help Fours follow through on their big ideas, and Fours help Threes become more self-reflecting. When each has the other type as a wing number, they can be highly ambitious and experience emotional depth together.

Trouble in paradise can occur when the Four feels like the Three is being disingenuous and pushes all of the Three's *shame* buttons, either in an argument or in making a casual observation. Meanwhile, the Three can get frustrated with their Four's constant emotions and need for reassurance. For the Three, it's easy to shut down their emotions and move on. This couple might have to go through some rough patches to do the work it'll take to stay together, but once they do, they will be unstoppable.

THREE/FIVE, THE EXTRO/INTRO COUPLE

On paper, it doesn't look like the marriage of an Enneagram Five and Three would work, but once you see this couple in action, it makes sense why they're attracted to each other.

Fives are steady, low-drama, and supportive, while Threes are social, full of ideas, and fast moving. These two types find each other endlessly fascinating. Threes don't often need another go-getter in their relationships, but they do need a supporter who is steady and kind. This is what ultimately attracts them to Fives. For their part, Fives are attracted to a Three's gumption, how easy social stuff is for them, and the ease with which they can have a conversation, with no awkward silences in sight.

The puzzle pieces come together for this marriage, but it's not without its challenges. The things that originally attract us to our spouse can become the very areas of contention later on in our marriage, especially when it's a case of "opposites attract."

Eventually, the Three will get annoyed with their Five's lack of social prowess and how often they don't want to attend events. The Five may get overwhelmed and annoyed by the constant stream of guests in their home, or the fact that their Three is always out someplace and never home. So much of this angst has to be ironed out by communicating expectations and compromising. Taking separate cars to events so the Five can leave early is a great compromise that my own parents used often. (My mom is a Three, and my dad is very likely a Five.)

Threes and Fives don't process their feelings. When there's a conflict, they both try to take emotion out of the equation wherever possible. This works well…until it doesn't. Repressed emotions tend to come out sideways in passive-aggressive and manipulative ways. Full healing cannot occur for the Three/Five couple until they do the hard work of cleaning out the infection and tending to their wounds. This process is hard for the couple because sitting in emotion and pain isn't natural for either of them.

THREE/SIX, THE GROUNDED DREAMER COUPLE

Although they share a stress/growth arrow—with the Three going to Six in growth and the Six going to Three in stress—this isn't a common pairing. Perhaps this is because Threes can smell insecurities from a mile away, and if they can't fix them, they have a hard time enjoying your company. For their part, Sixes can see through a Three's facade and aren't impressed by their success; if anything, the Six tends to view someone who's too successful or happy with suspicion.

However, when health and wings have been taken into account, this couple can make a great team. A Six spouse can bring out loyalty and thoughtfulness in a Three, and the Three can help the Six spouse become more confident and action-oriented.

THREE/SEVEN, THE PARTY HOST COUPLE

Threes and Sevens are a match in high energy, optimism, and a drive to plan the future. This couple will get a lot done in the most fun way, with the Three keeping the Seven on task and the Seven bringing endless adventure, creativity, and new ideas to the table. This couple enjoys each other and sees the value that they each bring to the relationship.

However, problems can occur because both Threes and Sevens have a propensity to gloss over pain points and bury their own emotions into doing or distracting. Neglecting the emotional issues this couple may face will make them susceptible to problems neither one of them wants to tackle. Unless one or both of them mature in this area to push past the discomfort and pain, the relationship will likely fall apart in an avalanche of bitterness and resentment.

THREE/EIGHT, THE BIG ENERGY COUPLE

Eights and Threes work well together when it comes to putting their noses to the grindstone and getting things done. Threes have the marketing and social components, while Eights possess the sheer strengths and drive. But we don't tend to see these two types in a couple because although both have high energy, when they are stressed, both withdraw, slow down, and isolate themselves.

Eights and Threes are also profoundly competitive, and a game night with these two can get pretty ugly pretty fast. Pain points can be obvious with two such strong numbers, but Eight/Three couples do exist and report passionate, energetic, and lovely marriages.

THREE/NINE, THE REST/OVERWORK COUPLE

Nines and Threes bring a great mixture of ambition and relaxation to each other. The Nine is often attracted to the Three's is endless energy, ease with people, and fascinating ambition, whereas the Three loves how the Nine listens first, judges sparingly, and helps the Three chill out.

Even though they work very well together, this pair can become frustrated with each other. The Threes don't understand Nines' lack of energy since this is something they only experience in stress. And Nines can easily be run over when their Three spouse plows ahead. Adding to these frustrations, neither type wants to rock the boat by bringing up the complaints, so they may each begin to experience resentment.

FOUR/FOUR, THE STRUGGLING ARTIST COUPLE

A Four/Four pairing will understand each other in a way no one else can, but such a couple is rare. Fours seem to be more attracted to each other as friends rather than romantic partners. Maybe this is because they sense that their capacity for both moodiness and selfishness would only hurt each other in the end. Or maybe one of them pushed and the other stayed away instead of pulling them back in, ending the relationship in mutual hurt and rejection.

However, a Four/Four couple can work with the help of wings, subtypes, and therapy. Fours give of themselves in a deep and meaningful way; as spouses, they will appreciate not having to force conversations, romance, and empathy on their own.

FOUR/FIVE, THE BOND AS OLD AS TIME COUPLE

Fives and Fours share depth and intensity that often draws them to each other. Fives are fascinated by Fours' talent, the way they feel instead of thinking their way through life, and how fun they are to talk to. Fours, on the other hand, find Fives mysterious and love how well they speak their mind and don't care what others think of them. Having the capacity to have the wing type of the other only adds to their chemistry, fascination, and mutual understanding.

But this relationship can cool off rather quickly. Fours have a drive for deep emotional connection, and although Fives want that too, the Four's yearning can feel almost demanding to them. What the Five views as space and boundaries, the Four might see as rejection and insensitivity, thinking others feel like they do. The Four can also start to feel like the Five is hiding their true depth from them, causing their emotions to spiral out of control.

If these two can genuinely try to understand and communicate their differences, they can have a rich relationship filled with inside jokes, knowing glances as they judge people, and many nights spent withdrawing together.

FOUR/SIX, THE STEADY AND TUMULTUOUS COUPLE

Fours and Sixes have a mutual appreciation of depth, feel existential anxiety, and experience self-doubt, all of which can create a deep bond between the pair. Sixes are naturally mistrusting, so the Four's focus on authentically is refreshing to them. Fours likewise appreciate the security that their Six partner gives them as well as empathy toward their own anxiety.

Troubles arise when the Six fears that the Four's emotions will drive them to leave, and the Six's motivation of security prompts them to start sabotaging the relationship early on. The Four will also feel like the Six doesn't trust them, or might feel trapped when the Six's aversion to risk is clear. Overall, once they are committed and understanding of each other's quirks, a Four and a Six make a bonded and compassionate couple.

FOUR/SEVEN, THE THEATER MASKS COUPLE

This is another *opposites attract* couple, as a Seven is one of the best partners to bring out the fun and enjoyment for life a Four can have. Likewise, a Four can help Sevens open up to those hard things they tend to gloss over and encourage them in their vulnerability.

However, a Four can feel misunderstood by their Seven and may feel like the Seven's life would be better if they were different, compounding the Four's own internal insecurities. Sevens can feel held down by a Four and a slave to the Four's ever-changing emotions. When the couple works together to truly understand and give each other freedom to be themselves, they bring out the best in each other.

FOUR/EIGHT, THE SENSITIVE AND TOUGH COUPLE

Fours and Eights are a more common pairing than you might suspect. Their relationship is intense, to say the least. Both Eights and Fours thrive on highs, whether that's emotional, physical, or literal. They both steer away from social norms, and when they argue, they go for the jugular. That being said, Fours love how unashamed, confident, and forward Eights are, while the Fours' mystical charm, poetic way of speaking, and emotional depth are fascinating to Eights.

Pain can occur when the Eight disappears in stress, leaving their Four depressed and feeling abandoned. Fours' emotions can become frustrating for the Eight, who will often wish their Four spouse had more of a backbone.

FOUR/NINE, THE EMOTIONAL SUPPORT COUPLE

Fours and Nines make wonderful friends but aren't often found as couples. Nines frequently find the Four's "I know my mind" attitude refreshing, and Fours love how caring and responsive Nines are. Romantically merging with an Enneagram Four's emotions can be quite the ride for a Nine, causing them to shut down emotionally. Feeling abandoned, the Four will be hurt and think they've been tricked into thinking the Nine was just like them, a true kindred spirit. The Four will believe the Nine wants to hide rather than develop a deep connection. If this couple can practice giving each other space while keeping their connection alive, they will have a long and happy relationship.

FIVE/FIVE, THE LOW DRAMA COUPLE

It's interesting to observe a double Five pairing. Fives often bond over a shared sense of, "Wow, finally someone who gets me!" They find each other's presence easy and non-demanding. Issues can come up when an almost roommate-like complacency occurs, so that they don't feel the need to communicate with each other deeply often. Fives' various interests of study can also take them down different paths, to the point where they can become annoyed with their spouse's *topic of the month*.

FIVE/SIX, THE BEYOND FEELINGS COUPLE

Sixes and Fives both understand that there is more to love than feelings, and since both of them have a committed nature, they make great partners for each other. Having each other's type as a wing adds to their insights as they learn how to motivate each other. However, Fives will need to be on their reassurance *A game* when married to a Six! Nothing is worse than having to beg an unwilling Five to give you reassurance, especially when the Six is likely to blame themselves for any withdrawing they might sense on the Five's part. Sixes will need to keep communication open and ask their Five what they're thinking before making assumptions.

FIVE/SEVEN, THE ALONG FOR THE RIDE COUPLE

With the low energy of Fives and the high energy of Sevens, this can make for an interesting pairing. Sevens can be attracted to how interesting, even-keeled, and practical the Five is. Fives generally enjoy the fun, optimism, and energy a Seven brings to their life. These two also share a stress/growth arrow, which can help them accept each other fairly well. As long as they both understand their differences and don't try to change their partner, they can thrive in a relationship full of witty banter, fun nights at home, and lots of freedom to be themselves.

FIVE/EIGHT, THE BLATANTLY HONEST COUPLE

Eights and Fives are noticeably different, but have one huge thing in common: they can handle the truth, and they expect it from the people in their lives. They're a common pairing, and I also think their differences are just fascinating to each other. Eights are usually extroverts while Fives are often introverts, but living together and going to each other's type in stress and growth can cause them to pick up the behaviors of their spouse.

A Five who is married to an Eight can come across as much more aggressive and assertive. An Eight might dig into their Nine wing and become more laid back with a Five spouse. Pain points can occur when either one believes their partner is wrong about something, and neither will concede to the other. There is also bound to be tension with two such different energy forces living in the same house. However, many couples make it happen by putting in the work to understand each other and have compassion for their spouse's view of the world.

FIVE/NINE, THE DOWN TO EARTH COUPLE

Nines and Fives are both independent, easily pleased, and low-drama people, so it's no surprise that they tend to attract each other. Fives love that Nines don't demand much of them, and Nines love that Fives don't tend to stir up unneeded conflict. Fives are steady, so Nines know what to expect. Nines are generally pleasant and easy to be around, so Fives feel at home in their company.

This couple can have their problems, however, as Nines want conflict resolved quickly, and Fives' contemplative nature doesn't lend itself to quick processing. The Nine may take the full blame for the conflict before the Five has even fully processed what's going on. This can lead to resentment on the Nine's part and a fully clueless Five. The Five might even think the Nine is stirring up needless conflict, which is devastating for the Nine to hear.

Both Fives and Nines withdraw when they feel disrespected or slighted, making the distance between them in conflict feel vast. It takes a lot of growth for them to stay present in conflict and have a fruitful discussion about their problems. This growth is vital to their marriage's success. It can be easy for Nines and Fives to live together peacefully while still feeling internal resentment for each other.

SIX/SIX, THE REALIST COUPLE

Two Sixes together amplify their mutual strengths and weaknesses. They are fiercely loyal and appreciate that characteristic in each other. They both take a no-nonsense approach to life and being in the head/pragmatist triad brings a natural empathy to their relationship. However, two Sixes can really hype each other up when it comes to fears and worse-case scenarios. Without proper insight from others, this couple can create a reality of their own that's planted in fear rather than truth.

With wings, levels of health, and subtypes taken into account, this couple is bound to look different from each other and can even help each other out in some areas. But they need to be careful not to encourage each other in stress and unhealthy coping mechanisms.

SIX/SEVEN, THE SAFE FUN COUPLE

Sixes and Sevens are a couple that doesn't make sense on paper, but in action, they balance each other out. Sevens enjoy how much they can trust a Six, and how they get each other from a head triad standpoint. Sixes seem to be endlessly entertained by Sevens, admiring their fearless approach to life. Obviously the very things that bring them together may eventually become pain points, but if they keep communication open and commit to learning from each other, they can have a wonderful marriage.

SIX/EIGHT, THE REACTIVE COUPLE

Both Eights and Sixes are *fiercely* loyal, which they tend to appreciate in each other. They can both be *all in* and trust that the other is too. Additionally, both also operate in a reactive conflict style, meaning they both want to be understood during conflict and disagreements can turn feisty in a heartbeat.

The Eight might roll their eyes at their Six spouse's caution, and Six may look on in horror when the Eight's reckless nature exerts itself, but overall these two get each other and trust each other on a level that is hard to replicate.

SIX/NINE, THE TRANQUIL ANXIOUS COUPLE

This is a quite common pairing, as Sixes tend to be attracted to Nines' easygoing, sweet, and safe presence. Nines are also no stranger to the Six's anxieties and worst-case scenario thinking, as they themselves experience these in stress. Decision paralysis can be real for this couple when the worse-case scenarios are many, and the Nine tries to be reassuring but usually isn't as decisive as the Six needs. They can stave off potential problems by not waiting until the last minute to make big decisions about expensive purchases, vacations, or other things that require some thought and discussion.

SEVEN/SEVEN, THE 100 MPH COUPLE

Sevens don't typically end up with fellow Sevens romantically, but it's not an impossible pairing to find. Sevens really appreciate a partner with a similar lust for adventure, stamina for fun, and independence. Their mutual optimism can be a gift—but it can also hurt both their marriage and them as individuals when hard things come up. Sevens have a habit of deflecting issues with distractions rather than working through them. The good times for this couple are *really* good, but when it comes to something serious, they may both run for the hills.

SEVEN/EIGHT, THE MATCHLESS ENERGY COUPLE

A Seven/Eight couple tends to lead to an active, fun, and nontraditional lifestyle, since neither of them likes to be told how their life *should* look. Having the ability to have a wing of the other's number, as well as Seven going to Five in growth and Eight going to Five in stress, helps this couple understand each other on multiple levels.

Problems can arise if the Eight assumes the alpha role in the relationship and tries to change the Seven into becoming more of a realist. This can cause the Seven to feel stuck and desperate for understanding outside of the marriage. Sevens also might not be as considerate and steady as their Eight spouse desires, which can cause growing bitterness. If both parties respect and value the other's strengths and are operating out of health, they both will feel happy and fulfilled in their relationship.

SEVEN/NINE, THE CONFLICT AVERSE COUPLE

Not an uncommon pairing, merging with a Seven can make a Nine look a lot like a Seven themselves. This couple will be incredibly supportive of each other, and a playful affection is usually at the center of their relationship. Nines will cheer on their Seven in all their grand ideas, and Sevens are great at calming nerves and getting the Nine out of their shell.

The trouble can come when it's time to make a decision. The Seven may act first and ask questions later, making the Nine feel like they don't matter. If the Seven does seek the Nine's input, the Nine may take *way* longer to make a decision than the Seven would appreciate.

Both of these Enneagram types do not like conflict and with an emphasis on the positive side of life, they may delay any conflict until it builds into a mountain too big to see around.

EIGHT/EIGHT, THE GO BIG OR GO HOME COUPLE

Two Eights together make for a passionate, independent, and energetic pairing. Eights tend to be attracted to other Eights for the pure strength they exude, as well as their honesty, justice-oriented focus, and hardworking nature—all things they value in themselves as well.

When two Eights get together, they can make a great team, but are not as affectionate as other couples tend to be. They are both independent people and value being able to be gone from their partner without feeling like they're doing something wrong.

This couple can get into trouble when they disagree about something big and neither will concede, or when they both reach seasons of stress and withdraw from each other, leaving them both feeling lonely and unloved.

EIGHT/NINE, THE TOUGH AND TENDER COUPLE

An Eight/Nine couple is a frequent pairing because although they are pretty opposite in almost every way, they meet each other as wings and in the gut triad. They recognize something in each other in the ways they think and operate. Their differences can complement each other, with one spouse being tough while the other is tender. The strengths of one will be the weaknesses of the other and vice versa. Nines feel protected by their Eight spouse, and Eights appreciate the ease of their Nine.

This couple will have their fair share of problems, especially if their communication isn't strong. I can't tell you how many Nines have messaged me to ask, "How do I get my Eight to listen to me?" The answer is, the Eight has to want to listen. You can't trick or manipulate an Eight into doing anything. So Nines need to be straightforward with their Eight spouse, who in turn needs to slow down and try hard to really listen.

NINE/NINE, THE GO WITH THE FLOW COUPLE

Two Nines together help each other achieve their common goal of being *undisturbed*, like living on an endless vacation. They both appreciate the other's down-to-earth nature, how their spouse doesn't start drama or conflict for no reason, and how they can often communicate without words. There is so much about two Nines being together that can feel like a dream, but we all know life is meant to be lived fully awake and alive. Two Nines together need to be careful that they don't settle for a life of no conflict instead of living a life they want.

● ● ● ● ● ● ● ● ●

There is no perfect Enneagram number, nor are there perfect pairings in marriage. Whether your spouse is interested in the Enneagram or not, they are always going to be the most trusted resource about themselves. Communication and asking those silly, awkward, and breath-holding questions are part of what it takes to truly get to know your spouse.

I know this chapter is far too brief to embody the immensely complex topic of marriage. If you would like to read more about different types in marriages, I recommend the Instagram page @enneagramandmarriage or the website www.enneagraminyourmarriage.com. Christa Hardin has devoted her career to helping marriages using the tools of the Enneagram. (For additional resources, see the book recommendations at the end of this book.)

14

PARENTING

As a parent you are never dealing just with the words and actions
of your children. You are always also dealing with the thing that
controls their words and behavior: the heart.
—*Paul David Tripp*

Parenting reveals a lot of things about your personality. Whether that's seeing your toddler act just like you, or handling the stress of caring for a wailing baby who's teething, the way you parent will reveal some truths about your motivations.

All of us will have different specifics, different children, and differing levels of comfort or discomfort in our parenting journey. But knowing what motivates us at our core gives us a good glimpse into how we may be prone to parent, and what our children may be feeling from us.

Most of us strive to be *good parents*, so hearing someone say that parts of our personality might be impacting our children negatively can be hard to take. However, I find it comforting to think of my own relationship with my parents when I am tempted to overanalyze my children's relationship with me. I can see my parents, their strengths and weaknesses, and what I have learned from them. Sometimes, their weaknesses hurt me, but ultimately, they had *no* impact on how much I love my parents.

● ● ●

PARENTING IS HUMBLING, AND YOUR CHILDREN CANNOT
BE SAVED FROM YOUR HUMANITY WITHOUT BEING
SEPARATED FROM YOU RELATIONALLY.

● ● ●

It can be uncomfortable to let your children learn from your weaknesses, have them choose something different based on how they saw you live, or even to know that your children may look back and remember all those bad moments with clarity. Parenting is humbling, and your children cannot be saved from your humanity without being separated from you relationally. In order for your flaws not to affect your children, you would have to stay away from them altogether. That, of course, is out of the question.

Even with your flaws and failures, your children still want *you*. Even if you hurt them, if you're reading this book trying to become a better parent, the chances are your heart is already for your children, and they want a relationship with you over everything.

It can also be comforting to know that all of us have both strengths and weaknesses. (See chapter 6, Our Parents' Enneagram Types, for more on the gifts that each type can instill in their children.)

It can be advantageous to look at parenting through two different lenses—what the healthiest version of yourself as a parent looks like, and what the unhealthiest looks like. Neither will describe you in full, but it will give you a clear goal, characteristics to nurture, warning signs, and characteristics to avoid.

ENNEAGRAM ONE

HEALTHY: THE CONSISTENT PARENT

As a parent, a healthy Enneagram One is consistent, whether that means they have dinner on the table at exactly 5:30 p.m. every day, they attend every tap dance recital without exception, or they discipline in the exact same way every time it's necessary. Ones find a way to do things, and they stick with it unless they are convinced of a better way. They are never inconsistent or flighty. This parenting style is good for children because it gives them stability, doesn't leave them guessing, and provides structure in a life that is ever-changing.

Enneagram Ones also go to Seven in growth, so they can be super fun as parents. Play, excitement, and spontaneity are all signs of a growing Enneagram One who is a gift to their children. There is a certain sense of calm when Enneagram Ones embrace fun and take themselves less seriously.

I will sacrifice anything for the emotional and physical health of my kids. I will always show up for my kids.
—*an Enneagram One parent*

UNHEALTHY: THE CRITICAL PARENT

An unhealthy Enneagram One will live with an air of frustration, and when this is pointed at their children, the parent comes across as critical and angry. The children are forced to tiptoe around the One's rules and try to keep them happy out of fear.

Adult children of unhealthy Ones report being hard on themselves, having people-pleasing behaviors, fixating on the areas where their parent was critical, and even having a version of an inner critic themselves even though they are not a One.

When Enneagram Ones are in a season of stress, we see them pick up many of the negative behaviors of Enneagram Fours. They may become hopeless, mopey, and depressive, focusing on their hurt and how everything is wrong.

IF YOU ARE AN ENNEAGRAM ONE PARENT...

Play is key. Lean into your growth number and embrace spontaneous trips, doing something fun *just because*, and all the play that your kids enjoy. This not only helps you engage with your children but unlocks something healthy and healing inside your own soul.

It can be a struggle not to let my rules come out as rigidity and anger toward my kids' mistakes. —*another Enneagram One parent*

ENNEAGRAM TWO

HEALTHY: THE COMFORTING PARENT

A healthy Enneagram Two is a nurturer and comforter in their very essence. They often report feeling *at home* in parenthood. Tending to their children's needs brings them a sense of purpose and belonging. Enneagram Twos have a natural ability to foresee needs that is helpful when they're parents. This gives their children a safe, attuned, and comforting nurturer who is always there for them.

Enneagram Twos go to Four in health, which gives them a flair of creativity and the ability to sit in pain without needing to fix it. This is abundantly helpful when the Two has teenagers with needs that are not as straightforward as a toddler's might be.

I enjoy my kids and being with them and do all I can to let them know they are loved. —*Mary, an Enneagram Two*

UNHEALTHY: THE SMOTHERING PARENT

An unhealthy Two may still appear to be a wonderful nurturer, but there is an air of pressure in their children being *everything* to them. For these Two parents, their children are their identity. The children fear the Two's retaliation and tears if they don't bend to their parent's subtle hints about their desires.

The Two's deadly sin of pride can keep them from seeing how unhealthy it is for them to prioritize their children above all else as well as the pressure it's putting on the children. Unfortunately, this sacrificial parenting style is often praised in Western culture.

Enneagram Twos go to Eight in stress, which means that when they sense they are losing control, they can get angry, or even spiteful and vengeful. Their children then obey and please them out of fear instead of the love that the Two craves.

When asked, several Enneagram Twos mentioned burnout and going to Eight in stress as their biggest parenting problems.

IF YOU ARE AN ENNEAGRAM TWO PARENT...

The best thing you can do for your children is to separate your identity from them. Being a parent is a wonderful thing, but it's not who you are. You are a child of God, a new creation. Being a parent is a job for you to steward. Your children do not owe you a relationship no matter how great of a parent you are. You can't control that. Don't let your children's sins later in life destroy your identity, but instead fix your identity firmly in Christ.

ENNEAGRAM THREE

HEALTHY: THE FUTURE-FOCUSED PARENT

Healthy Enneagram Threes are naturally encouraging and champion the God-given potential in their children. They see the abilities, gifts, and weaknesses of their children, and they want to set them up for success in the future, so they lovingly train, guide, and prepare them without any agenda of what they might become or how they might make the parent look more successful. Healthy Threes aren't afraid of failing, only doing what is right for their child in the eyes of God.

When growing, Enneagram Threes take on the strengths of type Six. They value loyalty over competition, they're better team players, and they gain a healthy amount of fear, which helps them to humbly come alongside those in their care.

I'm very proactive with parenting stuff. I'm not very reactive.
—*Jenna, an Enneagram Three*

UNHEALTHY: THE IDENTITY-FOCUSED PARENT

The unhealthy Three parent looks forward to their children's future and almost unconsciously chooses the route that looks most impressive as their children's future goal. Instead of loving encouragement, the child feels pressure to live up to their parent's dream. The weight of this image is placed on the child's shoulders, and they perform out of love or a sense of duty. When they grow up, many of these children later report that they did not even want the future their parent was manifesting for them, but because they were never given a choice, they really didn't see other options.

When the child rebels or fails, the Three's vision of themselves is shattered. They take their children's failures as personal failures on their part and replay over and over again what others must think of them.

When Threes are in seasons of stress, they will gain the negative characteristics of Nines, slowing down, numbing, and checking out. Threes become unrecognizable in stress and may even be detached from their surroundings.

> It's against my nature to let my children fail, so I tend to protect them too much sometimes. —*Olivia, a Three parent*

> I've been told that my expectations for my children are too high. —*Brynn, another Three*

IF YOU ARE AN ENNEAGRAM THREE PARENT...

Practicing an open-handed approach to your children's future will not only help you untangle your worth from their performance, but will save both you and your child a world of hurt. It's all right to hope for something and encourage your child in their strengths, but their future is ultimately up to them and may not align with your view of success.

ENNEAGRAM FOUR

HEALTHY: THE BE-WHO-YOU-ARE PARENT

A healthy Enneagram Four as a parent will be greatly attuned to their children and unfazed by the up-and-down emotions that come with growing up. They will delight in learning who their child is, be endlessly curious about them, and champion them in becoming their own unique person. Healthy Enneagram Fours are safe to the emotionally vulnerable—a huge asset in parenting.

As Fours grow, they take on healthy attributes of Enneagram Ones, becoming more consistent, logical, and organized, which helps children thrive in their environment.

When asked, several Enneagram Four parents mentioned their ability to understand and empathize with their kids' emotions being one of their biggest strengths. One notes, "It's not in my nature to shame my children because of how they're feeling."

UNHEALTHY: THE SELF-FOCUSED PARENT

An unhealthy Enneagram Four will come across as overstimulated by parenting and bothered by their children's needs. The Four's own emotions will feel loud and out of control, making them have little to no bandwidth for their children. These Fours may have bursts of creativity, fun, and caring as parents, but their lack of consistency leaves their children guessing and feeling uneasy. Overall, adult children of Enneagram Fours describe them as selfish, emotionally unstable, and hard to talk to because they monopolize the conversation with tales of themselves.

When Fours are in stress, they take up the unhealthy behaviors of Twos, becoming relationally clingy, manipulative, and needy.

> I find my own emotions to be my biggest struggle as a parent. Either I'm too overwhelmed with my own emotions to handle theirs, or I over-mesh myself in their emotions and don't let them work out things alone. —a Four parent

IF YOU ARE AN ENNEAGRAM FOUR PARENT...

Consistency and discipline are critical to your health as a parent. When passion wanes and you don't feel like doing what needs to be done, these two things are all that remain. You will often not feel like being a parent, and that's normal, but you will have to push through for the health and well-being of your children.

ENNEAGRAM FIVE

HEALTHY: THE TEACHER PARENT

Healthy Enneagram Fives are a wealth of accessible information to their children. They come down to their child's level and delight in learning with them. They don't get irritated by the child's lack of knowledge, but are fascinated by their innocence. Healthy Enneagram Fives establish healthy boundaries with their children to maintain their energy stores, but this can be a skill that takes a while to learn. Fives are also parents who are calm in crisis, thoughtful in discipline, and not overly reactive even when faced with lots of information or big emotions from their kids.

When Fives are growing, they gain healthy attributes of Enneagram Eights. They'll be more confident, action-oriented, and passionate, exemplifying knowledge in action for their children.

> I love how curious kids are! I get to learn with them and help them find the answers to their questions. —*Lila, a Five parent*

UNHEALTHY: THE ABSENT PARENT

An unhealthy Five will detach from their children in order to survive. Fives often have critically low energy stores, and withdrawing into their minds will make them highly self-focused. Even if they are not physically absent, they will be mentally aloof. Their children may grow up not even knowing who this parent truly is or anything about their past. Their inheritance will be a painful lack of parenting and attunement, leaving them to be a sponge for even the shallowest displays of affection.

Enneagram Fives pick up the worst traits of Enneagram Sevens when they are in stress, becoming distracted, hyper fixated, and indulgent, which only plays into their absence from their family.

When asked, several Enneagram Five parents mention noisiness and a lack of alone time as their biggest parenting struggles. One parent remarks, "It's hard to recharge yourself in an environment that feels overstimulating."

IF YOU ARE AN ENNEAGRAM FIVE PARENT...

Being present for your children doesn't mean you have to give 100 percent or nothing. You can demonstrate being available, attuned, and affectionate in your own way. Communicating and teaching your children about who you are and how you show affection will help them greatly in their future.

ENNEAGRAM SIX

HEALTHY: THE TRUSTWORTHY PARENT

A healthy Enneagram Six will be the most loyal and thoughtful parent, no matter who their child is or what they do. There is no losing the affection and support of a Six. They don't naturally see themselves as superior or all-knowing, making them notably humble parents. They want their children to be safe, to thrive, and to think for themselves.

In growth, Sixes gain the better attributes of Enneagram Nines, which gives them a slower, peaceful, and steady parenting style.

I help my children think through various possibilities and make thoughtful decisions. —*a Six parent*

UNHEALTHY: THE OVERPROTECTIVE PARENT

An unhealthy Enneagram Six may never leave their child's side, but rather than being a soft, comforting presence, their demeanor is anxious. Their children will not be allowed to experience falling and learning for themselves, which can lead to reckless behaviors later in their life. Adult children of unhealthy Sixes report being apathetic toward their parents' worries and rarely wanting to even speak to them as they think their parents are profoundly negative.

In stress, Sixes pick up the unhealthy behaviors of Enneagram Threes, which will give them a competitive, overworking edge and only heighten their energy toward preventing the worst.

I am constantly getting ahead of myself as a parent. If they just learned to crawl, I'm worried they won't learn to stand.
—*Amanda, a Six parent*

IF YOU ARE AN ENNEAGRAM SIX PARENT...

Slow and calm are your best friends. A packed schedule and fast pace rarely lead to a less-anxious Six. Give your kids a safe place to be free to roam and try to take life at a slower pace. It'll be good for your soul.

ENNEAGRAM SEVEN

HEALTHY: THE ADVENTUROUS PARENT

A healthy Enneagram Seven finds it easy to access their inner child and engage in play, make-believe, and adventures with their children. Unlike their unhealthy counterparts, this parent will have boundaries around their role as the parent and not let their children run them over. But they will balance authority and fun in a loving way. Sevens who are healthy want to give their child many fun childhood experiences while their innocence is still alive and well, so they try to make even the most mundane and boring things an enjoyable experience. This is their gift.

In health, Sevens gain the healthier traits of Enneagram Fives, which helps them find focus and consistency in their life, especially toward something that can be as mundane as parenting.

I'm good at planning fun and improvising when things aren't going as planned. —*a Seven parent*

UNHEALTHY: THE DISTRACTED PARENT

An unhealthy Enneagram Seven will still desire to give their children as many fun childhood experiences as possible, but these experiences will be inconsistent and tend to occur when the Seven is feeling distant from their children or bored themselves. In an effort to make their children happy, these parents may easily give in to their children's whims. Unhealthy Sevens are unusually distracted as parents. The pressures of adult life are uncomfortable, and they'll turn to one thing after another for distraction and comfort, often forgetting about their children's experience in the process. Their affection is sporadic, and their attention is even more so. Adult children of unhealthy Sevens report feeling like their parent was absent and unpredictable.

When Sevens are stressed, they gain the negative behaviors of type Ones, becoming highly critical of both themselves and others. They may engage in hyper-focus on what's wrong, often spending hours on cleaning or organizing.

My children who need consistency and schedules baffle me, and I really struggle to give them what they need in those areas.

—*Catherine, a Seven parent*

IF YOU ARE AN ENNEAGRAM SEVEN PARENT...

You need to set boundaries and focus on the here and now. Your children won't be happy adults if you give in to everything they want today, and your focus will not only benefit your children but will also help you grow.

ENNEAGRAM EIGHT

HEALTHY: THE PROTECTIVE PARENT

As parents, healthy Enneagram Eights are the definition of tough and tender. Their children will know that this parent is not to be messed with, but at the same time, they won't be afraid of the parent. Children know that their Eight parent will use their strengths *for* them, not against them.

Healthy Eight parents will be as quick to apologize to their children as they are to protect and defend them.

In growth, Eights gain the best qualities of Enneagram Twos, helping them become good listeners, softer, and more vulnerable, which makes them feel more accessible to their children.

I'm clear, direct, and my kids know what I'm asking for. They also know I'm always fiercely on their team.   —*an Eight parent*

UNHEALTHY: THE HARSH PARENT

An unhealthy Eight who's a parent can be particularly hard on their children. Their presence alternates from absent to scary, and there's not much in between. Eights dislike weakness, and an unhealthy Eight, in an effort to strengthen their children, will be harsh toward what they perceive as their children's weakness. Thus, their strong children become arrogant and harsh, and their sensitive children become scared and self-loathing.

In seasons of stress, Eights will take on the more negative aspects of Enneagram Fives, which plays into their absent periods in which they become withdrawn, fixated on projects or tasks, and guarded emotionally.

When asked, several Enneagram Eight parents say anger is their biggest parenting problem. One admits, "I blow up...I don't like it, but it happens."

> It's not natural for me to praise all the tiny accomplishments that my children make. I'd rather be coaching them toward making big strides and meeting goals. I'm not impressed by your finger painting—sorry! —*Kelly, an Eight parent*

IF YOU ARE AN ENNEAGRAM EIGHT PARENT...

You need to remember that strength is your default, so you need to *work* toward softness, especially toward your children. Slow down with them, listen, and meet them where they are.

ENNEAGRAM NINE

HEALTHY: THE EMPATHETIC PARENT

The healthy Enneagram Nine parent is truly empathetic toward their children. Their drive toward having a connected relationship with their own parents makes them also want to be deeply connected and attentive to their children. They are curious about them and enjoy them as they are, but are also able to separate their identities from what their children do. Healthy Enneagram Nine parents help their children feel understood and safe, but won't let their children run the show and have everything they want. They're dedicated to that balance.

When Nines are growing, they gain the best parts of Enneagram Threes, becoming more confident, action-oriented, and unafraid to assert their boundaries. All of these qualities help to balance out their gentle, humble nature and make them parents their children not only love but respect.

When asked, several Enneagram Nines mention their mediation skills and empathy being huge assets to them as parents. As one remarks, "Gentle parenting is very natural for me."

UNHEALTHY: THE PUSHOVER PARENT

An unhealthy Nine's fixation on peace turns toward their children's happiness and view of them as a parent. This fixation prevents them from asserting their own needs and boundaries in an appropriate parent-child relationship and instead gives control to the child. Adult children of Nines note they lack respect for their parent and also feel like they have to walk on eggshells to make sure they don't say things that upset them.

In seasons of stress, Nines gain the more negative traits of Enneagram Sixes. They experience heightened anxiety, worst-case scenario thinking, and less control over their outward responses toward what causes them anxiety.

> I hate feeling unheard. So if my kids aren't listening to me, it's very triggering.　　　　　　　　　　　　　　　—*Lee, a Nine parent*

IF YOU ARE AN ENNEAGRAM NINE PARENT...

Remember that boundaries are not mean and asserting your own presence helps your children to understand that they have permission to assert theirs.

• • • • • • • • •

We all will operate on a spectrum of healthy and unhealthy as parents. None of us are entirely healthy 100 percent of the time, so we will have some mix of healthy and unhealthy behaviors throughout our parenting. Keep in mind that fixating on how your children will remember you is fruitless and often leads to more trouble than it fixes. What *will* help your children is to see you trying, fixing your eyes on Jesus, and being quick to apologize and grow. Your children ultimately want healthy parents, and working on your health is just as much for them as it is for you.

If you are blessed to become a parent, your life will change during your adult years. There are added complications, anxiety, stress, joy, love, and blessing, all mixed together. Psalm 127:3 tells us that children are a blessing, so their addition to your life *is* a blessing. It can be hard to feel that way sometimes when children bring up some of the worst in our own personalities. Their own personalities might not always be easy for us to deal with as parents, but that doesn't subtract from the blessing they are.

15

CENTERS OF INTELLIGENCE: TRIADS

"**W**hy do you always take things so personally?"

"Don't you care at all?"

"What's wrong with you?"

"What do you mean, you need more time to think?"

These questions are conflict starters. We all have heard or said at least one of them, or something similar. They indicate a distinct misunderstanding about how we receive and process information, but it's hard to not assume that this process is universal and impersonal. This makes the mechanisms we use to receive and process information pivotal in understanding ourselves and others.

Centers of intelligence was a theory that was well-developed in Eastern culture before someone saw a pattern within the Enneagram. The centers of intelligence illuminated how we all process with our head center, heart center, or gut center—through thinking/analysis, emotions/connecting, and action/instinct, respectively.

HOW THIS PLAYS OUT

We see centers of intelligence come into play when we receive any type of information. While all of us use all three ways of thinking, we also tend to favor one or two, depending on our particular Enneagram type.

• • •

WHILE ALL OF US RECEIVE AND PROCESS INFORMATION USING OUR HEART, HEAD, OR GUT, WE TEND TO FAVOR ONE OR TWO OF THESE, DEPENDING ON OUR ENNEAGRAM TYPE.

• • •

When we look at the Enneagram and the centers of intelligence, we see that Two, Three, and Four favor the heart center; Five, Six, and Seven favor the head center; and One, Eight, and Nine favor the gut center. Since these types are grouped in threes, we refer to these as center of intelligence triads, or simply triads.

HEART CENTER

Those who are strongest in their heart center will receive information by asking, "How does this make me feel?"

HEAD CENTER

Those who are strongest in their head center retreat into analysis, asking lots of "Why?" and "What about?" questions in order to gain more information to analyze the situation. These questions may be asked internally or verbally.

GUT CENTER

Those who favor the gut center ask questions like, "What needs to be done?" or "Is this right or wrong?" This indicates an instinct-based thought process.

RECEIVING VS. PROCESSING INFORMATION

To further understand how triads work in practical application, let's take a look at how we receive information compared to how we process information.

When we receive information, it takes milliseconds for our brains to understand it, whether it's a situation, a conversation with someone, or something we're reading. Our brains work so well that it can be hard for us to pinpoint and differentiate this state from *processing* because it happens so fast!

● ● ●

THE MOMENT OF RECEIVING INFORMATION WILL BE ACCOMPANIED BY A DEEP EMOTION, A GUT RESPONSE, OR A NEED TO GATHER MORE INFORMATION.

● ● ●

But which center you use to receive information directly impacts how you process it. The moment of receiving information will be accompanied by a deep emotion, a gut response, or a need to gather more information in order to analyze what you've just received.

Processing information is what we do to cope with our initial response to receiving information. Most of us use a different center of intelligence to process information than we do to receive it.

For example, for an Enneagram Three, there can be a sharp shift from "Oh, no, I feel horrible about this!" (a heart response) to "What do I need to know to solve or reshape this?" (head processing). An Enneagram Nine in the same situation could shift from "What do I need to do here?"(gut response) to "I hate what needs to happen!" (heart processing).

As with every processing and coping strategy we use, the goal is balance and growth. We need to feel, think, *and* act, but it takes work to get there. By learning about your natural bent and shedding light on your blind spots, you can receive information as an invitation to grow and participate in the hard work of balance.

● ● ●

LEARNING ABOUT YOUR FAVORED CENTER OF INTELLIGENCE AND SHEDDING LIGHT ON YOUR BLIND SPOTS WILL HELP YOU REACT FROM A POSITION OF GROWTH.

● ● ●

This is how each Enneagram type first receives information and then processes it:

ENNEAGRAM ONE (GUT TO HEAD)

Enneagram Ones are considered part of the gut triad. They receive information as right or wrong, and although they may think this reaction is logical, they actually aren't using their head to come to this conclusion but their gut instinct. Their gut is working to keep them aligned with their core motivation to be good and right.

However, Enneagram Ones move on to process the information with their head. They want facts, they want more communication, and they want to double-check their gut instinct. Ones are the only type in the gut triad for whom this is a natural instinct.

Ones can get stuck in an analysis and action mode in which they analyze the information, plan for action...and then repeat the process.

Ones tend to be weak in the heart center, unable to clearly see the situation from another point of view or accurately assess how it might be making others feel before moving forward. Being weak in this center specifically can attribute to a lot of hurt feelings in others; meanwhile, the One feels superior for dealing with things logically and without emotion.

If you're a One, how do you push into growth in your heart center? In the midst of instinct, reaction, and analysis, you must ask, "How does this make me feel?" The answer may not come as quickly as you'd like, but something like a wheel of feelings or emotions could be a helpful tool.

Another good exercise would be to ask others how your actions have made them feel while trying not to become defensive or offended, which would prevent them from being open and honest.

ENNEAGRAM TWO (HEART TO GUT)

Twos are considered to be part of the heart triad. "How does this make me feel?" is the first and foremost question they ask themselves as they receive information. Being part of the heart triad means they have to fight against taking things personally. Not everything happens to evoke an emotional response from the Two, and not everything deserves the energy of one.

However, Twos quickly move on to process information with their gut, asking, "What action is needed here?" If the information made the Two sad, then those in the sad situation probably need something to cheer them up. If the information made the Two happy, their gut instinct asks, "What should we do to celebrate?" This is how their mind automatically processes information. Twos don't sit around and wallow in the emotion they feel; they let the emotion inform them of what needs to happen next.

Twos tend to struggle in their head center. They may think *a lot* and get stuck. They'll think over interactions until they've read way too much into them, or they will dwell on something that *could* happen until they drive themselves (and everyone around them) crazy.

If you're a Two, to push toward growth in your head center, you need to distract yourself when you get stuck in a thought spiral of unhealthy thinking. Watch something on TV or a funny YouTube video, read a book, go for a walk, or go to bed. You're not going to help yourself by continuing to think about the problem. You may return to it later, but you need some distance. This way, logic and facts will become clear.

Ask a friend who is strong in their head center to listen to you verbally process and give you feedback. This can help train you to think more like they do if they show you how to untangle your thoughts.

ENNEAGRAM THREE (HEART TO HEAD/GUT)

As part of the heart triad, Enneagram Threes receive information by the way it makes them feel, particularly if the information makes them feel valued or not. Threes can take offense at any information that does not make them feel valued. Like Twos, they need to put the brakes on this response.

What's interesting about Threes in particular is that even though they are in the heart triad, they are considered to be emotionally repressed. After initially receiving information in their hearts, they quickly pass it on to the head or gut, so their main center is also their weakest.

Processing with the head or gut means Threes typically push away whatever emotion pops up and try to make their action plan as logical and emotion-free as possible. Emotion is messy; thinking and acting are efficient. Threes like that.

If you're a Three, you can push into growing in your heart center by acknowledging how much your initial feeling response impacts everything else. You may think you're removing emotion entirely, but it's not gone, just suppressed.

Staying in that emotion—even if it feels like the worst thing in the world—will enable you to better process the information. This is where a counselor, a close friend, or journaling come in handy. Have an ear that you can bring your emotional response to so you can iron it out before putting it away. It won't consume you or define you, processing doesn't make you weak, the discomfort will leave eventually, and you will be better for it.

ENNEAGRAM FOUR (HEART TO HEART)

Enneagram Fours are considered to be a part of the heart triad, but they are the only type that both receives and processes information through their heart center.

When something first comes up, they'll ask, "How does this make me feel?" If the answer they come up with is "sad," they will then ask, "How does *that* make me feel?" They might feel lonely, shunned, disappointed, inadequate, or some other emotion. Fours can appear to be dwelling in emotion, especially negative emotion. But they can also dwell in positive emotion.

Fours will take one emotion to its furthest logical conclusion, and if they're healthy, they'll let it go. As a Four, I know from experience that the journey isn't fun, but any counselor or therapist would tell you that processing emotions like this does reduce a lot of unhealthy emotional coping in the future.

Fours will be weaker in either their head center or gut center, depending on their level of health and which wing they lean toward. (See more on wings in chapter 19.) If they have a Five wing, they may be stronger in their head center; if they are healthier and going to One in growth, they'll be stronger in their gut center.

If you're a Four, you need to practice distancing yourself from the emotional spiral you can get caught up in and gather more facts to access the head center. Research the problem, devise a next step, and get second opinions. Shelving your emotions until you know more is *really* hard, but it is the best decision to make when there are unknowns that are causing you pain. The more you practice distancing yourself from your emotional processing to gather facts, the easier it'll be to resort to that in the midst of great emotion.

To access the gut center, Fours need to get physical. Prioritize exercise—even if it's just short sessions three times a week—do breath prayers, get massages, and try to take inventory of how your body feels. You also need to work on trusting your instincts. Try to separate how you feel about something from what you know to be true. Sit in the tension and let your gut inform your feelings.

ENNEAGRAM FIVE (HEAD TO HEAD)

Enneagram Fives are considered to be part of the head triad, receiving information through the lens of analysis and facts. They'll weigh a situation by what they know and what they need to find out.

Fives also process information through their head center. First, they ask, "What do I know? What more do I need to know?" Once they have the details, they ask, "What is this information telling me about what I know to be true, and what I may need to learn more about?"

Fives will then process with their gut or heart centers, depending on their wings and level of health. A Four wing can give a Five more access to the heart center, and growing to Eight will give them more access to the gut center.

If you're a Five, to grow in your heart center, you need to follow up some of your analysis with questions about how this information is impacting you or others emotionally. If this information is bad for someone, will they be sad? Angry? How do *you* feel about them feeling this way?

To grow in your gut instinct, spend some time each day engaging your body in exercise or some other physical pursuit to stop the constant absorption of information. Your mind has a tendency to wander, so practicing anything that helps you slow your mind and keep your body busy will be helpful here. Ask yourself, "What is my gut telling me?" when you have the urge to learn more before making a decision. Your gut is significant and strong, but you need to trust it occasionally in order to fully appreciate it.

ENNEAGRAM SIX (HEAD TO GUT/HEART)

Enneagram Sixes are considered to be part of the head triad, receiving information as something to be analyzed and thought through. However, just like their arrow counterparts, Nine and Three, Sixes' primary center is also the one where they are weakest.

You may think anxiety comes from the head, but it actually comes from the heart or gut. The head relies on facts, while the heart or gut can have just a twinge of a bad feeling and run with it, no facts involved.

After receiving information as something to be thought about, Sixes quickly move on to, "How does this make me feel? What is my gut telling me about this?" The two instincts often inform each other, making up a Six's inner committee. There's a general sense of dread or worry that they aren't thinking of all possible scenarios, and that feeling gives them the energy to take some sort of preventative action.

If you are a Six, you can grow in your head center by returning there. Once you start feeling and preparing for action, ask yourself, "What do I know? What do I need to know? What are the facts? Who can I ask?"

Your feelings and gut instinct don't get to decide what is fact, and they do a poor job of predicting the future. What you probably need in these moments is reassurance, more details, and positive information.

ENNEAGRAM SEVEN (HEAD TO HEART)

Sevens are considered part of the head triad, where they receive information as something to analyze. This may surprise others because Sevens seem to be action-oriented and feeling people. However, a flood of analysis occurs when Sevens receive information. They will move on rather quickly to feeling, asking, "How do I feel about this information?" Does it excite them? Make them want to hide? Make them want to plan? Depending on the answer to that question, Sevens tend then to return to the head to gather more information and plan for what will make them feel the most pleasure. Some call this *dopamine chasing*. The Seven may plan a vacation, ignore the information altogether, or gather more information that will change their emotional response from sad to happy.

If you are a Seven, you need to grow in your gut instinct for the problems that give you an adverse emotional reaction. Asking, "What do I need to do here?" might help you push past the uncomfortable emotion and find the right action before returning to your mind.

ENNEAGRAM EIGHT (GUT TO GUT)

Enneagram Eights are considered to be a part of the gut triad, receiving information through the reaction of action. Their gut is oriented toward *doing* and because they process the information through their gut as well, Eights are hard to slow down when their gut tells them that there is something to be done.

The question, "What needs to happen here?" will often feel obvious to Enneagram Eights—almost infuriatingly so. When no one else seems to be taking action, Eights take it upon themselves to be the example. It's a misconception that an Eight wants to be the person to steam ahead and call the shots. They'd actually rather be left alone for the most part. But their gut won't let them sit idly by when there is something that needs to happen, especially if no one else is willing to do it.

If you're an Eight, you need to grow in the head center, gathering more information before acting, and the heart center, asking, "How do my actions make others feel?" You can gain a plethora of empathetic processing power by going to Two in growth. (See chapter 7, Seasons of Stress and Growth.) Slowing down when your instinct is telling you to *do something* can be difficult, but you need to learn to hit the brakes and ask a couple of questions before charging ahead.

ENNEAGRAM NINE (GUT TO HEART/HEAD)

Enneagram Nines are considered to be part of the gut triad, where they receive information as an instinctual *good or bad*. However, like their arrow counterparts, Three and Six, they do not process with their strongest center. In fact, most Nines silence their gut altogether and move on quickly to feeling and thinking.

When heart processing, the Nine may ask, "How does this make me feel? Is this stealing my peace? Does this make me happy?" On the other hand, with head processing, the Nine may ask, "What do they think about this? Did I react the right way? Did I do the right thing? Did my reaction cause conflict"

If you're a Nine, you will experience growth by returning to your gut instinct and learning to trust it. This may make you uncomfortable at first because the gut is solely *your* experience. It doesn't consult others or care about keeping the peace. Asking questions like, "What was my initial gut response to this?" and giving yourself time to consult your gut before responding can be helpful in learning to trust what it says.

● ● ● ● ● ● ● ● ●

In adulthood, there are a lot of interactions to manage—at home, at work, or even going to the grocery store. There is always someone to talk to about something. There may be a problem to solve, or some kind of information that needs to be passed on.

Determining where you lean on the centers of intelligence will not only help you understand yourself better, but will also help you with all your interactions with people who may not receive or process information the way you do. It's human nature to regard anything different with an air of suspicion or judgment, but it will serve you well to be sensitive and curious here.

16

WORKPLACE STANCES

Don't judge each day by the harvest you reap but
by the seeds that you plant.
—*Robert Louis Stevenson*

It's estimated that around 90,000 hours of your life are spent at work. With so much of our time and energy being spent earning a living, knowing how our personality is paying into common workplace problems and how to better understand our coworkers can be life-changing.

One of my favorite Enneagram theories happens to play heavily into the work environment. It's called stances or Hornevian groups. These groupings are based on how we position ourselves toward others in order to get our needs met. Theorized by the German psychoanalyst Karen Horney, these three strategies include compliance, aggression, and withdrawal.

● ● ●

PEOPLE USUALLY USE ONE OF THREE STANCES OR STRATEGIES TO GET THEIR NEEDS MET: COMPLIANCE, AGGRESSION, AND WITHDRAWAL.

● ● ●

Karen Horney did not merge her model with the Enneagram; this was accomplished by many Enneagram teachers who saw how perfectly this model, another triad, fit with this typology. Enneagram teachers have called this theory "stances" because they describe our general posture or disposition toward others. We take our particular stance in order to get our needs met.

I find the theory of stances to be particularly helpful in the workplace, where we may not be able to know everyone's Enneagram type, but their disposition is relatively easy to decipher. This gives us a practical resource to move forward in understanding them.

Stances are more about how others experience us rather than how we see ourselves. Even though they are positions we use in order to get our needs met, they just feel like autopilot to us. However, they are loud to others, especially in times of conflict.

If the stance for your particular Enneagram type doesn't make sense to you, read the other descriptions of stances. Depending on your wing, you could be using another stance or a blend of two stances. For example, if you are a Four with a Three wing or a Nine with an Eight wing (4w3, 9w8), you could be considered withdrawn-aggressive. A 5w6 or 9w1 might be withdrawn-compliant. There are several possibilities for your type, depending on your wing or whether you are in a season of growth or stress.

Here is a brief overview on stances.

THE COMPLIANT STANCE: ONE, TWO, SIX

People operating under the compliant stance get their needs met by moving toward others. Their view of who they are and how they're performing is found outside themselves, in how others are reacting to them. So they will move toward people to please them, fix conflict, and communicate needs in order to establish their own goodness, lovability, or need for security.

The compliant stance struggles to say "no." In work environments, they often have poor boundaries with authority. They are extremely responsible and thrive off of knowing others think they are proficient and dependable.

If they feel they have been used or disrespected, they will be indignant and angry. This can be hard for them to hide, but being the good, responsible workers that they are, it often comes out in passive-aggressive ways, not outright hostility.

● ● ●

IN A WORK ENVIRONMENT, THE COMPLIANT STANCE THRIVES IN A TEAM ENVIRONMENT WHERE THERE IS LOTS OF OPEN COMMUNICATION AND FEEDBACK.

● ● ●

In a work environment, the compliant stance thrives in a team environment where there is lots of open communication and feedback. In any work environment they find themselves in, they will always seek more communication and feedback on their work, which can make others think they are clingy and need hand-holding to do their job.

THE WITHDRAWN STANCE: FOUR, FIVE, NINE

Those in the withdrawn stance get their needs met by withdrawing internally. Whether they are thinking, feeling, or numbing will depend on their core type, but when they feel disrespected, their instinct is to run rather than attract or freeze.

The withdrawn stance is overstimulated by the world in general and has a lot of natural boundaries to keep themselves feeling safe. They naturally assume others have these boundaries too, and they don't often communicate what their boundaries are. This can lead to all sorts of problems because while they may feel disrespected when their boundaries are crossed, the offending party didn't even know they were crossing this silent boundary.

When they feel disrespected, those with the withdrawn stance may still be kind and outwardly pleasant, but internally, they will be completely shut down toward the offending party. It takes a lot of work for them to give second chances as they tend to believe others are showing their true colors and don't anticipate change.

The withdrawn stance has the least amount of energy on the entire Enneagram. They can be extroverted but the large majority are introverted individuals.

● ● ●

IN A WORK ENVIRONMENT, PEOPLE IN THE WITHDRAWN STANCE TEND TO BE PRETTY INDEPENDENT WORKERS WHO DON'T GO ABOVE AND BEYOND.

● ● ●

In a work environment, people in the withdrawn stance tend to be pretty independent workers who don't go above and beyond. The work laid out for them often tends to be a boundary they keep. They prioritize a work-life balance and are relatively drama-free in an office environment.

Others can think those with the withdrawn stance are too quiet, not team players, and kind of weird…at first. It can take a member of the withdrawn stance a long time to warm up to a new work environment

THE ASSERTIVE STANCE: THREE, SEVEN, EIGHT

People with the assertive stance get their needs met by standing firm in conflict. To others, this can feel like pushing back. When disrespected or stuck, the assertive stance's first instinct is to fight. This stance comes across as confident and energetic.

With their wide bandwidth and general take-charge attitude, they tend to be hard workers and hold themselves to a high productivity level. They also expect this same standard from others, which can cross boundaries when they expect other types to have the same stamina they do.

The assertive stance values honest, direct communication and does not want to waste time wallowing in emotions or tiptoeing around issues. For the most part, they will assume others are fine unless they speak up.

● ● ●

THOSE WITH THE ASSERTIVE STANCE VALUE HONEST, DIRECT COMMUNICATION AND DO NOT WANT TO WASTE TIME WALLOWING IN EMOTIONS OR TIPTOEING AROUND ISSUES.

● ● ●

Although you may assume people with the assertive stance gravitate toward leadership, they often don't want to be the leader. They understand the work, time, and energy that goes into leadership roles, where the pressure to perform can be suffocating at times. However, they won't be led by someone who is incompetent, which by default can make them step up to be the leader if there is no one else.

People know that someone with the assertive stance is often the first to say something if there is silence and will be the first to raise their hand if there is hesitation. Others may take advantage of this and use it to get out of doing things they'd rather not do, thus putting a larger workload on those with the assertive stance.

• • • • • • • • •

COMMON DESIRES

We can see some common desires among different Enneagram types and their stances that can help us interact with them in the workplace.

ONES, TWOS, AND SIXES WANT COMMUNICATION

Operating under the compliant stance, these types want to know very clearly what's expected of them, they want feedback, and they need to know if you approve of the work they did. For the other two stances, this can seem like over-communication.

• • •

ONES, TWOS, AND SIXES DO NOT LIKE TO BE SET UP FOR FAILURE SIMPLY BECAUSE YOU DIDN'T COMMUNICATE SOMETHING TO THEM.

• • •

Reassurance is huge for the compliant stance. They also want to be prepared for what's expected of them. They do not like to be set up for failure simply because you didn't communicate something to them. Communication feels like respect to this stance.

FOURS, FIVES, AND NINES WANT WORK-LIFE BALANCE

Using the withdrawn stance, these types do a lot of living inside their own heads. They want the freedom to experience life at their own pace in the spaces they're comfortable with. For Fours, this means being able to express and create their own identity. Even if they love their job, people with the withdrawn stance have a pull toward their home life—where they have control—that is stronger than the other stances.

● ● ●

WHEN FOURS, FIVES, AND NINES FEEL PRESSURE TO MAKE THEIR JOB THEIR TOP PRIORITY, OR DON'T FEEL FREE TO EXERCISE THEIR WORK-LIFE BALANCE, THEY SHUT DOWN.

● ● ●

When they feel pressure to make their job their number one priority, or don't feel free to exercise their work-life balance, they shut down, and morale goes out the window. This is especially true when they are expected to come in early, stay late, or work on their days off. They need the clear-cut boundaries of a schedule, and they need others to respect their time by not expecting more than what was asked of them.

THREES, SEVENS, AND EIGHTS WANT PRODUCTIVITY

Those with the assertive stance need things to keep moving. They don't care how it gets done as long as it gets done. They all share a mutual hatred for stalled projects, boredom, or waiting for no reason.

● ● ●

THREES, SEVENS, AND EIGHTS SHARE A MUTUAL HATRED FOR STALLED PROJECTS, BOREDOM, OR WAITING FOR NO REASON.

● ● ●

In a workplace, those who are not productive feel disrespectful to these three Enneagram types, especially if they are hindering the work they are trying to do. Threes, Sevens, and Eights have a lot of task energy, and as long as they believe in the goals or feel respected within their work environment, they are hard-working individuals.

COMMON PAIN POINTS

Within these stances, we also find common pain points around boundaries. These pain points ultimately make them miss the other stances' points of view and create a harder work-life balance for themselves.

ONES, TWOS, AND SIXES STRUGGLE TO SET WORKPLACE BOUNDARIES

Those in the compliant stance want to be responsible and trustworthy. They may falsely assume that taking time off, delegating, and saying "no" means they are not good workers—and your view of them as a good worker means everything to them. They tend to take on too much and then not let any of it go, causing them to feel burnt out and resentful toward everyone else because they're not doing *their part*.

● ● ●

ONES, TWOS, AND SIXES MAY FALSELY ASSUME THAT TAKING TIME OFF, DELEGATING, AND SAYING "NO" MEANS THEY ARE NOT GOOD WORKERS.

● ● ●

Things can get really testy if they feel underappreciated for all the extra work that they are doing, or if they begin to feel used. Growing in boundaries and work-life balance will require these types to do some deep work on where their identity comes from and who they are, even if others think they aren't doing enough.

FOURS, FIVES, AND NINES STRUGGLE TO COMMUNICATE THEIR BOUNDARIES

People with the withdrawn stance harbor hurt over crossed boundaries. They struggle to imagine a life with fewer boundaries, or those who do not have a strong pull toward home. When others ask more of them than they are willing to give, they feel disrespected and misunderstood, causing them to pull away from their workplace relationally and mentally.

● ● ●

WHEN OTHERS ASK MORE OF FOURS, FIVES, AND NINES THAN THEY ARE WILLING TO GIVE, THEY FEEL DISRESPECTED AND MISUNDERSTOOD.

● ● ●

There is nothing more unprotected or uncommunicative than someone with a shut-down withdrawn stance, which their assertive and complaint stance coworkers find hard to bear. It's only when the withdrawn stance person braves having their boundaries heard and does the hard work of communication that they can work in harmony with others.

THREES, SEVENS, AND EIGHTS STRUGGLE TO RESPECT OTHERS' BOUNDARIES

Types with the assertive stance assume others have as much energy as they do. This leads to people around them feeling disrespected or to uneven work environments in which most employees have the assertive stance because the strengths of the other two stances are not valued. This creates a workplace with poor communication and no work-life balance, yet lots of individual productivity.

● ● ●

IT'S HARD FOR THREES, SEVENS, AND EIGHTS TO IMAGINE LIFE WITH LESS ENERGY; THEY THINK WORKING HARD MEANS GIVING THEIR ALL, NO MATTER WHAT.

● ● ●

Those with the assertive stance can struggle as they attempt to deal with their coworkers and employees. It's hard for them to imagine life with less energy; they think working hard means giving their all, no matter what. It's only when the types with this stance do the hard work of putting themselves in others' shoes and adjusting their expectations that they can truly build a work environment based on mutual respect and trust.

17

INDIVIDUAL ENNEAGRAM TYPES AT WORK

We won't have pure motives until we see Jesus face to face,
but in the meantime, we can be aware that the
visible can overwhelm the invisible.
Gradually, we can learn to live in the tension between
outward success and inward fulfillment,.and we can experience
increasing levels of gratitude and passion.
—*Sam Chand*

The workplace, finding a job, changing jobs, and overall work/life fulfillment are huge challenges that mark our adult years. Like marriage and parenting, the challenges we face and the joy we find in this facet of our lives can be impacted by our personality. Self-awareness in this area is key to making the best choices for you and what you ultimately want out of a career.

For our last chapter in the section on adulthood, we turn to how each individual Enneagram type operates in the workplace.

ENNEAGRAM ONE

As a coworker or employee of an Enneagram One, you'll probably feel like they take a lot of unnecessary steps to get things done and are overly preoccupied with rules and orderliness. Try to have grace for the One you're dealing with, as they're not trying to control you as much as they're trying not to get in trouble with their inner critic. They also *do* probably know the best way to accomplish a task or goal, and although it may take extra time, you can count on them to do it well.

Ones like work environments that are consistent and stable, with rules that make sense. They also like environments that they can improve and provide an added value.

If you're managing a One, they'll do really well with tasks in which you need to find and correct errors. Make sure they know your expectations because clear communication feels like respect to them. At the end of the day, try to give your One employee the respect that their quality of work deserves, and you'll see them shine.

ENNEAGRAM TWO

Twos at work will pride themselves on making their coworkers' lives better, knowing all the workplace secrets, being a behind-the-scenes puppet master, and bringing everyone together. If morale is bad, a Two will almost take it personally, or at least make it their goal to do their part to improve the situation. For instance, they will bring in cookies or dough-nuts to share.

Much like Threes, Twos thrive on praise and admiration in the work-place, but they go about getting it in different ways. The Three wants to be the boss, but the Two wants to be the boss's favorite.

Twos do best in environments where they feel supported. They may quit many jobs early on if they sense a lack of support or if they don't feel loved. They don't feel work is worthwhile without relationships, so Twos don't tend to work for themselves.

ENNEAGRAM THREE

The American workplace was made for Threes, and Threes might believe it's vice versa. The workplace is a goldmine of praise, fulfillment, and value, and it's easy to assume your job title as your identity. Threes have the most energy when there is a task to complete, but this is also when they're the least aware of themselves. They confuse completed tasks, a heavy workload, and a pat on the back with emotional fulfillment. However, the pleasure they derive from praise is fleeting, and there is always more to be done, leaving the Three never completely satisfied.

Being the coworker of a Three can prove challenging at times. Few numbers can keep up with their energy, and when their image is on the line, Threes have high standards for your work. If you're managing a Three, you're bound to appreciate how they get stuff done, but you may need to encourage them to take a vacation or go home when the workday is over.

ENNEAGRAM FOUR

Fours thrive in work environments where they're free to feel, create, and inspire. They'll want to be liked and noticed for what they uniquely contribute. They tend to have a hard time with the boss's favorite. A lot of Fours end up working for themselves because they love the freedom to follow their creative highs. They also love highly emotional jobs in which they can use their talents and feel a sense of connection, such as counselor, 911 operator, or pastor.

If you're managing a Four, you will need to give them set rules and expectations because it's sometimes hard for them to feel like doing more than is expressly expected of them. You'll also do well to give your Four a project with a clear outcome and let them decide how to work on it. You'll be surprised by how they bloom when given freedom to create.

ENNEAGRAM FIVE

A Five is a great employee, but not always fun as a coworker. They will work hard to gain independence and not have to work *with* you. Don't take this personally. Fives need space and freedom in order to thrive in their work environments.

As a supervisor, a Five will delegate social aspects of their work to an assistant, if that's an option. They'll want to communicate indirectly through emails so they can take their time to respond. They'll be highly knowledgeable and good at what they do, but their office door will usually be closed.

If you work with a Five, it's best to make your expectations clear, and always tell them how long a meeting will take.

ENNEAGRAM SIX

Sixes experience an internal paradox of being action-paralyzed when they achieve success, yet getting things done against incredible odds when their backs are against the wall. This happens because Sixes struggle with self-doubt when they believe their best decisions might be behind them, but are able to see an issue from many different worst-case scenarios and plan for them accordingly in stressful times.

In a work meeting, the Six will be the one who raises their hand and says, "Yes, but..." or "Have you considered that this may not work?" A natural worst-case-scenario thinker, a Six's doubt might be annoying to more ambitious or confident types, but we need Sixes' cautious attitude nonetheless.

ENNEAGRAM SEVEN

A Seven at work is a breath of fresh air for morale. They bring a positive outlook, enthusiasm, and joy that few can match. However, managing a Seven can be much like trying to train an older cat. Sevens naturally set themselves up as benign on a peer level with everyone, making people beneath their social level feel honored and those in authority feel frustrated.

Sevens assume they're generally likable, so they don't feel the need impress their boss to be liked. That being said, Sevens are a wealth of great ideas, are fun to work with, and thrive in fast-paced environments.

ENNEAGRAM EIGHT

Contrary to popular opinion, Eights do not need to be *in control*; they just don't want to be under someone else's control. This is often why we find Eights in leadership roles and why they can feel challenging in work environments where rules, boundaries, and control are inevitable.

Eights are hard workers; they roll up their sleeves and get things done. They don't dillydally, waste time, or procrastinate when it comes to work—and they expect the same from their coworkers or subordinates.

ENNEAGRAM NINE

For Nines, success in the workplace is all about how the job makes them feel. Nines are great at all sorts of jobs, and their ability to merge can be a gift when it comes to morale, support, and dedication. They don't tend to like surprises or sudden change in their workplace and find clearly defined rules comforting.

Nines, however, can be easily overwhelmed by jobs in which they feel unfairly pushed, have heavy workloads, or they don't believe their personal well-being is taken into account. Nines are prone to stay in bad jobs for far too long, hoping that things will change if they wait it out and that they will be able to avoid conflict.

• • • • • • • •

Finding a workplace that gives us life, joy, and purpose doesn't normally happen by accident. In fact, it can take a lot of trial and error for us to find the right jobs. Money aside, if we spend the majority of our adult life working, then enjoying our work is indispensable to our quality of life.

● ● ●

FINDING WORK THAT GIVES US LIFE, JOY, AND PURPOSE CAN TAKE A LOT OF TRIAL AND ERROR. MONEY ASIDE, ENJOYING OUR WORK IS INDISPENSABLE TO OUR QUALITY OF LIFE.

● ● ●

What each Enneagram type needs in any work environment can be boiled down to three main categories:

+   The cause for which they are working
+   The people with whom they work

+ The kind of work they're actually doing

Noticing what each type needs in these categories can help them make decisions about the workplace they need in order to fulfill the needs that motivate them.

ENNEAGRAM ONE

Ones value improving, communication, and the freedom to implement improvements.

+ The cause: Ones do best when their work is improving or benefitting people's lives or the world at large.

+ The people: No matter the personality of their coworkers, Ones will do well if they have clear and consistent communication of expectations and feedback.

+ The work: Ones are problem solvers, and they need some sort of work environment where they have the freedom to improve systems. If they notice something that could be done better, do they have freedom to offer that feedback and help implement improvements?

ENNEAGRAM TWO

For Twos, work and life in general is all about the people.

+ The cause: The Two's cause is people and relationships. They need the work they do to benefit people or the relationships they hold dear.

+ The people: Twos want the people they work with to like them, and they would miss you if you left. Twos need to feel like they're part of the group and cared about as an individual.

+ The work: Twos can do almost any sort of work, but if they notice someone needs help, they want their help to be warmly received and appreciated.

ENNEAGRAM THREE

Threes esteem opportunity, encouragement, and accomplishment.

+ The cause: Threes need personal improvement, opportunity, room to improve, and a way to find success in the work they do.

+ The people: They want the freedom to improve people. If they notice that someone isn't reaching their potential or is slowing productivity, the Three wants to be able to offer feedback and suggestions.

+ The work: Threes need work that is seen either by themselves or others. They need boxes to check, quotas to meet, and a way to go above and beyond.

ENNEAGRAM FOUR

Fours treasure a cause, community, and creating.

+ The cause: Fours need to be a part of something bigger than themselves to work for or toward. Simply making money isn't enough.

+ The people: Fours need to feel seen by the people with whom they work. They want to feel like they're part of the group and cared about as a person.

+ The work: Fours need creative freedom within the type of work they do. They want to be able to make the environment or job their own and do things in their own way.

ENNEAGRAM FIVE

Fives value independence, learning, and trust.

+ The cause: The type of cause a Five will support will vary with each individual, but a lot of the time, you'll find that a roof over their head and food on the table is enough of a cause for them.

+ The people: Fives want trust and freedom to be independent at work. If they are given tasks, they can be trusted to complete them without micromanagement or interference.

+ The work: Fives want to have the opportunity to learn more in their field and grow in their knowledge. They want a job where they aren't surprised by the expectations day to day.

ENNEAGRAM SIX

Sixes want to be proactive, trusted, and honest.

+ The cause: Sixes want to feel proactive in the world, but they are often fine doing work that keeps them and their family secure.

+ The people: If Sixes feel distrusted, especially if they believe this is unjustified, their morale tanks. They want to feel trusted because they know they are trustworthy. They want people to trust them more than they want people to like them.

+ The work: Sixes honestly don't care what type of work they do as long as it's a job that isn't precarious.

ENNEAGRAM SEVEN

Sevens have a high regard for excitement, comradery, and freedom.

+ The cause: Sevens want work they can feel good about that ideally incorporates things they like to do so it doesn't feel like work.

+ The people: Sevens appreciate inside jokes and a positive workplace. In general, Sevens want to like their coworkers, but they don't need to be lifelong friends.

+ The work: Sevens don't want to feel trapped by their job; they don't want to feel like they are forced to be there. They also like a workplace that is constantly changing and evolving.

ENNEAGRAM EIGHT

Eights appreciate the cause, independence, and hard work.

+ The cause: Eights want to work for something bigger than themselves and counteract some of the injustice and evil that's in the world.

+ The people: Eights prefer little to no supervision and the ability to do their work on their own time. They also require the freedom to ignore incompetent people and don't want them in a position of authority over them.

+ The work: Eights are hard workers and don't want work that feels inconsequential or boring.

ENNEAGRAM NINE

Nines want to be kind, valued, and peaceful.

+ The cause: Nines are adaptable and don't necessarily *need* a big cause to work toward, but they are deeply tenderhearted toward causes.

+ The people: Nines want to be surrounded by people who are willing to assume the best and slow to dish out harsh reprimands. Nines also feel valued when their voices are both heard and sought out.

+ The work: Nines are highly adaptable to any type of work. However, they tend to do best when the work is collaborative, or they are fully trusted to do it themselves.

● ● ● ● ● ● ● ● ●

Regardless of Enneagram type, anyone who is emotionally unhealthy will not have an ideal workplace experience. Each type wants to be trusted and liked in some capacity, but in order to have a healthy workplace, you yourself need to be healthy.

The first step is always awareness and acknowledgment of our problems, but after that, we need to allow wise voices to give us feedback in our lives. We need God to do a new work in our hearts. Becoming familiar with who He is and what He says will bring us closer to Him.

Our work life is not as important as the health of our soul.

For we are his workmanship, created in Christ Jesus for good works, which God prepared beforehand, that we should walk in them.

(Ephesians 2:10)

SECTION FOUR:

ADVANCED ADULTHOOD (RHYTHM/WINTER)

Old age may have its limitations and challenges, but in spite of them, our latter years can be some of the most rewarding and fulfilling of our lives.

—*Billy Graham*

Winter is the season in which we get to reap the rewards of our hard work from seasons past. Life's pace slows down...but somehow, time is flying by faster than ever before. Some falsely believe that the work of growth grows stale in these years—and it can—but those who make a habit of self-reflection and keep a humble heart are still in the midst of becoming all God has created them to be.

There is some debate about when traditional adulthood ends and advanced adulthood begins. I think some of the discussion exposes our angst and fear about aging. None of us are truly fine with the idea of being advanced in years ourselves. In Western culture, it's difficult for us to think about the end of life.

I think it's helpful to think of advanced adulthood as beginning around age sixty, or once both of your parents have died if you're over fifty, whichever comes first. Victor Hugo said, "Forty is the old age of youth; fifty the youth of old age."

Making it to advanced adulthood is a blessing, a time for sharing late harvests, mending fences, and completing projects. Adolescence is full of angst and adulthood is full of labor, but in advanced adulthood, we reap the rewards of everything we have grown in the prior years. Hopefully, we get to experience retirement, rest, family, and friendships that have lasted a lifetime.

The Enneagram doesn't stop impacting our realities once we are classified as *old* or *elderly*. How we handle the last season of our life will be impacted by our personality, as with every season that came before it.

● ● ●

HOW WE HANDLE THE LAST SEASON OF OUR LIFE WILL BE IMPACTED BY OUR PERSONALITY, AS WITH EVERY SEASON THAT CAME BEFORE IT.

● ● ●

Hollywood boils this over-sixty age group to only two or three kinds of people—classically angry, wise, or young at heart—but in reality, they are simply being who they've always been, just in a different season.

In advanced adulthood, we may have done so much growing that our core behaviors no longer have their loud or negative flare, which can make us believe our personality has drastically changed. The reality is we have merely learned to temper it.

SECURITY AND MISSING PIECE ARROWS

As we age, we have more access to balance in life—a balance that touches wings, subtypes, and even arrows. The theories of security and missing piece arrows are part of that balance, and those arrows are most likely to be accessed in our advanced adulthood.

Your missing piece arrow is considered to be the best quality of your stress number. That type's behaviors and characteristics happen to be what your core Enneagram type needs the most in their growth journey. You can access this missing piece once you have matured thoroughly in your growth number, which acts as a ladder to the missing piece.

Once you have reached that point, your missing piece will balance out some of the harsher and more negative traits of your core personality.

● ● ●

YOUR MISSING PIECE—THE BEST QUALITY OF YOUR STRESS NUMBER—WILL BALANCE OUT SOME OF THE HARSHER AND MORE NEGATIVE TRAITS OF YOUR CORE PERSONALITY.

● ● ●

On the other hand, although your security arrow is the same number as your growth arrow, you access it by using your growth type's more average to negative behaviors around those with whom you are most comfortable. Thus, your behavior at work or with a new love interest will reflect your Enneagram type, but your behavior at home or with your family may reflect your security arrow. You subconsciously know the latter won't leave you and will tolerate such behavior. Security is a positive feeling, so these behaviors are confusing, but nonetheless, they are truly negative.

For example, when Fours are around the people they are most secure with, they may act like average Ones—having high standards for their loved ones, being openly critical, and even increasingly bossy.

● ● ●

WHEN ACCESSING YOUR SECURITY ARROW, YOU EXHIBIT THE NEGATIVE BEHAVIORS OF YOUR GROWTH TYPE AROUND THOSE WITH WHOM YOU ARE MOST COMFORTABLE.

● ● ●

The Enneagram type you are prone to exhibit in a season of stress and your missing piece arrow point to the same number; likewise, your security arrow and your Enneagram type in growth will be the same number. However, the security and missing piece arrows have different triggers.

Stress and growth are seasons of life, and the behaviors of our stress and growth arrows will show up in those seasons. Regardless of what season you're in, security behaviors are triggered by certain relationships, and the missing piece is an overarching goal and characteristics that your Enneagram type needs.

The following chart provides a visual explanation of each arrow and when it's accessed.

	Stress	Growth	Missing Piece	Security
Stress Arrow	X		X	
Growth Arrow		X		X
Seasons	X	X		
Triggered by Relationships				X
Triggered by Overarching Goal			X	

Here's what security looks like for each type:

ENNEAGRAM ONE

In security, Ones will take on more average to unhealthy traits of Sevens. They may be extra wacky, silly, or nonsensical; they may even fail to follow through on some things they said they were going to do.

Games especially can bring out a joking demeanor that borders on harassment and is anything but fun to the One's target.

> I've been told by family members that I don't know when to let a joke go, and my hyper side is something only they see.
> —*Boyd, a One*

ENNEAGRAM TWO

In security, Twos will start to act out in the average to unhealthy characteristics of Fours. They may overshare, refuse to be cheered up, and speak in dramatic language, perhaps saying things like, "I'll always feel this way."

Around their family or friends, Twos may overdramatize stories to gain sympathy or feel the need to exaggerate their mood for their pain to even be noticed.

> I didn't understand why my family thought I was an Enneagram Four until I understood the security arrows. They are the ones who see my dramatic, overly emotional side.   —*Natalie, a Two*

ENNEAGRAM THREE

In security, Threes will start to act out in the average to unhealthy behaviors of type Six. They will voice their precautions, overprepare, and more easily access internal anxiety.

Threes appear to be almost bulletproof to everyone except those who know them best. Threes don't let anyone else see their internal fears, so they tend to pour out without restraint around people with whom they feel safe.

I originally didn't think my husband could be an Enneagram Three because, to me, he didn't seem confident enough. Sure, he always did fine, but I was who saw the nerves before the interview or big presentations. Remembering how I saw him when we first met really helped me see what everyone else sees.   —*Una, a One*

ENNEAGRAM FOUR

In security, Fours will act out in the average to unhealthy behaviors of type One. They will be openly critical, hold their loved ones up to a high standard, and find themselves slipping into bossy behaviors. To an Enneagram Four's family or friends, the phrase *frustrated idealist* may feel more apt than *suffering artist* or *hopeless romantic*.

I used to think I was just bossy around my family because I'm the oldest child. Now I understand how my arrow to One plays a really big part in how I interact with those I'm closest to.
—*Kelly, a Four*

ENNEAGRAM FIVE

In security, Fives will act out in the average to unhealthy behaviors of type Eight. They may state their opinions in an aggressive manner, start arguments, or display other distrusting behaviors.

At times, Fives can even seem arrogant, controlling, and overbearing to their family or friends. They make themselves feel more competent by making others feel smaller.

I never noticed how argumentative my wife felt like I was until I heard about security arrows. I always knew I was opinionated, but I didn't think she thought I was angry or hostile when stating my thoughts.   —*Luke, a Five*

ENNEAGRAM SIX

In security, Sixes will start to act out in the average to unhealthy behaviors of type Nine. They will want to retreat and check out from life; they may not feel like asserting their presence is worth the effort.

Sixes have to keep a tight hold on their security, which means they don't trust many people. Those they *do* trust bear the brunt of their laziness because their trust involves letting others do things for them. They can be both endearing and annoying.

> I always thought this was part of being an introvert, but now I can see the decision fatigue I suffer from being responsible all day and how I lay the burden of my fatigue on my roommate.—*Cate, a Six*

ENNEAGRAM SEVEN

In security, Sevens will start to act out in the average to unhealthy behaviors of type Five. After being joyful all day, the Seven will withdraw, often with little or no communication. This is different from Sixes numbing out and expecting others to make all the decisions. Sevens will quite literally disappear and dive into some project for hours on end.

> I'll go hiking, and when I get back to my parents' house, I'll get overstimulated by their presence pretty easily. So I'll just retreat to the basement or my room for a couple hours to recoup. My mom says this hurts her feelings at times because I was just gone and now I need more alone time. —*Matt, a Seven*

ENNEAGRAM EIGHT

In security, Eights act out in the average to unhealthy behaviors of type Two. They are prone to becoming overly involved in the lives of their loved ones, often jumping in to fix a situation before they know all the details—or if it's even theirs to fix. An Eight's mama or papa bear mode is meant to be protective, but it can be destructive and rash instead.

> I have teenagers and have always identified with the term "mama bear." My daughter at one point said she doesn't tell me about some things that hurt her because she doesn't know what I'll do, and that made me really rethink some of my reactions in the past. —*Peg, an Eight*

ENNEAGRAM NINE

In security, Nines act out in the average to unhealthy behaviors of Threes. They are often competitive and even a little boastful about their achievements or strengths.

This can come out as joking about their spouse's flaws at a party, becoming excessively competitive during a board game, or not so silently comparing themselves to a sibling.

My husband is a Nine, and I always thought he was merging when he would meet my competitiveness and teasing on family game nights. Apparently, it is part of his own Three-ness. —*Jill, a Three*

● ● ● ● ● ● ● ●

Here's what the missing piece can look like for each Enneagram type:

ENNEAGRAM ONE

Ones ultimately need type Four's emotional connectivity and ability to see the beauty in everything. They need to discover that there's no shame in big emotions and no reason to pick out tiny flaws in precious moments. This allows Ones to rest in the beauty of the moment, critic free.

ENNEAGRAM TWO

Twos need type Eight's confidence in themselves and a backbone. They need to be able to say no when someone asks for *just one more thing*, take full ownership of their own worth and importance, and stand confident even when relationships fail.

ENNEAGRAM THREE

Threes need type Nine's ability to empathize rather than conform, rest in what's already been done instead of what needs to happen, and listen to hear instead of compare. They also need to rest in the stillness of an unhurried moment.

ENNEAGRAM FOUR

Fours need to learn to love others and themselves the way Christ does—unconditionally. When they pick up their missing piece from type Two, they will no longer wonder if someone will discover that they are fatally flawed, beat themselves up for not reaching their potential, hold people at arm's length, or envy the ease with which others seem to live.

ENNEAGRAM FIVE

Fives need type Seven's drive to get out, have fun, and fully participate in life rather than merely observe. They need to experience the great joy of a shared life and the adventure that can be had when everyone throws their ideas out there.

ENNEAGRAM SIX

Sixes need type Three's ability to trust their inner compass and have confidence in themselves. They need to stop asking for a second opinion and living under the burden of past mistakes that could not be prevented. They need to try to have faith even in the unknown.

ENNEAGRAM SEVEN

Sevens need type One's ability to find divine purpose within their everyday responsibilities and joy within a job well done. They need to find fulfillment and delight right here, right now. Nothing else needs to happen or be added.

ENNEAGRAM EIGHT

Eights need type Five's humility and objectivity. They need to second guess their gut responses, ask more questions, pay close attention to others, and respond instead of react.

ENNEAGRAM NINE

Nines need type Six's ability to assert their opinions and grow in adversity, not hide and numb while hoping for better days. They need to pay attention to their gut response, show up, and stop assuming that others don't want to hear their voice.

● ● ● ● ● ● ● ● ●

It makes sense to discuss security and missing piece arrows in advanced adulthood because this is the season when we typically have many people in our lives whom we have known for a long time. We feel secure with these people—not just our spouses but also our children, best friends, longtime coworkers or colleagues, and even grandchildren.

You are probably aware of these behaviors even if it's just a vague feeling that you're acting your worst around your favorite people. This is the paradox of security. It's a good feeling, but with it comes complacency and negative traits because you know your closest relations aren't going anywhere no matter how you behave.

God called us to be aware of this paradox when Jesus explained the greatest commandments:

> You shall love the Lord your God with all your heart and with all your soul and with all your mind. This is the great and first commandment. And a second is like it: You shall love your neighbor as yourself. On these two commandments depend all the Law and the Prophets.
> (Matthew 22:37–40)

Jesus taught us the Golden Rule: "*Whatever you wish that others would do to you, do also to them*" (Matthew 7:12; see also Luke 6:31).

When we treat others how we want to be treated, there isn't room for the pent-up frustration or angst that you didn't lash out on others all day to be thrown instead toward the people you love most.

As children, we were trained to conform, temper our true selves, and hide our dirty laundry at home. The problem with conformity is that your unacceptable behaviors never completely go away; they are just pushed into the corner of our lives where the people who accept us fully live. Even when these people love us despite our flaws, God doesn't want us to be lazy in our growth as His beloved children. If we truly want to treat others how we want to be treated, we need to be aware of our negative tendencies and open to being called out on them.

● ● ●

EVEN WHEN PEOPLE LOVE US DESPITE OUR FLAWS, GOD DOESN'T WANT US TO BE LAZY IN OUR GROWTH AS HIS BELOVED CHILDREN.

● ● ●

These security behaviors are best dealt with after substantial awareness and growth in who we truly are and how God sees us, which is why they are often tackled in advanced adulthood. By this season, we are prone to have enough character that we can be ourselves no matter who is around.

The missing piece, likewise, is something we reach only after tangible growth in all other areas of our lives. Some people, sadly, never reach their missing piece, but those who do often find it in advanced adulthood. After steady and continuous growth through adolescence and adult life, we now get to reap the rewards of our efforts.

In my coaching sessions, I have witnessed the most tears from my clients when discussing the missing pieces. (The tears that flow when talk turns to parental orientations is a close second.) It stings to hear the things we lack so desperately, but it's also a relief to know they are within our reach.

I think this is part of what we fear when we believe that personality assessments *put us in a box*, that people don't change and our flaws are permanent.

On the contrary, throughout your lifetime, you will change, grow, and conquer your worst pain points with God's help, without losing who He created you to be. It is in turning our eyes to Jesus and forgetting *ourselves*—our excuses, our ruts, our sin—that we can find our true fulfillment and joy in Christ. We will be complete on the day we see Him face to face.

WINGS

There's a beauty to wisdom and experience that cannot be faked.
It's impossible to be mature without having lived.
—*Amy Grant*

A wing is one of the two numbers on either side of your core Enneagram number, which adds some flavor to your personality type. Your core number won't change and your main motivation, sin proclivities, and personality will come from that type. However, your wing can influence your overall personality and how it presents itself.

There's a lot of different theories about wings, but the viewpoint we hold to is:

+ Your wing can only be one of the two numbers on either side of your number. For example, a Five can have a Six wing (5w6) but not an Eight wing.

+ You have access to both of the numbers on either side of your type, though most people only have one dominant wing—dominant more of one number's behaviors over the other, not dominant over one's core type. It is possible to have equal wings or no wing at all, although this is rare.

+ Your dominant wing number can change from one to the other throughout your life, but it's speculated this might only happen once.

● ● ●

THROUGHOUT LIFE, YOUR DOMINANT WING WILL ACT AS SOMETHING THAT PROTECTS AND SHIELDS YOU FROM HAVING TO BE TOO VULNERABLE TOO QUICKLY.

● ● ●

Throughout most of your life, your dominant wing will act as something that protects and shields you from having to be too vulnerable too quickly. For example, as a Four, I'm quiet and hard to read, but when people meet me, they may think I'm a Five because I will dive into any conversation about things I'm interested in with a lot of passion. This Five wing is distracting and protects the vulnerabilities that my Four-ish behaviors show all too clearly.

Five-ish characteristics point toward a deep need for competency, something I care about that doesn't make me feel vulnerable. On the other hand, my Four-ish traits show a deep need for authenticity and a feeling of *glorious purpose* that I would rather not advertise. I don't want anyone taking advantage of that information.

A lot of people may even test as their wing number because these are the traits and qualities others may see in them. A Nine with an Eight wing may hear about their confidence and boldness all the time, so it can be hard for them to claim the meekness of Nines.

Another facet of wings is that we all have access to two of them, and we usually will see characteristics from both throughout our life. But for the majority of our lives, we will have a dominant wing that we rely on the most to shield us and use a lot of that type's behaviors. We may use the other one, which I affectionately call the *baby wing*, in certain situations or to access only a few behaviors from that Enneagram type.

● ● ●

WE MAY USE THE BABY WING IN CERTAIN SITUATIONS OR TO ACCESS ONLY A FEW BEHAVIORS FROM THAT ENNEAGRAM TYPE.

● ● ●

This can feel confusing to some types because their most dominant wing may have quieter traits—traits like being observant, conflict avoidance, having anxiety, or a draw toward creative arts—while the smaller wing may host louder traits such as confidence, success orientation, perfectionism, or a need to be heard.

Online and in books, you will find various descriptions of wing traits for each type. I've written some of these myself. However, no Enneagram teacher or coach can fully encapsulate how your wing might be showing up in your life. There are just too many factors involved to say definitively, "*This* is how your wing number's behaviors are interacting with your core type." There is your history, your surroundings, your lifestyle, your culture, and everything else to consider. So descriptions and lists need to be read with a grain of salt.

Even so, I think it's helpful to think of each type and the influence of its wings like this:

EACH TYPE WITH ONE WING

ENNEAGRAM ONE

Unlike your type One motivation for integrity and goodness:

+ Your Nine wing makes you seek inner peace.
+ Your Two wing makes you want to be loved, feel wholly accepted by others, and worthy of love.

ENNEAGRAM TWO

Unlike your type Two motivation for love and relationships:

+ Your One wing makes you want to be right or do good.
+ Your Three wing makes you desire to have your worth seen and affirmed by others. You may worry that you don't have any self-worth.

ENNEAGRAM THREE

Unlike your type Three motivation for worth and self-importance:

+ Your Two wing traits are things you do because you want to be loved. You may be afraid that you are not worthy of love.

+ Your Four wing gives you a drive to be authentic and shine as an individual.

ENNEAGRAM FOUR

Unlike your type Four motivation for authenticity and a unique identity:

+ Your Three wing gives you the desire to have your talents, authentic self, and skills seen and affirmed by others.

+ Your Five wing makes you want to be seen as competent and intelligent.

ENNEAGRAM FIVE

Unlike your type Five motivation for competency and objective truth:

+ Your Four wing seeks to have others affirm you as an authentic individual.

+ Your Six wing traits are those things you do to gain security in your job or relationships.

ENNEAGRAM SIX

Unlike your type Six motivation for security and guidance:

+ Your Five wing is motivated by competency. You may be afraid you're not really competent at all.

+ Your Seven wing provides an inner longing for satisfaction in life and a deep contentment that you're afraid you may never have.

ENNEAGRAM SEVEN

Unlike your type Seven motivation for satisfaction and freedom:

+ Your Six wing inspires you to seek the security that proves you're not alone.

+ Your Eight wing makes you seek an autonomy or independence that protects you from being controlled by others.

ENNEAGRAM EIGHT

Unlike your type Eight motivation for independence and control:

+ Your Seven wing gives you an inner longing for satisfaction and a deep sense of contentment without fear it could be taken away at any moment.

+ Your Nine wing makes you seek inner peace for its own sake.

ENNEAGRAM NINE

Unlike your type Nine motivation for peace and equilibrium:

+ Your Eight wing encourages you to seek autonomy or independence to prevent you (or those you love) from being controlled and harmed.

+ Your One wing motivates you to be right or do good because you're afraid you're neither right nor good.

BALANCE IN LATER YEARS

Wings are something that can fluctuate during our lifetime, and it's possible to have balanced wings or no wings at all. However, it is theorized that balanced wings are most common during the later years of our life.

Balance can be a sign of maturity and wisdom, something that comes not just after living many years but also making a lot of mistakes. Our personalities at their most unhealthy and excessive will not be tolerated by everyone. We learn to correct our behaviors when we are hit with the backlash of our peers and stumble over our blind spots.

You don't have to have balanced wings to be healthy, and your maturity journey is never over this side of heaven, but balanced wings can be a sign of the type of maturity that many years can bring.

Your core Enneagram type will always host your most dominant strengths and pain points. It will always point to your arrows for stress and growth. However, both of your wing numbers will bring traits to your core type to make you more balanced, content, and effective in your purpose.

EACH TYPE WITH BOTH WINGS

ENNEAGRAM ONE

Ones with balanced wings (1w2/9) will have their inner drive for perfection and rightness tempered by a need to create peace and be loved. Their inner and outer voice becomes kinder as they grow in both wing behaviors. The need for love drives them to action that their need for peace might have prevented them from taking. And their peacemaking skills will help them repair mistakes with urgency that their need for love might let them overlook.

Type Nine's desire for peace and type Two's desire for love balance type One's need to be right and create perfection. The One's strengths of amplifying goodness, tasting the sweetness of grace, and solving problems is only made more effective by Two and Nine traits.

ENNEAGRAM TWO

Twos with balanced wings (2w1/3) have their need for love balanced by the motivation to do right and gain worth. Motivated by love, Twos may overlook hurts for the sake of love and not claim their worth because taking care of themselves could conflict with making others feel loved.

Type One's traits of focus, integrity, problem-solving, and seeking not only goodness but holy perfection help Twos decide what is actually theirs to do as well as their moral obligation. Type Three's confidence, success orientation, encouragement, and drive help Twos live for their own dreams instead of living through others.

Twos are better able to love and receive love when they know they deserve it, know what to do, and know when to say no—all things that come with balanced wings.

ENNEAGRAM THREE

Threes with balanced wings (3w2/4) have their need to prove their self-worth balanced by their need to love others and be authentic. Leaning to only one wing or the other can make Threes feel like they are always doing things for others, or only ever trying to cultivate their authentic image. But with both wings, Threes have a balance of servanthood and self-care, of using their talents for others and cultivating their own dreams, of making others feel loved without losing themselves.

Threes are better able to live out their success orientation and worth when they are balanced by love and authenticity. These two wings will help them live with integrity and have people in their lives who can appreciate their success.

ENNEAGRAM FOUR

Fours with balanced wings (4w3/5) have their need to find their authentic self balanced by knowing their worth and finding competency. Both of these wing traits bring Fours more confidence to bring their skills and abilities to the outside world when they are mature. The skills of type Three are more success oriented and loud, whereas type Five's skills will ensure that the Fours are doing their homework and not experiencing false confidence.

Fours are more effective people when they stop cultivating their vision of who they *could* be and instead act on what talents and gifts they have right now. A Five wing will fill them to the brim with information that begs to get out, and the Three wing will give them the confidence to use their capabilities.

ENNEAGRAM FIVE

Fives with balanced wings (5w4/6) have their need for competency balanced by the motivation for security and authenticity. Security will ensure that the Fives are taking care of their physical needs as well as their families, and authenticity will help them build a life that they actually enjoy instead of falling into the rut of a cycle of work and sleep.

Their authenticity drive will take care of the Fives internally, while their security drive will take care of their more physical needs, giving them more stamina for the mental space they love to occupy. Fives are more effective in life when they make choices that echo who they are and keep them secure.

ENNEAGRAM SIX

Sixes with balanced wings (6w5/7) have their need for security balanced by a desire for competency and satisfaction. A Six with balanced

Five and Seven wings experiences the ultimate balance on the Enneagram, accessing both the most naturally outgoing and reserved types. I think this is why my type Six clients will typically answer a question with, "Well, it depends..."

Action and thinking, alone time and socializing, gaining knowledge and using that knowledge in real life—all of these are balanced when a Six uses both wings together.

These wings temper out the Sixes' pain point of getting stuck in thought. The Five wing will compel them toward facts, and the Seven wing pushes them toward action. Sixes are more effective in the world with balanced wings because of the confidence they gain from both Seven's energy and Five's objectivity.

ENNEAGRAM SEVEN

Sevens with balanced wings (7w6/8) have their need for satisfaction balanced by a motivation toward security and independence. Rather than fighting against each other, these wings create balance in Sevens, giving them the freedom they desire and the safety and thoughtfulness they need.

Sevens are more effective when they have both wings because they are more considerate and less conflict avoidant, more safety conscious and more energetic, more loyal and more protective.

ENNEAGRAM EIGHT

Eights with balanced wings (8w7/9) have their need for independence tempered by a motivation toward satisfaction and peace. Satisfaction gives them a goal and helps them point their energy in a specific direction, while their drive for peace can coexist with their desire for justice and helping others. It also helps them with their relationships.

I don't think it was an accident that God designed Eights with access to both the most energy and least energy on the Enneagram. As Eight (core type) and Seven (wing) are the two highest energy types, and Nine (wing) and Five (stress arrow) are the two lowest energy types, these differences play tug-of-war until the Eight achieves a healthy balance.

ENNEAGRAM NINE

Nines with balanced wings (9w1/8) have their need for peace balanced by independence and doing what is right. Both of these paradoxes to peace help Nines claim their space in the world and not let others run over them. Thus, their conflict avoidance will not damper their quality of life.

The Eight and One wings balance each other out by finding the middle ground between perfection and shamelessness, quantity of work and detailed work, and acting without thinking and overthinking. With this balance, Nines are more effective in the world because they access energy and find a cause that makes them want to live wide awake.

• • • • • • • • •

As you navigate life and your wing behaviors play out, you will find it easier to achieve wing balance as you age. Perhaps you've been using both wings on and off for a long time. Perhaps maturity and growth have brought you to that point.

However it comes to pass, we know that our goal should be balance, using the best traits of all nine Enneagram types. These are all the strengths God has given to us.

> Now there are varieties of gifts, but the same Spirit; and there are varieties of service, but the same Lord; and there are varieties of activities, but it is the same God who empowers them all in everyone.
>
> (1 Corinthians 12:4–6)

20

GRIEF

How lucky I am to have something that makes
saying goodbye so hard.
—*Alan Alexander Milne*

I was feeling chaotic, and my inner world felt noisy. I'm afraid I was snippy with my children and not thoughtful toward those around me. A fear threatened to swallow me. *Is this who I am? Why am I behaving like this?*

As I sat with God's Word and slowly reflected on Ephesians 3:16— *"That according to the riches of his glory he may grant you to be strengthened with power through his Spirit in your inner being"*—I asked God to tell me what was going on in my inner being. Why did I feel so chaotic yet so fragile?

In the clearest voice, I heard, "You're grieving."

Now this should not have come as a surprise to me. Just days before that moment, my grandmother died after a sudden and unfair battle with amyotrophic lateral sclerosis (ALS). I had spent the day before weeping on and off. I knew I was in the throes of grief, but I was still learning just what that meant.

Grief is not just tears and aching for what is lost. It is like being punched in the gut, losing your ability to breathe, hurting, yearning, and healing ever so slowly. When others bump into you, you're tender and caught unawares, so you may yelp in pain. You may be sensitive and your thoughts may be a jumbled mess. Going about everyday life feels so counterintuitive, but breakfast still needs to be made, diapers still need to be changed, and clothes still need to be washed. Or perhaps you need to put on a brave face and go to work.

● ● ●

THE CONFUSING AND MESSY TIME OF GRIEF CAN BE MADE EVEN MORE TURBULENT WHEN WE DON'T UNDERSTAND OUR OWN REACTIONS.

● ● ●

No one escapes life without going through some form of grief. This often confusing and messy time can be made even more turbulent when we don't understand our own reactions. In this chapter, we'll take a deep dive into how each Enneagram type typically responds to grief and how God brings comfort to each.

In chapter 16, we discussed stances as they relate to the workplace, so if you skipped over that, you'll want to return to it for a fuller understanding of this theory. Stances are also useful when we talk about grief and moving forward.

The three stances are:

+ Compliant (types One, Two, and Six)
+ Assertive (types Three, Seven, and Eight)
+ Withdrawn (types Four, Five, and Nine)

COMPLIANT STANCE

Those in the compliant stance will initially take too much responsibility for what happened. They may run over the moments or weeks in their minds over and over to try to find what they did wrong; generally speaking, they will blame themselves. They may also struggle with not giving themselves enough time to grieve before they're back in action. Being in the compliant stance means they place a lot of their worth into how people see or react to them.

- Enneagram Ones need to be seen as good. They respond to grief by thinking, *This is my fault. I need to fix this.*

- Enneagram Twos need to be seen as helpful. They respond to grief by thinking, *It's my fault. I must control how people respond to me in this.*

- Enneagram Sixes need you to stay with them so they'll have security. They respond to grief by thinking, *This must be my fault. I must regain control by making sure this doesn't happen again.*

Jesus meets each of these types as they grieve, taking all of the guilt and shame with Him to the cross and lovingly speaking to each individual.

- Ones, your grief is not wrong. Grief can feel horrible and still be 100 percent appropriate and right. Something terrible has happened; your anger and your tears are proof of your love and belief in the sanctity of life. *"Are not five sparrows sold for two pennies? And not one of them is forgotten before God…Fear not; you are of more value than many sparrows"* (Luke 12:6–7).

- Twos, your neediness in this time does not make you worth less than others. Let your brothers and sisters in Christ fulfill the biblical call to help you in your time of need. *"Rejoice with those who rejoice, weep with those who weep"* (Romans 12:15).

- Sixes, this situation does not mean that you now need to live burdened by control, or that you must plan, prepare, and make sure this never happens again. Fear will try to convince you to take control and tell you that God cannot be trusted, but those are lies. You don't need to carry this burden. *"Come to me, all who labor and are heavy laden, and I will give you rest. Take my yoke upon you, and learn from me, for I am gentle and lowly in heart, and you will find rest for your souls. For my yoke is easy, and my burden is light"* (Matthew 11:28–30).

ASSERTIVE STANCE

Because assertiveness is typically something that you use to push outside yourself, those in the assertive stance will be more likely to look for blame outside themselves. They are also the most independent types on the Enneagram, so the tragedy feels like it has victimized their very identity.

- Enneagram Threes need to be successful. They respond to grief by thinking, *This is others' fault. I must make sense of this or disregard it.*

- Enneagram Eights need to be autonomous. They respond to grief by thinking, *This must be others' fault. I must not appear weak. I must regain control by focusing on what I can control.*

- Enneagram Sevens need to be free. They respond to grief by thinking, *This must be others' fault. I must try to find the positive. I must run away from grief because if it catches me, I may never recover.*

Jesus meets each of these types as they grieve by taking their guilt and bringing justice for their loved one. If someone is to blame, their sin was forgiven at the cross, or they will face punishment. Justice is coming.

- Threes, grief is not a failure; what you lost was never yours to win or fail by. *"In his hand is the life of every living thing and the breath of all mankind"* (Job 12:10).

- Eights, grief is not a weakness, nor a signal of your loss of control; it's an indication of your deep love for the one you lost. *"My flesh and my heart may fail, but God is the strength of my heart and my portion forever"* (Psalm 73:26).

- Sevens, grief will not kill you. Although you feel the extremes of sadness now, after this trial, your heart will once again feel light. *"So also you have sorrow now, but I will see you again, and your hearts will rejoice, and no one will take your joy from you"* (John 16:22).

WITHDRAWN STANCE

Those in the withdrawn stance are neither aggressive toward others nor compliant with them, but rather move away from people. The three Enneagram types in this stance—Fours, Fives, and Nines—are more self-focused. They are born with a backpack full of boundaries, and when they feel like a boundary has been crossed, they withdraw. Their view of themselves has a lot to do with how they handle grief:

- Enneagram Fours need to be authentic. They respond to grief by withdrawing, deeply wanting to be understood, and letting grief define them.

- Enneagram Fives need to be competent and know everything about what caused the death. They respond to grief by withdrawing and thinking, *I must understand why this happened and regain my control with knowledge.*

- Enneagram Nines need peace. They respond to grief by withdrawing, both fully feeling and fully pushing away pain in their effort to restore peace.

While those in the compliant or assertive stances either initially blame themselves or others for causing their grief, the types in the withdrawn stance may teeter-totter between those two responses, but initially, they blame God. God crossed their boundaries by taking a loved one—and that's really where God will meet them. He tells us, "I love your loved one more than you do. They were not yours to begin with, they were Mine. And now they've come back to Me."

Unlike what you can do on your own or what others can do for you, God can actually take your anger and sadness. He knows why you're grieving, and He grieves with you. This is what I believe His message would be to each one of these types:

- Fours, grief does not define you. What happened is meaningful and tremendously painful, but you are God's, and that is your ultimate identity. You are not just someone who lost a loved one; you are God's child. *"Know that the LORD, he is God! It is he who made us, and we are his; we are his people, and the sheep of his pasture"* (Psalm 100:3).

- Fives, grief is not proof of your incompetence or lack of knowledge. After all, Solomon in all his wisdom wrote the book of Lamentations. Grief is a symptom of being human. Don't be afraid to mourn. *"Blessed are those who mourn, for they shall be comforted"* (Matthew 5:4).

- Nines, grief will not destroy your peace. You can trust the keeper of peace to restore what has been taken and heal your broken heart. *"He heals the brokenhearted and binds up their wounds"* (Psalm 147:3).

GRAPPLING WITH GRIEF

Within grief, we grapple with the injustice of losing someone who shouldn't be gone. The fact of death is not something that sits well with the human heart because we were not created out of dust to die, but to live with Christ.

● ● ●

DEATH DOES NOT SIT WELL WITH THE HUMAN HEART BECAUSE WE WERE NOT CREATED OUT OF DUST TO DIE, BUT TO LIVE WITH CHRIST.

● ● ●

When we feel like something has been taken away from us unfairly, we can become bitter, thinking our "rights" have been taken away by God. It's part of the power struggle we foolishly attempt to instigate with our all-powerful, all-knowing God.

For each Enneagram type, we learn to give into humility and submit to Christ when we give up our way in favor of His will. This is not something that is easy by any means, but it brings peace.

+ Enneagram One: Give up your right to fix this.

+ Enneagram Two: Give up your right to be the one who helps.

+ Enneagram Three: Give up your right for this not to slow you down.

+ Enneagram Four: Give up your right to be understood.

+ Enneagram Five: Give up your right to understand what happened.

+ Enneagram Six: Give up your right to prevent it from happening again.

+ Enneagram Seven: Give up your right to be okay.

+ Enneagram Eight: Give up your right to control what happened.

+ Enneagram Nine: Give up your right to not have grief invade your peace.

21

DEATH

As believers in Jesus Christ and those who find comfort
in His trustworthy ways, even impending death should
not be able to deliver a spirit of fear to our hearts.
Death will simply transport us to Him.
—*Carol McLeod*

As we age and those around us start to die, we have to face something that American culture never taught us how to handle. Death is inevitable, and no human life is untouched by its sting. Each Enneagram type will tend to view death—their own and others'—with different biases and degrees of avoidance or acceptance.

All of us have specific, often traumatic memories of death becoming real to us. Whether it was unexpectedly losing someone close to you, an open-casket funeral no one prepared you for as a child, or even hearing that someone you admired has died, the thought of death can be scary. Our very soul cries out against death because we are not made to die.

Rather than living forever as God intended, original sin caused Adam and Eve to be cast out of the garden of Eden so they could no longer eat from the Tree of Life. (See Genesis 3:22–24.) Our longing for immortality and our true habitat of Eden is evident in our youth-oriented culture.

• • •

**RATHER THAN LIVING FOREVER AS GOD INTENDED,
ORIGINAL SIN CAUSED ADAM AND EVE TO BE CAST OUT OF EDEN.
OUR LONGING FOR IMMORTALITY AND OUR TRUE HABITAT IS EVIDENT
IN OUR YOUTH-ORIENTED CULTURE.**

• • •

Death and dying are not comfortable topics for Western culture. They are considered taboo, sad, and, in some cases, too grotesque to bring up. We like to live life as if there were no end.

Perhaps you are even hesitant to read this chapter.

I won't lie and say this chapter is a light read, nor is it a fun topic, but it is a necessary one. And if you are reading this before you are in your advanced adulthood, you are ahead of the game on processing some of these ideas and letting your heart take comfort in where you are going after death.

Scripture tells us, *"And the dust returns to the earth as it was, and the spirit returns to God who gave it"* (Ecclesiastes 12:7). When we die, our souls are united with God in heaven; we get to *go home* because we belong with God. We do not cease to exist, but rather we enter into a new life. Jesus said, *"I am the resurrection and the life. Whoever believes in me, though he die, yet shall he live, and everyone who lives and believes in me shall never die"* (John 11:25–26).

Jesus talked a lot about heaven and hell. He is fully aware of the reality of both, and we are not. He wanted to lend us some of His awareness, knowing that it would change how we lived.

What we know from Jesus about the reality of death is that heaven is true paradise (see Luke 23:43) where we get to be with God in a perfect relationship.

Behold, the dwelling place of God is with man. He will dwell with them, and they will be his people, and God himself will be with them as their God. He will wipe away every tear from their eyes, and death shall be no more, neither shall there be mourning, nor crying, nor pain anymore, for the former things have passed away.

(Revelation 21:3–4)

Let not your hearts be troubled. Believe in God; believe also in me. In my Father's house are many rooms. If it were not so, would I have told you that I go to prepare a place for you? And if I go and prepare a place for you, I will come again and will take you to myself, that where I am you may be also. (John 14:1–3)

When you are tempted to fear or even dread death, take those fears to Jesus. He is the orchestrator of your life, your death, and eternity. He wants to teach you to count death as a grace so that like the apostle Paul, you can say that you *"would rather be away from the body and at home with the Lord"* (2 Corinthians 5:8).

● ● ●

WHEN YOU ARE TEMPTED TO FEAR OR EVEN DREAD DEATH, TAKE THOSE FEARS TO JESUS. HE IS THE ORCHESTRATOR OF YOUR LIFE, YOUR DEATH, AND ETERNITY.

● ● ●

We all wrestle with death, and God wants to be with us in those moments. I won't pretend to be done with my own battles, nor am I an expert on the topic of death, but I do want to share what I know about how our specific takeaways may look different than those of our spouse, brother, or friends, depending on our Enneagram type. In this way, our struggles as we try to come to grips with death may not be so scary or isolating, and we can have a firm grasp on grace for those around us.

As we have learned, each Enneagram type has a dominant center of intelligence—head, heart, or gut—and we receive information from those centers.

For those in the gut triad—Ones, Eights, and Nines—learning of death feels instinctively *wrong*. They tend to default to action and protective measures for themselves and those they love, trying to make sure that they will never be the cause of someone's death. This can result in a lot of controlling tendencies around safety, nutrition, health, and other relationships as these types try to cover all the bases of prevention in order to feel *right* again. When talking about death, Eights, Nines, and Ones tend to use words like *final, permanent, gone, done,* and *end.*

For those in the heart triad—Twos, Threes, and Fours—the thought of death feels profoundly personal. A lot of their thoughts around death are about how people will think of them after they die, and what will happen to those they love and everything they've built. They dwell on the feeling part of death, and most of their thoughts are of their own death. When talking about death, Twos, Threes, and Fours tend to use words like *sadness, forgotten, grief, nostalgic, final words, love,* and *peaceful.*

For those in the head triad—Fives, Sixes, and Sevens—most of their initial thoughts about death revolve around *how* one dies. They fixate on the pain and how to avoid having a painful accidental death. To them, death is not something to be fully prevented or taken personally, but something that is inevitable and can be analyzed. When talking about death, Fives, Sixes, and Sevens tend to use words like *pain, prevention, quick, painless, peaceful, private,* and *gone.*

As we age, our specific encounters with death shape our views. Observing the ways in which different cultures react to death, the death of a child or parent, or our own near-death experience can make us take a step back and reevaluate our default center of intelligence reaction toward death. By the time we reach advanced adulthood, we will have had opportunities to challenge and change these default reactions.

● ● ●

WE ALL NEED TO ENCOUNTER THE THOUGHT OF DEATH WITH A BALANCED PERSPECTIVE AND HAVE OUR REACTIONS BE INFORMED BY OUR FAITH. GOD IS OUR BEST GUIDE.

● ● ●

We all need to encounter the thought of death with a balanced perspective and have our reactions be informed by our faith. This is a deeply personal and individual journey, and God is definitely our best guide. When we look at specific Enneagram types and their default reaction toward death, we see a base reaction that is formed in self-preservation, not one that is founded in faith and total trust in God's goodness. None of us are born with that kind of faith.

When you read these reactions, particularly for your type, use a critical eye and spot where you might be clinging to ego and false understanding instead of the hope in the cross of Christ.

ENNEAGRAM ONE

Type One's biggest fear is being bad, corrupt, or beyond salvation, so causing a death or dying in a shameful way are big things they want to avoid. This avoidance may be passive as they try not to think about death, or active as they think about safety and prevention a lot. Much of this has to do with their particular subtype and wing. For instance, a 1w9 may be more attracted to avoidance whereas a 1w2 or Sp subtype will be more likely to take an active approach.

Whatever the One's approach, they may hold the false assumption that they have a responsibility that defies even God's will, that they could make a mistake so huge, they would become unredeemable. While this may feel true if something horrible does happen, we know that no one is beyond the reach of God's grace, not even a disgraced One.

ENNEAGRAM TWO

Type Two's biggest fear is being rejected and undeserving of love. Twos know that others find them lovable when they include the Twos in gatherings, name their children after them, remember them on their birthday and holidays, and call or text them *just because*. They hope that they will be remembered fondly after death.

Twos spend a lot of their life subconsciously making sure they will be not only loved and adored but honored after death, that the list of their good deeds and generosity will be carved into their tombstone for everyone to read, and that there won't be a dry eye at their funeral. Someone remembering them with anything other than adoration feels like rejection. So Twos will try to hide all of their more negative emotions and thoughts in an effort to control how others see them.

This amount of control and fear is not God's heart for us. The responsibility for others' emotions and how they think of you is a heavy yoke, and God wants to exchange His light yoke for the one you are tempted to think is your only option.

ENNEAGRAM THREE

Type Three's biggest fear is being worthless, a failure, or disposable. Words like *legacy*, *achievement*, and *leader* are all music to their ears. Threes don't like to spend a lot of time thinking about death because the emotions around death are complicated and unpleasant. Even if they do receive all the praise and admiration they would desire after death, they won't be there to hear any of it, making the whole process rather anticlimactic for them.

Nevertheless, Threes want to be the *best* or *win* at whatever they're attracted to. They may want to live longer than everyone else in their family ever has, leave their children more money than their parents left them, or control every aspect of their funeral. They may even daydream about the sad eyes and wonderful words spoken about them. Threes don't often speak of this aloud, but this is the thought process they are tempted to have when they really have to think about death after a lifetime of pretending it won't affect them.

We know that God is bigger than our failures, and He is the victor over death. It is messy and sad now because we live in a cursed world, but resting in what is to come is truly where we find Threes at their healthiest.

ENNEAGRAM FOUR

Type Four's biggest fear is not having a unique identity, not living up to their potential, or being exposed as fatally flawed. Because Fours live with deep emotions and aren't afraid of sadness, death tends to be something that crosses their mind often. How they'll die, what others will think of their life, and whether they'll feel like they are living within their purpose before death are all thoughts that could cross the Four's mind on any given day. Fours idealize not only their life and future, but also their death. This can cause a great deal of existential anxiety as they feel like they need to make these ideals come true with no real roadmap or motivation to do the work it would take to make it happen.

God has the ideal prepared for Fours. The glint of gold He put in their hearts will be fully realized and fully born in heaven. The anxiety that comes with marking this life as ideal is not one He wants Fours to bear. He will use them like a bright, shining star in this life, but He will fulfill their starry-eyed big dreams in the next.

ENNEAGRAM FIVE

Type Five's biggest fear is being incompetent, inept, and exposed as not having enough. Consequently, the idea of dying in a way that was brought about by their own stupidity or causing a death out of lack of knowledge can keep Fives awake at night. They tend to think of death analytically, as a fact of life, but the manner of death being unknown can give Fives a rather morbid curiosity about the options for dying. They can try to prepare themselves for certain possibilities and try to find ways to avoid deaths they consider to be undesirable.

Death can happen in an instant, and it's not something we get a second chance at doing better once we gain more knowledge. The anxiety that can come with this unknown is where faith in God's total control comes in. God's control tends to be something Fives need to wrestle with before they can truly rest in it. They need to know why God is worthy of trust and how far His control reaches. This journey will look different for each Five, so I recommend looking to the people you trust for resources and answers in these areas.

ENNEAGRAM SIX

Type Six's deepest fear is being insecure in life, truly alone and without support. Sixes probably think about death more than other Enneagram types do, which isn't surprising given their propensity toward worst-case-scenario thinking and their analytical approach toward the realities of death. Sixes are on a prevention mission most of their life—not just for themselves, but mostly for the people who bring them security. Sixes often grapple with the idea of dying when they are children and so reach a certain peace about that, but losing the people they are loyal to is something else entirely. This is one of the reasons getting married or having kids can feel terribly costly to a Six. They are adding more people to their life whom they can't live without. The more people they love, the greater the opportunities for devastation. This reality is sometimes disorienting to Sixes and can cause a great deal of anxiety.

Truly handing over the lives of their loved ones and their own security to God is a lifelong journey for Sixes. It's something they need to pray through, meditate on, and give up multiple times a day. What Sixes are truly longing for is a security and wholeness that is only found in heaven, which can feel so distant and mysterious that they are tempted to place their hope in the here and now. Sixes are pragmatic. They want proof; they want to feel the holes in Jesus's hands and feet—something I think Jesus will gladly let them do in heaven.

ENNEAGRAM SEVEN

Type Seven's biggest fear is being in unfixable pain, deprived, or stuck. Pain and Sevens are not compatible, and nothing is more heartbreaking than seeing a Seven in horrific pain. The thought of death, even the death of a possibility or a dream, is devastating to a Seven, especially when it's impossible to put a positive spin on the reality and move on from there. When Sevens are in the pits of deep grief, depression has no better friend. When all hope is lost, a Seven's very soul seems to have shriveled and died with whatever they're grieving.

Sevens will take chances with their own death. They would rather die trying than live a boring life, but they can't bear the thought of loved ones mourning them and the pain for everyone touched by their lives. Sevens don't spend much time thinking about their funeral or anything that follows the moment that they die. Likewise, Sevens don't like to consider the death of their loved ones until it occurs, and when it *does* happen, they want the open wound/grief stage to be over *now*. (See chapter 20 on Grief for more on how Sevens respond to death.)

God wants to meet Sevens in their avoidance of the bad part of death with the beauty of true grief. Their pain honors what they lost. Jesus knew the importance of the valley and submitted to grief before raising His dear friend Lazarus from the dead. (See John 11:32–44.) Patience is a good pairing to Sevens' resilience.

ENNEAGRAM EIGHT

Type Eight's biggest fear is being controlled by others or unable to protect those they love. Eights can feel controlled by the inevitability of death, the reality of sickness, and things beyond their control that cause death. Because Eights' defense mechanism is denial, the rest of us may think they feel impervious to death. They have a larger-than-life, death-can't-touch-me vibe, even if that's not how they truly feel. This air of confidence is a coping skill that keeps them sane. When the death of a loved one or anyone they felt protective toward impacts the Eight's life, we tend to see them withdraw in their vulnerability and come back with even more resolve to protect those they love from death.

God offers a comfort that is vital to the health of Eights—the permission to fully trust the one who is in control. It isn't the Eights. Trusting God, especially with their loved ones, is an everyday decision and battle for Eights but a worthy one nevertheless.

ENNEAGRAM NINE

Type Nine's biggest fear is loss or separation. When your motivation is peace, you need to have happy memories, no regrets, and reconciliation. Nines feel haunted by the finality of death and how it threatens them with eternal/internal conflict. If someone they love dies, the memories become bittersweet, the ache of *could have* and *should have* is heavy, and any unresolved conflict or pain becomes an unsightly scar. Nines have a lot of fears when it comes to death, and this can make them shut down toward the topic. It can be too painful for them to think about, and they feel paralyzed to do anything about it.

God doesn't promise us a peaceful life, not every conflict in this world will be resolved, and death is not the final ending but rather a beginning. God welcomes Nines to come close so He can comfort them in the pain of this life and help them not only survive it but grow through it. His presence is enough of a balm to keep Nines sane through the uncertainty, conflict, and inevitable pain, if only they will run to Him with the pain and not hide.

●●●●●●●●●

From birth to death, our personalities define the perch from which we view life. Each view is worthwhile and necessary, but also carries its own pain points. None of us walk through this life without scars, and our personality can often dictate how we view them.

Learning about the Enneagram has helped me to view not only myself with curiosity, but also those around me. It has helped me realize the wounds that formed them and the strengths that I may not understand but that we need in the world. It has enabled me to see others with grace instead of confusion.

● ● ●

YOUR LIFE IS A MAGNIFICENT TAPESTRY IN THE OVERARCHING WORK OF CHRIST. GOD IS MAKING ART OUT OF EACH ONE OF OUR STORIES.

● ● ●

Your life is a magnificent tapestry in the overarching work of Christ. Although we may see chaos if we turn the tapestry over and view the underside, God is making art out of each one of our stories. May we find beauty in the color of thread we get to be and value our place among the fibers that shine God's glory.

But you are a chosen race, a royal priesthood, a holy nation, a people for his own possession, that you may proclaim the excellencies of him who called you out of darkness into his marvelous light. (1 Peter 2:9)

EPILOGUE

Throughout our lives, our personality will be both our greatest pain point and our greatest strength. More so than any other typology system, the Enneagram encapsulates how both of these can be true.

We can also see that we relate to every type in many different ways, which can be a mess that we need to untangle. I think it can be helpful to assess both what we know to be true about our own Enneagram type and what we know to be true about our life, and compare.

+ What is your core type?

+ What wings do you have access to?

+ What is your stress and growth number?

+ What is your subtype?

  » If it's self-preservation, you may relate to Sixes because of that mutual drive for security; if it's social, you may relate to Twos because of that drive to put others first; and if it's one-to-one, you may relate to Eights' confidence and assertiveness outside their main relationships.

+ What are the other two numbers in your stance?

+ What are the other two numbers in your triad?

+ What numbers are your parents or guardians?

+ What is your birth order?

  » Which Enneagram type relates most to the stereotyping of that birth order?

+ What types might you speculate were your first friends?

  » If those friendships ended badly, might that be why you struggle with those types now?

+ What type is your significant other?

  » If you are a one-to-one subtype, for example, you may especially relate to this type.

Looking back at this list, can you find every Enneagram type? If you can, this may be a big reason why you relate to descriptions, memes, and stories about other types. We all impact each other in one way or another.

When God created us, He gave us specific skills, temperaments, and longings. Each of us has a different purpose and plan to show His glory to the world. One of the mistakes we make is that we are partial to our own temperaments, longings, and skills. We may either compare these to others' attributes to make us feel better about ourselves or fixate on how our skills aren't *as much* as what others have. Both of these comparisons are prideful and a distraction from using what God has given us for His glory.

● ● ●

BY GOD'S GRACE, WE ARE ALL GROWING, AND GOD DESIRES ALL OF US TO BE EQUIPPED WITH EVERY GOOD WORK.

● ● ●

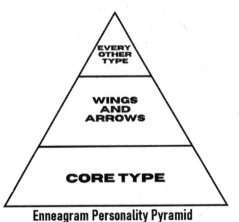

We know that by God's grace, we are all growing, and God desires all of us to be equipped with every good work. This may be one of the reasons why we feel like we can relate to most if not every Enneagram type. It's a sign of maturity and growth.

The Enneagram personality pyramid graphic illustrates how we

Enneagram Personality Pyramid

all start out with our core personality—the Enneagram type that we use the most—at the base.

Additionally, we have access to our stress and growth numbers as well as the wing numbers on either side of our core type. The four other types shown at the top of the pyramid will be pretty hard for us to access.

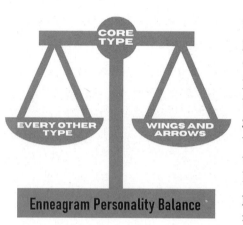

Enneagram Personality Balance

However, as we grow, we start to look more like the Enneagram personality balance graphic, with our core type still being how we process the world, but holding all the other types in balance. This gives us access to every good and wonderful gift of each type for the times when we most need them. Excess and extremes are easy—perhaps even on autopilot for most of us—but balance is hard. Balance does not happen by accident, but comes when we work at it, aided by the Holy Spirit.

If you desire growth and change in your life, I would implore you to focus on your Savior. Your personality can answer a lot of questions, but God made your personality and holds the keys to everything you seek. The Enneagram can be helpful, but without God, the answers it gives you will never point you to a soul-satisfying end. You are your biggest problem, and you cannot be your own Savior.

● ● ●

THE ENNEAGRAM CAN BE HELPFUL, BUT WITHOUT GOD, THE ANSWERS IT GIVES YOU WILL NEVER POINT YOU TO A SOUL-SATISFYING END.

● ● ●

Here are some ways we can grow by fixing our eyes on Jesus:

1. Get to know Him through prayer, reading His word, and being with His people.

2. Let yourself be seen by Him in earnest prayer and seen by His people in a community setting.

3. Be active and vocal about your desire for change. Ask those wiser than you for book recommendations, mentorship, and their honest feedback on your life. Pride will get you nowhere, but humility can move mountains.

As you grow in Christ, the rest of your life won't be solved and you'll have to face consequences, but you will find treasure when you can sing "It is well with my soul" through every storm.

Being knit together in love, to reach all the riches of full assurance of understanding and the knowledge of God's mystery, which is Christ, in whom are hidden all the treasures of wisdom and knowledge.

(Colossians 2:2–3)

ABOUT THE AUTHOR

Elisabeth Bennett first discovered the Enneagram in the summer of 2017 and immediately realized how life-changing this tool could be. She set out to absorb all she could about this ancient personality typology, including a twelve-week Enneagram Certification course taught by Beth McCord, who has studied the Enneagram for more than twenty-five years.

Elisabeth quickly started her own Enneagram Instagram account (@Enneagram.Life), which has grown to more than 75,000 followers. Since becoming a certified Enneagram coach, she has conducted more than four hundred one-on-one coaching sessions focused on helping her clients find their type and apply the Enneagram to their lives for personal and spiritual growth.

She has also published nine devotionals, one for each type, and a study guide companion to these works.

Elisabeth has lived in beautiful Washington State her entire life and now has the joy of raising her own children there with her husband, Peter.

To contact Elisabeth, please visit:

www.elisabethbennettenneagram.com

www.instagram.com/enneagram.life

www.facebook.com/enneagram.life.coaching

BOOK RECOMMENDATIONS

I'd like to thank all of these teachers and leaders in Enneagram research for their influence on my own work and consequently on this book. None of us have discovered or worked with the Enneagram all alone; it's a community work.

I also want to note that although I think many of these books are helpful in learning about the Enneagram, I do not endorse or support a lot of the theology to which some of the teachers who wrote them ascribe.

BEGINNER

My 60-Day Enneagram Devotional Series:
The Perfectionist: Growing as an Enneagram 1
The Helper: Growing as an Enneagram 2
The Achiever: Growing as an Enneagram 3
The Individualist: Growing as an Enneagram 4
The Thinker: Growing as an Enneagram 5
The Guardian: Growing as an Enneagram 6
The Enthusiast: Growing as an Enneagram 7
The Challenger: Growing as an Enneagram 8
The Peacemaker: Growing as an Enneagram 9
All nine books were written by me and published by Whitaker House between 2020 and 2022.

Marilyn Vancil, *Self to Lose, Self to Find: Using the Enneagram to Uncover Your True, God-Gifted Self* (New York: Convergent Books, 2020).

Kim Eddy, *The Enneagram for Beginners: A Christian Guide to Understanding Your Type for a God-Centered Life* (New York: Zeitgeist, 2020).

Ian Morgan Cron and Suzanne Stabile, *The Road Back to You: An Enneagram Journey to Self-Discovery* (Downers Grove, IL: InterVarsity Press, 2016).

Elizabeth Wagele and Renee Baron, *The Enneagram Made Easy: Discover the 9 Types of People* (New York: HarperCollins Publishers, 1994).

INTERMEDIATE

Stephanie Barron Hall, *The Enneagram in Love: A Roadmap for Building and Strengthening Romantic Relationships* (Emeryville, CA: Rockridge Press, 2020).

Drew Moser, *The Enneagram of Discernment: The Way of Vocation, Wisdom, and Practice* (Beaver Falls, PA: Falls City Press, 2020).

Adele and Doug Calhoun, Clare and Scott Loughrige, *Spiritual Rhythms for the Enneagram: A Handbook for Harmony and Transformation* (Downers Grove, IL: InterVarsity Press, 2019).

Suzanne Stabile, *The Journey Toward Wholeness: Enneagram Wisdom for Stress, Balance, and Transformation* (Downers Grove, IL: InterVarsity Press, 2021).

Ian Morgan Cron, *The Story of You: An Enneagram Journey to Becoming Your True Self* (New York: HarperCollins Publishers, 2021).

Beth McCord and Jeff McCord, *Becoming Us: Using the Enneagram to Create a Thriving Gospel-Centered Marriage* (New York: Morgan James Publishing, 2020).

Suzanne Stabile, *The Path Between Us: An Enneagram Journey to Healthy Relationships* (Downers Grove, IL: InterVarsity Press, 2018).

ADVANCED

Beatrice Chestnut, *The Complete Enneagram: 27 Paths to Greater Self-Knowledge* (Berkeley, CA: She Writes Press, 2013).

Richard Rohr and Andreas Ebert, *The Enneagram: A Christian Perspective* (Chestnut Ridge, NY: Crossroad Publishing, 2016).

Don Richard Riso, *Personality Types: Using the Enneagram for Self-Discovery* (New York: Houghton Mifflin Co., 1996).

Helen Palmer, *The Enneagram in Love and Work: Understanding Your Intimate and Business Relationships* (New York: HarperCollins Publishers, 1995).

Helen Palmer, *The Enneagram: Understanding Yourself and the Others in Your Life* (New York: HarperCollins Publishers, 1988).